Teeny's Tour of Pie

A COOKBOOK

MASTERING THE ART OF PIE IN *67 Recipes*

TEENY LAMOTHE

WORKMAN PUBLISHING • NEW YORK

Library of Congress Cataloging-in-Publication Data is available.

ISBN 978-0-7611-7336-6

Design by Becky Terhune
Principal photography by Sara Remington
Food Stylist: Lillian Kang
Prop Stylist: Christine Wolheim

Photo Credits
Front cover spot: Katie McKenzie. **Back cover spot:** Aaron Morris. **Background image:** Melissa Lucier. **Inside front and back covers:** Michael DiMascio.

Clare Barboza: p. 165 (bottom). **Mary Costa:** p. 233. **Courtesy of Emmy's Organics:** p. 91. **fotolia:** p. iii, kiboka; p. viii (top), Constantinos; p. viii (bottom), DBtale; p. xv (background), LeitnerR; p. 3 (right) Cpro; p. 5 (right), VL@D; p. 6 (left), michaeljayberlin; p. 9 (top left), Igor Normann; p. 9 (middle left), Brent Hofacker; p. 9 (bottom left) Iryna Melnyk; p. 28 (top left), Mark Carrel; p. 46, robynmac; p. 49 (bottom middle), Magdalena Kucova; p. 58, robynmac; p. 69, M. Schuppich; p. 75, siwaporn999; p. 76, irmaiirma; p. 82, Kelpfish; p. 87, inerika; p. 96, fuzzyfox; p. 105 (top second from right), Nicole Taraftu; p. 105, pomegranate Gorilla; p. 115, irmaiirma; p. 124, Grigoriy Lukyanov; p. 127, Michael Gray; p. 133, irmaiirma; p. 152, irmaiirma; p. 158, HandmadePictures; p. 160, irmaiirma; p. 161 (top second from right), posh; p. 161 (middle right), arinahabich; p. 209 (top second from left), arinahabich; p. 224, gitusik; p. 244, volgariver; p. 262, LaCatrina. **Julien Guttman:** p. 260. **Cathie Harvey:** p. 10. **David Harvey:** p. 1 (middle left and bottom right), p. 9 (second from right), p. 248 (left), p. 249, p. 259 (top left). **Courtesy of High 5 Pie:** p. 64 (top), p. 65 (top), p. 66. **Courtesy of I Heart Pies:** p. 232. **© Katie Parra Photography/katieparra.com:** p. 1 (top left, top right, top second from right, bottom second from right), p. 2, p. 9 (butter and bottom right), p. 49 (top left, top right, bottom left, middle right), p. 209 (top left), p. 225, p. 261 (top), **Melissa Lucier:** p.vii, p.xiv, p. 7 (right), crumbs on pp. 28–42, p. 59. **Aaron Morris:** p. 259 (top right, bottom right). **Sharin Nathan:** pp. 142–143. **Courtesy of Petsi Pies:** p.116 (top right). **Jillian Perez:** p. 174 (top and bottom), p. 175 (bottom). **Sara Remington:** p. i, p. 8, p. 9 (middle right), pp. 17–24, p. 49 (blackberries and pumpkin pie), p. 49 (bottom right), p. 60, p. 72, p. 80, p. 98, p. 105 (bottom left and right), p. 110, p. 122, p. 136, p. 139, p. 148, p. 155, p. 156, p. 161 top second from left and bottom left, p. 168, p. 184, pp. 190–191, pp. 206–208, p. 209 (middle left and bottom left), p. 212, p. 218, pp. 228–230, pp. 236, p. 241, p. 247, p. 254. p. 259 (second from top right and bottom left), pp. 270–271. **Sarah Roth:** p. 194, p. 195 (bottom), p. 196. **SHED:** p. 64 (bottom) **© Nydia Blas Williams:** p. 90.

Unless noted above, all other images are courtesy of the author.

Workman books are available at special discounts when purchased in bulk for premiums and sales promotions as well as for fund-raising or educational use. Special editions or book excerpts can also be created to specification. For details, contact the Special Sales Director at the address below, or send an email to specialmarkets@workman.com.

Workman Publishing Co., Inc.
225 Varick Street
New York, NY 10014-4381

workman.com

WORKMAN is a registered trademark of Workman Publishing Co., Inc.

Printed in the United States of America
First printing February 2014

10 9 8 7 6 5 4 3 2 1

To my mamma, the best pie baker I know

Acknowledgments

When pursuing pie, it's essential to find someone who is willing to eat at least one slice of every single pie that is presented to them and then give honest and helpful feedback. It helps to have someone who is willing to discuss soupy fruit filling strategies over the dinner table, and who will draw up very scientific charts in order to avoid devastating crust disasters. Someone who will ignore the fine dusting of flour over everything and instead simply appreciate that there's pie for breakfast every morning. A very special, love-of-your-life someone who talks you through the tragedies and celebrates the victories; a follower of dreams who refuses to let you be anything less. Aaron, thanks for being that someone.

It's also essential to have a loving and supportive family that doesn't think twice about your traveling for a year to figure out how to make pie and champions your every choice. It's especially helpful to have a mom who is both sweet and unflinchingly strong, who will teach you everything she knows about making pie. Special thanks to the whole fam, but most especially Mom, Jay, and Dave. I would never have made it this far without them.

It also helps to have a slew of incredible friends, old and new, who are willing to test recipes, eat endless pie, lend out their kitchens, and edit run-on sentences. Thank you, thank you, thank you: Jenn, Duncan, Magoo, Effie, Carly, Jenny, KaySway, Lord Weisshammer, Krissy, Arnie, Matty, Dan, Sam, Ian, Lyss, Carlnina, Adria, Mallory, Katie, Justin, Pat, Marsha, Mr. Trisher, Whitney, Josh, Julien, Ross, Leah, Erin, Jeremy, Sami, and the Morris family.

It also takes the generosity of strangers who are willing to share their homes, their kitchens, and whatever knowledge, however slight or epic it may be, they possess on the subject of pie. Thank you with a big exclamation point to the Magee family, Dani Cone, Anna Bicknell, High 5 Pie, Felicia's Atomic Lounge, Emmy's Organics, Petsi Pies, Renee McLeod, Rachel, Allison, Gillian, Sweet Sensations Pastry, Sharin Nathan, PieLab, Shanijah, Kita, Bob Roth's New River Groves, the Roth family, Alla, Rose, the Weiner family, Pie Shop, Mims Bledsoe, Belinda, the Golan family, I Heart Pies, and Emily and Nick Cofrancesco.

You also need very important people who can see a beautiful book amid the ramblings of a vagabond baker who mostly just wants to make pie. Thanks to everyone at Workman Publishing, most especially Kylie Foxx McDonald, Becky Terhune, Liz Davis, Beth Levy, Anne Kerman, Selina Meere, Jessica Wiener, and Molly Kay Frandson, for making me part of your cook-bookery family.

Contents

IN PURSUIT OF PIE   viii

CHAPTER 1

Tools of the Trade   1

CHAPTER 2

The Elements of Crust   9

CHAPTER 3

Fall: Pies to Frolic With   49

CHAPTER 4

Winter: Pies to Hibernate By   105

CHAPTER 5

Spring: Pies to Chase Away the Chill   161

CHAPTER 6

Summer: Pies to Picnic With   209

THE END, WHICH IS ACTUALLY A BEGINNING   259

INDEX   263

CONVERSION TABLES   272

In Pursuit of Pie

From: **TEENY LAMOTHE**
Subject: Pie education
Date: August 3, 2011 8:33:40 PM EDT
To: Dani Cone

Dani Cone
Owner/Lady Baker
High 5 Pie
1400 12th Avenue
Seattle, Washington 98122

Hi Dani,

My name is Teeny Lamothe and I want to be a lady pie baker. I want to learn everything there is to know about pie, one pie shop at a time, and I want to start with yours.

For as far back as I can remember, I've been baking. It started with my mom (quite the lady baker herself), who used to provide me with miniature-size tins of whatever she was making so that I could bake right alongside her. Over the years, not only have my tins gotten bigger, but so has my passion for pie. It's a tricky thing, though, turning a passion into a career, and the path toward reaching the goal of one day owning and operating my own pie shop remains unclear. I have a lot more to learn about the art of baking, as well as the ins and outs of running a business.

This is where you come in. You are a lady pie baker with the wherewithal to own and run your own pie shop, and it's you that I want to learn from. I have this irrepressible, old-world, romantic notion in my head that apprenticing is the fullest way to learn a trade: to be in a shop, learning and doing, working under a master/mentor who can provide invaluable real-world know-how.

I'm taking my education into my own hands, and embarking on what I'm fondly referring to as my "Tour of Pie." I'd like to spend a year traveling America, hopping from pie shop to pie shop, spending a month or so at each bakery, and soaking up as much experience and advice as possible. It's an ambitious project, and all the details have yet to be worked out, but it seems to be the most hands-on way to educate myself in all things pie. Total pie immersion, if you will.

While all that seems pretty perfect from my perspective, you may ask, "What's in it for me?" Well, I'm offering a free set of helpful and dedicated hands. I'm fast in the kitchen, a quick learner, and I don't need much work space. I will do anything that needs to be done, even the things that nobody else wants to do, and all I'm looking for is advice and some awesome lady baker mentoring in return. I'm also going to be blogging online about my journey, and will be able to provide as much publicity as I can muster for all the shops along the way.

I would love for High 5 Pie to be one of those pie shops. In looking over your website and reading what I can about you and your shop, I think you would be the perfect fit. Your commitment to fresh produce and homemade pastry is something I truly aspire to emulate. I sincerely hope that this idea is something that interests and inspires you, because the idea of being able to apprentice with you at High 5 Pie is definitely something that inspires me.

Please let me know if you're interested in hearing more, and even if you're not interested, I'd love to hear from you all the same. Thank you for inspiring me, and I hope we have the chance to collaborate!

Best,

Teeny Lamothe

IN THE BEGINNING

Baking has always been part of my life. It's been something that my family has done for generations; from bread to cookies, from cakes to most especially pies, the women in my family have been wonderful bakers. I spent countless hours of my childhood covered in flour, happily looking on while my grandma kneaded bread dough or my mom rolled out the perfect pie crust. I had my own miniature rolling pin that I brandished with glee and tiny pie tins that I got to press all of the leftover scraps of dough into all by myself. Pie was always my family's dessert of choice, which meant it wasn't relegated to one or two random holidays a year. Instead, we had pie all year long made with whatever fruit was currently growing in our garden. My grandma, who I'm sure learned from her mother, taught her three girls to make and love pie, and in turn my mom taught me.

I'd done a fair amount of baking alongside my mom all through high school, but it sort of fell by the wayside when I went away to college. I went halfway across the country, from my hometown of Littleton, Colorado, to Ithaca, New York, where I was much more interested in pursuing an acting career than baking the perfect pie. And as soon as I graduated I moved, full of high hopes, to Chicago, where baking was more or less forgotten. Occasionally I brought out the rolling pin my mom had gifted me when I moved into my very first grown-up apartment, either to make a pie for the odd picnic or to bake an apology pie. But for the most part baking sat in the very back of my mind, relatively untouched, for a few years.

I loved living in Chicago. By the time I was twenty-six I had made wonderful, lifelong friends, was participating in new and exciting theater, and had recently realized that I was in love with one of my very best friends, Aaron (don't worry, the feeling was mutual . . . this isn't a story of unrequited love). Everything was going swimmingly, but something that I couldn't quite put my finger on seemed to be missing. Then, in early October 2011, a tiny pie pumpkin showed up in my CSA box and changed everything.

As I peered at our bounty of veggies I had no inkling of the impact that pumpkin would have on my life. I simply knew that we had been given an adorable pumpkin that came with a recipe for pie; and Aaron, best-friend-love-of-my-life, and I loved pie. Using a childhood recipe and inexpertly channeling my mom's knack for rolling out dough, I managed to make a pretty presentable crust while Aaron followed the CSA recipe to make a delightful filling of roasted pumpkin, honey, and fragrant spices. We whisked, mixed, and baked ourselves a perfect pumpkin pie—and a new tradition of Sunday evening baking was born.

PIE TIMES

Each Sunday that fall we filled our apartment with the quintessential smells of autumn and with old-timey music that demanded we dance to it in our stocking feet. The oven kept our tiny kitchen toasty all throughout the blustery Chicago winter, and the weeks flew by because mornings were filled with coffee and breakfast pie. We had friends who gladly trooped through the winter snow to share in slices of Bourbon Bacon Pecan Pie and apple pie; friends who brought with them good conversation and more often than not whiskey and apple cider.

Sometime during those first few baking-filled months, my mom sent along the tiny tins of my childhood, and I would break them out whenever there was excess dough or filling, baking one or two "Teeny Pies" along with the large one. Soon one pie a week had turned into two or three; we passed the winter with apples, pumpkins, sweet potatoes, and a fairly consistent sugar high, until I met the spring with the vague idea of a lady bakership floating in my head. The lease on our apartment would be up in July, Aaron was leaving for the year to get his master's in education from Harvard, and while I loved the family I'd been nannying for, the upcoming fall seemed like the perfect time to try something new.

I was intrigued by the idea of going to pastry school and learning anything and everything about baked goods, but I also knew that I wanted to focus mainly on pie, and that wasn't necessarily possible in a superstructured school environment. I wanted to navigate myself away from being a home baker and closer to becoming a professional pie baker, perhaps one day even a pie shop owner. I wanted time to focus solely on pie, and I wanted some really stellar bakers to teach me what they knew, not only about baking but about what it meant to own and operate a small business. I just had no idea how to accomplish such a thing.

BUTCHER, BAKER . . . LADY PIE-MAKER?

Since I'd begun thinking about baking professionally, I'd fallen in love with the idea of becoming a baker's apprentice. Apprenticing seemed romantic, taking up a vocation and learning from the best of the best. It also seemed like a good way to build a small and supportive group of people who loved pie as much as I did. I was determined to learn from female bakers specifically; I wanted to study under strong women who'd had the gumption to open their own shops, in the hopes that one day I might be like them. I wanted to learn from ladies who were helping to reintroduce pie to a cupcake-crazed world by using their grandmothers' and great-grandmothers' timeless recipes. And I figured that by turning a single apprenticeship into a series of apprenticeships, I could travel and collect multiple pie mentors along the way. The "Tour of Pie"—an apprenticing odyssey that would take me from pie shop to pie shop and various points in between—began to take shape.

The plan was to get in touch with as many popular pie shops as I could and offer myself as an unpaid hand eager to do anything and everything pertaining to pie. I would travel from place to place, picking up new skills and honing those that I already had. I'd meet pie people from all over, draw inspiration from working with them, and hopefully make a few friends along the way. I'd also get to delve into all of those mysterious, region-specific pies, like shoofly and chess pies, depending on how far and wide I managed to travel.

Because I was forgoing a traditional pastry school education, complete with a pastry school degree, in favor of a vagabond year of baking, I thought it only fitting to work toward a degree of my own invention: a "lady bakership." I created a list of "lady bakership lessons" (you'll find them sprinkled throughout the book)—essentially the skills and knowledge I needed to acquire and goals I had to achieve in order to become an outstanding pie baker. I also wanted to become proficient enough in small business management to embark on the next insanely intimidating step of the adventure: becoming the owner of a pie business. It was through completing this path to pie, and ultimately to pie business, that I would officially become a Lady Pie Baker.

EPIC ADVENTURE OR EPIC FAIL?

Once I'd decided to go ahead with this rather harebrained but altogether thrilling idea, I drafted and redrafted several versions of my "pie proposal of epic proportions." I tried to infuse it with the right amount of warmth, passion, and can-do spirit—without sounding like a crazy person. But the moment I sent the email (to thirty different pie shops, all told) I wanted to snatch it back. I had put some pretty big hopes and dreams on the line, and everything felt much safer while it sat as a draft in my outbox. Was I ready to make myself so vulnerable, to leave a city I knew so well and move from town to town, effectively starting over month after month? And especially to leave behind my dear friends, to try to forge new friendships with complete strangers?

It turns out I'd have plenty of time to wonder: Days and then weeks went by with no response to my beautifully crafted pie plea. I could only conclude either that change wasn't in the cards for me, or that bakers simply didn't check their email. I kept my fingers crossed for the latter. After three torturous weeks of waiting I'd had a few sincere apologies from shops that didn't have the time or space to host an apprentice, but no one had said yes. I was checking my email constantly, getting more anxious each day, when I finally got the answer I was looking for. Dani Cone, owner of Seattle's High 5 Pie and author of *Cutie Pies*, got in touch with a resounding YES! With that the tour had a beginning, and there was no turning back.

A PIE FAREWELL

July was suddenly upon us, and Aaron and I began packing up our apartment. Aaron headed to Cambridge, Massachusetts, while I stayed in Chicago another month, attempting to line up a few more bakeries and prepping for the trip. I began a blog, figuring it would be a fun way to stay in touch with my friends. I titled it *Teeny Pies,* with the tagline, "Saving the World, One Pie at a Time," never imagining how many people would end up reading my blog over the course of the next year. As the end of the month got closer and closer, I decided the best way to kick off the tour and say good-bye to all my friends was to have a huge party: a pie party, where there would be food, drinks, and copious amounts of pie. Friends could preorder from a three-pie menu (Bourbon Bacon Pecan, Sweet Potato, and Bluebarb), or have slices of what was available day-of. Two of my best Chicago friends, Jenn and Duncan, lent me their kitchen for the baking and the rest of their apartment for the party, claiming a Bourbon Bacon Pecan Pie as the only form of payment.

The day before I started the great bake-off, the fridge was packed with fresh fruit and freshly made crust dough, ready to be rolled out. Bags of flour, sugar, and pecans lined the counter next to the empty pie tins that were just waiting to be filled. I had a handful of helpers the next day, washing and chopping fruit, frying bacon, and "sampling" the bourbon. The summer heat soon made the kitchen absolutely unbearable, but by taking frequent breaks to go stand in front of the oscillating fan, we managed to coax twenty-five nine-inch pies, countless star-shaped crust cookies, and dozens of Teeny Pies out of one tiny little oven. We decorated the tables with aprons and other pie paraphernalia; freshly baked pies rested on every available surface. I looked around, surrounded by the people I loved, all rooting for me to succeed, and it finally felt real: The Tour of Pie was under way.

AND SO IT BEGINS . . .

I could not have imagined at the start of all of this that my pie journey would culminate in the writing of a cookbook. Now that it's here in front of me, I'm thrilled to be able to prattle on about pie. This book is many things. First and foremost it's a cookbook with pie recipes of my own invention as well as recipes from the bakers who generously opened their doors to me during my apprentice year. It's also a traveler's log chronicling the time spent in each of those wonderful shops and the things I learned along the way. But most important, it's *your* guide to adventures in pie. I hope you'll use it often: Smear it with butter, dust it with flour, stain it with berry juice, and most of all, make a lot of pie.

A FEW HUNDRED WORDS ON BAKING SEASONALLY

I am one of those people who firmly believe that to bake the best pie possible, you must use seasonal ingredients whenever you can. This means using fresh, plump pie pumpkins in the fall and the sweetest of strawberries in the summer. Raspberries and blackberries should be plucked from their well-protected, prickly bushes when they are the perfect combination of sweet and tart. Pecans, cream, and sugar can help chase away the new chill brought on by fall, and rather than trying to force unripe berries or pitted fruits to taste good in the dead of winter, you can experiment with sweet potatoes mixed with a touch of honey and cinnamon. Each season comes with its own set of perfect ingredients.

I grew up in a family of enthusiastic gardeners. There were raspberries and chokecherries growing just steps away from my back porch. Our little Colorado suburb was tucked right up against the foothills of the Rockies, and the looming mountains were only a half hour's drive away. My grandparents, uncle, and aunts all lived twenty minutes from us, and everyone got together at least once a week, oftentimes more, to share a meal or to make jam or pickle cucumbers. It was wonderful growing up in such a tight-knit family.

My childhood backyard was nice in that generic grass-and-a-few-trees sort of way, but the garden was truly wonderful. Large stalks of rhubarb grew with abandon in a rather forgotten corner, while the strawberries had their very own patch and required constant weeding throughout the summer to prevent bindweed from overtaking them on a weekly basis. Pumpkins plumped and rounded all through August and September before my brother and I carved them with ghoulish faces in October. The smaller, sweeter, and far less interesting pumpkins, according to our adolescent selves, were our mom's responsibility—to be used for roasted seeds and pumpkin pie.

My grandmother grew the plums, blackberries, and gooseberries, while my aunt provided the apples and sour cherries. Anything we didn't use by the end of the season we canned and stored for the frigid and fruitless winters. Surrounded by this homegrown bounty, I came to understand that good pies (good anything, foodwise) came from fresh, in-season ingredients. I learned when to bake with berries, pitted fruits, or pumpkins based on what was ripe in the backyard. By tasting, testing, and trying all sorts of fruits and veggies from our garden, I discovered the seasons with my senses.

While I was on the Tour of Pie a few friends asked why I chose to be in the northern states when it was cold and the southern states when it was hot, rather than the other way around. They were curious to know why I didn't turn this trip into an opportunity to take a vacation from the normal seasons.

The truth is, I wanted to experience Atlanta in the middle of July, because it would ensure that I was there during the height of peach season. And I managed to be in Seattle while the wild blackberries were still ripe and found myself apple-picking my way through an Upstate New York fall. I wasn't interested in taking a vacation from the seasons; I was interested in embracing them.

I don't think you have to grow all of your own fruit in order to make good pies (although I do dream of the day when I can have a garden that will rival my mom's), but I do value seasonal baking. By using ingredients that are at the peak of ripeness, the bulk of the work is already done for you; you can simply enjoy the wonderful, robust flavors that shine through.

Tools of the Trade

I *moved to Chicago straight out of undergrad,* and somehow I managed to accumulate an entire dowry's worth of stuff during the four years I lived there. By dowry, I mean you could have married me off to the highest bidder and we wouldn't have had to register for a single thing. I had linens, a hope chest, the family china, and every kitchen gadget imaginable. I even had an egg machine that apparently cooked eggs twelve different ways. Needless to say, when it came time to pare down my life to a single bag

Crust making!

before beginning my year of pie baking, I became a bit panicked. Once I stopped hyperventilating, however, I realized that aside from a few baking clothes all I really needed were three things: a rolling pin, a pie plate, and a pastry cutter. Those are the only truly essential kitchen tools you need to make pie (and even the pastry cutter isn't entirely essential because a fork or your fingers will do in a pinch). There are countless other gadgets and tools—outlined below—that will make your pie baking easier or more fun, but in the end all you really need are those three little things, and all of them fit in a suitcase.

ROLLING PINS

In order to make a pie you will need some sort of rolling device. The most obvious choice is a rolling pin. That doesn't mean I haven't used an especially tall water glass or an empty wine bottle when there was a desperate need for pie and not a single pin to be found. But a rolling pin is best.

If you're looking to purchase a rolling pin

before embarking on your own pie adventure, you have some options to consider. In my world there are two types of pins: wooden rods and rollers.

ROD ROLLING PINS, also known as French rolling pins, are simply solid pieces of wood that have been whittled down to a cylindrical shape and in many cases have tapered ends that help with pivoting. When you roll out crust with a rod pin you are using the weight of your palms to guide the pin, and therefore the dough, into the shape you are trying to achieve. The difficulty with this pin comes with knowing how much pressure to apply, because too much weight with soft dough will drive your crust into the counter and leave you with a sticky mess. Your hands are also in direct contact with the rolling surface, so they can cause the dough to warm faster than it will when you use a roller pin. I find that these pins are easiest to use when you've let your crust chill in the fridge overnight (something I generally advocate anyway). The longer the dough sits in the fridge, the firmer it gets, and then you can use as much pressure as you need to roll out your crust without fear of squashing it. Rod rolling pins are lovely, and if you're feeling particularly Parisian, you should go for it and get one.

ROLLER ROLLING PINS are the ones with a large cylindrical roller and an internal axle that attaches to two smaller handles at either end. I find these pins really easy to use, because it seems as though the pin does most

of the work. As opposed to using only your hands and your weight to push the dough into a circular shape, you can exert half the effort and the pin will help with the other half. However, you do have to concentrate on rolling fairly evenly with roller pins; otherwise you'll end up with a crust amoeba.

I have one of each of these pins, and I tend to switch it up every other pie so neither pin feels neglected; I wouldn't want feelings of jealousy to flare up. Essentially, they both work really well . . . you just have to go with what works best for you.

Rolling pins are made of all sorts of materials. Glass, plastic, Teflon, marble, and wood are all pin possibilities. I definitely prefer wooden pins, because they are light enough to use for long periods of time and heavy enough to get the job done. There is an added bonus to using a wooden pin that I think makes them particularly wonderful: The more dough you roll out, the softer and more lovely your pin becomes. With every roll, the oils from the fats in your dough are absorbed by the wood. So, if you are in fact using a wooden rolling pin, never use soap and water to wash it. A simple wipe-down with a damp towel should do the trick. If you want to get fancy, you can oil your rolling pin with bee's oil to keep it in top shape. I prefer to make more pie instead.

PIE PLATES

Pie plates, I think, come down to personal preference. Disposable aluminum pans are fine to use, and can be found at any grocery store, but they are kind of a one-pie deal. So I would recommend buying an actual pie plate if you're planning on making this particular deliciousness part of your life. Non-disposable pie plates come in a variety of shapes and sizes and are made out of lots of different materials. I like a simple nine-inch plate without handles, and most often I use metal or ceramic rather than glass. (When I've used clear glass plates, the bottom crust always seems to take longer to bake through, which sometimes turns the filling to mush. Metal and ceramic, on the other hand, tend to heat more evenly so it's much easier to achieve a crispier bottom crust with shorter bake times.)

Shiny metal pie plates do not bake the bottom crust as well because the metal deflects the heat, which is why I prefer metal plates with a darker, nonstick finish. Bake

a few pies in different plates until you find one or two that you can't live without. I just recently got my first ceramic pie plate and I am smitten with it. Whichever pie plate makes you want to make endless amounts of pie is a keeper.

LITTLE PIES, aka Teeny Pies, are my favorite size pie to make. I haven't met a single person who can contain his or her excitement at these itty-  bitties' general adorableness. At just five inches across from edge to edge, they are the perfect size for an indulgent large dessert for one; split down the middle, they make a lovely treat for two.

Each of the recipes marked with a in this book makes between four and six 5-inch pies. Because I tend to make so many Teeny Pies at a time, for these I like to buy disposable plates in bulk from The WEBstaurant Store (webstaurantstore.com). They have crazy deals where you can buy hundreds of pans for less than twenty bucks, but if you're looking to live a simple life that doesn't include large sleeves of pie pans crammed in every available cupboard, Amazon.com sells a useful little set of four nonstick mini pie plates as well as smaller quantities of disposable pans. Regardless of which direction you choose, just make sure the tins measure five inches across the top.

PASTRY CUTTER

My mom taught me to make crusts using a pastry cutter, and since then my kitchen drawers have always contained at least one. They are super helpful when you're making only one or two pies at a time because they make quick work of cutting the butter or shortening into the dry ingredients, helping to achieve those perfect pea-size bits. Having spent the year in borrowed kitchens, however, it turns out most people have no idea what a pastry cutter is or what one looks like. Most likely you've seen them in the baking section and simply passed them over. Also sold as pastry blenders, they are a pretty simple tool: Thin strips of metal or wire stretch in an arc and attach to two ends of a handle, almost as if you'd untwisted the head of a whisk and affixed it to the handle of a snow shovel. They are reminiscent of a miniature potato masher and are used similarly; however, rather than mashing your fats they cut into them.

Pastry cutters are helpful but not imperative to the pie-making process. If you don't have one, don't panic! You can use a fork, two knives, or even your fingers instead; just be aware that you may struggle to break up the cold, hard fat and that the heat from your hands may affect the temperature—and thus the flakiness—of the dough.

ELECTRIC MIXER AND/OR FOOD PROCESSOR

Having lived the life of a vagabond pie baker where it was impossible to pack my KitchenAid into my carry-on—despite how much I would have used it—I've come to the conclusion that neither an electric mixer nor a food processor is necessary to the pie process. Will they make your life easier? Of course. Are they a valuable investment? Yes! Should not having them be the deciding factor for whether or not you make a pie? Of course not! If you need to grind graham crackers or crush a cupful of nuts, stick them in a ziplock bag and roll over them with your rolling pin.

If you need to cream butter until it's light and fluffy, stir it with a wooden spoon until your arm feels like it will fall off. You could also consider getting a handheld mixer and tiny food processor if you'd like a little extra assistance without the expense.

MEASURING CUPS, MEASURING SPOONS, AND BOWLS

I use both plastic and metal measuring cups and spoons. I don't think there is much of an advantage to using one or the other. I know my mom prefers to have long skinny spoons so they can fit through nearly any spice lid the world has to offer, but I rarely worry about that. I do think, however, you should have at least one stellar stainless-steel bowl. Not only can you put them in the fridge to chill when making crust or whipped cream, but you can use them as a double boiler—which is absolutely essential when working

with chocolate or making a curd. If you don't have a stainless-steel bowl, it should be on the top of your wish list.

It's also important to understand that liquid measuring cups are slightly different from dry measuring cups. So, you should have a set of dry measuring cups for your dry ingredients and at least one 1-cup liquid measuring cup for all of your liquid ingredients.

CRUST COVER

Crust covers are just what they sound like—a simple ring of metal or silicone that you place atop your crust to prevent it from burning. They're pretty useful if you're like me and have a tendency to forget you have a pie in the oven—at least the outer crust won't get scorched. A cover is also great for those pies that have an extended bake time in the oven. Your decorative crimp won't get too toasty while you let the bottom crust crisp and the insides fully bake. A quick substitute would be a few strips of aluminum foil carefully folded over your crimp.

THE BIRDS AND THE BEADS

PIE BIRDS were really not on my radar until I began the Tour of Pie. Pie birds are little ceramic birds that are placed in the middle of a pie and act  like a chimney to help steam escape so the filling doesn't bubble and boil over. Rather than having to cut steam vents directly into your crust you can use a pie bird instead; instructions are on page 23.

    PIE BEADS, which are also known as pie weights, are super helpful when prebaking a crust (see page 25). Some pies, such as lemon meringue or any sort of cream pie, require a prebaked shell. If you don't have any pie  beads handy, dried beans make a quick and inexpensive substitute. The pie beads or dried beans are placed in the unbaked foil- or parchment-lined crust to prevent it from shrinking and puffing during baking.

FINE GRATER OR ZESTER

This may be the one and only kitchen implement that you simply cannot replace with anything else. Citrus zest is one of those magical ingredients that I fell in love with when I began baking. Not only is it always pretty, it packs a pretty serious flavor punch without adding any excess liquid. This can help you avoid having a soupy pie without having to sacrifice any stellar flavor. A very fine grater or an "official" zester is necessary to get those little citrus shavings I'm sure you'll also come to love and enjoy. Microplane is a brand I count on.

    In a pinch you can substitute almost everything in this section and make yourself a decent pie, so don't hesitate to start baking!

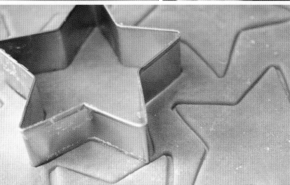

CHAPTER 2

The Elements of Crust

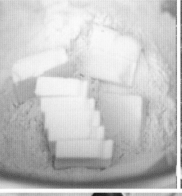

One of my most vivid childhood memories is of perching on a tall kitchen stool next to my mom, wielding my miniature rolling pin in an entirely sincere attempt to imitate her fluid crust-rolling movements. My mom's knack for making a good pie crust always made anything *not* homemade seem a bit silly. She would roll out the crust with ease, occasionally letting me help by using my little fingers to crimp the edges, and would always press the leftover dough into the tiniest of tins, sprinkle it with cinnamon sugar, and

Baking as a wee tot

bake it off for snacking later. My mom is the reason I never felt any trepidation when endeavoring to make a pie. When I moved to Chicago she sent a kitchen start-up kit that included a pastry cutter, a rolling pin, and a pie plate. She encouraged the baking of pies for birthdays, apologies, and holidays; anything and everything was a good enough reason for pie.

In pie everything starts with the crust. It is the foundation, the base, and can make all the difference between a mediocre, slightly soggy, sometimes surprisingly chewy slice of pie and one with a light and flaky crust that's still sturdy enough to envelop a decadent filling. When you start with a good crust, everything else seems to fall into place. Had I not grown up baking with my mom, I imagine I would have had a healthy dose of fear when it came time to attempt my first pie crust. Instead, I just did it, and then kept on doing

it until I got good at it. It took time and patience, and I definitely threw away plenty of overworked dough, but in the end I learned how to make a crust I could proudly call my own. I started with my mom's favorite recipe, which calls for shortening, all-purpose flour, and warm water. While I found a certain ease with that recipe, Aaron wanted a crust with a little more character and brought home a bag of whole wheat flour to play with. So in went the whole wheat flour. To complement its slightly nutty flavor, I added a little butter for richness and vodka to help with the flakiness (don't worry, the alcohol cooks out). I tinkered and tweaked until my taste buds (and Aaron's) were satisfied.

With my signature recipe in my back pocket, I was especially excited to see how other bakers tackled this most essential pie element. Each of the shops on my tour had their own special way of doing things, whether it was using a very specific type of flour; vinegar instead of vodka; all butter, all shortening, or some combo of the two. No matter what ingredients or methods they chose, they all shared an unwavering pride in their crusts. Which is the way it should be: There is something undeniably rewarding about mixing together a batch of crust from scratch.

At least, it's undeniably rewarding until it doesn't work; dealing with temperamental dough is just the worst. After my Tour of Pie, I moved with Aaron to Washington, D.C., and during my first few weeks of living there, every batch of dough I made was incredibly difficult to roll out. Each one fell apart before I could even get it into the tin, and soon I was banging my head against my new cupboards in frustration, taking (large) sips of (cheap) vodka to get through

the traumatic process. Aaron suggested I change one variable at a time, and he drew up a pie chart to help me figure out what the problem was. I tried combining flours. I tried using different mixing methods. I even tried leaving water out on the counter to let the chlorine evaporate before using it, which in retrospect was the silliest of everything I tried. It turns out that because my D.C. kitchen was smaller than my previous one in Chicago, it tended to retain any and all excess heat and humidity in the air, making for some very melty crust dough. The solution was to start refrigerating my shortening and letting my dough rest in the fridge a little longer. With those few changes, my crusts began to roll out beautifully.

I was surprised that such a small detail, like the few degrees difference of my tiny kitchen, could make such a huge difference in my dough. But I learned a valuable lesson about the importance of trial and error and also of sticking with it. Making a homemade crust is something I got better at and more confident about over time, and I'm sure the same will be true of you. To give you a head start, here are a few things I learned that will help you turn out perfect crust every time:

THE 5 COMMANDMENTS OF CRUST

1. **START WITH INGREDIENTS THAT YOU LOVE.** I have a crush on whole wheat flour because I love the nutty flavor and toothsome texture it imparts. However, whole wheat flour can be temperamental on its own, so I like to tame it with some all-purpose flour. For fats, I go with butter, which makes the crust tasty, *and* shortening, which makes it flaky. After testing and tinkering with different flours, I've homed in on a few favorites, which you'll see described in the box on page 13.

2. **GIVE YOURSELF ENOUGH TIME.** I find that when I rush, I end up adding too much flour or too little fat and in the end am left with a stubbornly unworkable lump of dough. Most crust recipes call for a chilled resting period for your completed dough as well, and I've found that this step is essential. Once I've made several batches of dough and wrapped the individual disks in plastic wrap, I let them sit in the refrigerator for at least an hour (and usually overnight) before attempting to roll them out. The longer the dough rests in the refrigerator, the easier it becomes to work with. If you try to roll out a crust when it's too warm, it will fall apart and you'll end up just getting frustrated. You can even make it the day before you plan on baking, as I often do, to give it extra time in the refrigerator.

3. **CHILL A COUPLE OF YOUR KEY INGREDIENTS.** I've had people swear that a good pie crust is absolutely impossible unless you use the coldest possible ingredients. This is somewhat true: Cold ingredients do make the dough easier to work with in the long run. But they don't have to be rock solid or absolutely frigid to make a good dough. It's all a balance when you're working with pastry. I never like to fist-fight with frozen butter in order to obtain those perfect pea-size pieces, but at the same time, the colder the butter, the more it maintains its shape, which ultimately leads to those flaky layers we all adore. So I tend to split the difference by storing my butter and shortening in the refrigerator to keep them cold, then letting them warm on the counter for five minutes before making dough. That way they're not stubbornly stiff when I go to cut the fats

into my flour. I also prefer to use ice water and/or chilled vodka rather than tepid tap water. While I was in Ithaca, New York, on the Tour of Pie, my friend Alyssa put her flour in the freezer to chill it before we made our crust. It's not a practice I picked up because I happen to have the smallest, most jam-packed freezer in the world, but it's certainly something to keep in mind if you have the space.

4. **DON'T OVERWORK YOUR DOUGH.**

It's incredibly squishy when you mix it up, and I am all for using your hands to work everything together, but resist the temptation to knead the dough. It's not that kind of dough, so the more you touch it, squish it, squash it, and roll it around the stronger the gluten becomes and the tougher your crust will be.

5. **KNOW WHEN TO THROW IN THE TOWEL,** dump the whole mess, and start fresh. One of the most valuable lessons my mom ever taught me was that if you've reached a breaking point because your dough is still too sticky or overly crumbly and you're considering brandishing a rolling pin at the next person who walks into the kitchen, put the pin down, take a deep breath, and know that it's okay to scrap it and begin again.

Whole Wheat Flour Made Easy

The low gluten content of whole wheat flour can make it challenging to work with. The recipes in this book take that into account with the addition of all-purpose flour, but there are a few different whole wheat flour options that can also make your life a little easier.

I like to use white whole wheat flour whenever possible. First, it's fairly light in color and therefore doesn't darken too quickly during baking. It's also usually close in texture to all-purpose flour, so you get that wonderful flavor without the denseness that some whole wheat flours can impart. Trader Joe's 100% White Whole Wheat is my top pick because it produces a light and flaky crust with a hint of whole-wheat goodness; I also like Gold Medal White Whole Wheat and King Arthur Unbleached White Whole Wheat. If I can't find any of those options, Gold Medal's Stone Ground Whole Wheat Flour is my go-to.

KEY INGREDIENTS AND TECHNIQUES

FAVORED FLOURS

My go-to Whole Wheat Crust (page 28) is made with equal parts whole wheat and all-purpose flour. The whole wheat is slightly nutty and, I think, especially nice with sweeter, fruitier pies. Although whole wheat flour is heartier than its all-purpose cousin, it's still possible to achieve a flaky crust with it, and in my opinion the flour helps make it more substantial. However, whole wheat flour contains less gluten than all-purpose flour, which means this dough doesn't bind together as readily or provide quite as much elasticity as an exclusively all-purpose-flour dough. But no matter; if you give the dough enough time to rest in the refrigerator, it's just as easy to roll out.

That said, sometimes a crust that's incredibly flavorful all by itself isn't what you're looking for, especially when you're pairing it with something fairly subtle (such as banana cream pie) or something particularly complex that would compete with a more robust crust (like the Reuben Potpies on page 253). In those cases you may wish to use one of the all-purpose crusts on pages 29 to 31. For more information on the specific brands of whole wheat flour I prefer, see the box on page 13.

ABOUT FATS

As far as fats are concerned, I like a mixture of shortening and butter for all of my pie crusts (except for Mom's All-Shortening Double Crust—because it's great and, hey, it's my mom's): The butter provides the flavor and the shortening provides the flaky tenderness that makes a crust truly wonderful. When choosing butters, it's generally better to use unsalted, because then you know exactly how much salt is going into your dough and can guarantee it will taste the way you want it to. But if salted butter is all you have in the fridge, don't hesitate to use it; simply use half the salt that's called for in the recipe.

Crisco is my shortening of choice, and after a recent bout with a million melty crusts I started storing it in the fridge rather than the pantry. Depending on the warmth of your kitchen you can decide where to store your shortening, but it will keep equally well at room temperature and chilled. If you have an aversion to either butter or shortening, you can simply substitute one with the other in whatever measurement the recipe calls for.

Lard is another fat option, but one that I know little about firsthand. Neither my mom nor my grandmother used it for her pie crusts, and as a result I never use it either. Lard is rendered pig fat, and when rendered correctly it tastes like nothing. Similar to shortening, it's simply used to make a flaky pastry dough. A lot of recipes call for half lard and half butter, which makes for a flaky yet rich flavor. Leaf lard is the most common kind of lard used in baking because when it's rendered correctly there isn't even the slightest hint of pork flavor. Lard can be used in place of shortening or butter in any of your favorite crust recipes.

BRING ON THE BOOZE

Because pie crust technically needs only three ingredients—flour, fat, and a liquid binding agent—there are hundreds of variations to build on the basics, with the addition of salt, sugar, eggs, vinegar, and so on rounding things out. While I was experimenting with different recipes and developing my signature crust, I came across an article in *Cook's Illustrated* that claimed vodka is the secret to a flakier crust. Vodka, it turns out, evaporates faster than water at high temperatures, so

LIQUOR FOR THE LITTLES?

Worried about the littlest pie lovers getting tipsy on your crust? No need to fret—the bake times and temps ensure that any and all alcohol gets baked out by the time your pie comes out of the oven. The only evidence that there was any vodka at all will be your delightfully flaky crust. Cheers!

when it's used in pie crust it helps produce a much flakier final product. Because I was focused on using whole wheat flour, it seemed like the perfect solution to achieving a lighter, flakier crust than if I were to use only ice water. Vodka works really well in a crust that contains whole wheat flour, but it's just as good in a crust made of all-purpose flour alone. If you have an aversion to using vodka, you can use all ice water instead of half vodka and half ice water. If you do decide to use vodka as one of your liquids, the quality of the liquor doesn't matter whatsoever. There's absolutely no residual taste left in the crust once you've baked it . . . plus a few sips here and there will steel your nerves for the rolling-out process!

MIXING METHODS

If you're making a single batch of dough, the simplest way to combine wet and dry ingredients is with a pastry cutter (see page 5). Once you've mixed the dry ingredients together, you'll want to add your fats and break them up by cutting into them with the pastry cutter until each piece of butter and/or shortening is the size of a small pea and coated in flour. At that point you'll add the liquids and begin to gently press the dough together with a rubber spatula or your hands, gathering the tiny crumbs from the bottom of the bowl and continuing to press them into a large ball of dough.

A WORD OF CAUTION

The danger in using a mixer or a food processor is the possibility of overworking your dough. That's why it's important to mix only as long as it takes to bring everything together. If you've pulsed one too many times or mixed too long and the dough comes out the consistency of mashed potatoes, I'm sorry to say it but . . . you should start over.

If you're making more than one batch of dough in a day, it's faster and easier on your hands to use a stand mixer or a food processor. For a mixer, use the paddle attachment to combine the flour, salt, sugar, and any other dry ingredients. Then cut your cold fats into small squares and add them to the bowl. It's best to mix everything together on a low setting, letting the paddle break up the fats into the desired size. At this point you can slowly add your liquid and mix until everything just comes together. If you're using a food processor, you'll want to mix the dry ingredients together and then pulse in the fats only as many times as it takes to get them to the size of small peas. Then, transfer the whole mix to a large bowl and slowly add the liquid, using a spatula or your hands to press the dough into a large ball.

Regardless of your mixing method, once your dough comes together, you can shape it into a ball if you're making a single-crust batch of dough, or separate it into two balls if you're making a double-crust batch of dough. Press the ball(s) into flat disks, wrap in plastic, and chill immediately. (The dough disks will keep this way for several days in the refrigerator or you can freeze them as directed on page 26.)

READY TO ROLL

Once you've successfully made your dough and let it chill out for a while in the fridge, you're ready to roll it out.

1. Sprinkle your counter and rolling pin with a generous pinch of flour [A]. (You'll want to use up to 3 tablespoons for each dough disk (or batch of Teeny disks.)

2. Unwrap the disk of dough, place it on the floured surface, and roll it out in an X pattern: Starting in the middle of the disk, roll once diagonally to the top right section and back down to the bottom left section of the disk [B]. Again, starting in the middle of the disk, roll once to the top left section and back down to the bottom right section.

3. Lift up the dough, sprinkle the counter with flour if necessary, and turn the dough 90 degrees. Starting in the center, roll another X pattern before turning your dough again.

4. Continue to roll out the dough from the center of the disk in a uniform X pattern, turning regularly until the disk is about 6 inches across [C] (about 3 inches across for Teeny Pies).

5. Carefully lift the dough from one side and drape it over your hand while you sprinkle the counter with more flour. Gently place the dough downside up on the newly floured surface.

6. Continue to roll and turn the dough in this X pattern until it forms a rough [D]

Flour Is Your Friend

- Keep the bag of flour next to you and sprinkle some on the counter whenever the dough gets sticky. I like to use all-purpose flour when I'm rolling out my dough, even with my whole wheat crusts, because it has a much finer consistency, but if whole wheat flour is all you have, it will work just as well.

- Rotate and flip the dough often so that it has little opportunity to stick. After every few rolls, pick up the dough, sprinkle the counter with flour, and begin rolling again with the dough downside up (i.e., on the "wrong" side).

- On your first few tries rolling out the dough, you'll probably produce more of an amoeba shape than a circle. That's okay. Keep at it and remember to rotate the dough often and flour the surface regularly, which will make the whole production a little less sticky.

circle about 11 inches across (about 6 inches for Teeny Pies). You're looking to create a vaguely circular shape that's slightly larger than your pie plate. The crust should have a ¾-inch overhang, which gives you plenty of dough to tuck under and creates a much fuller and more toothsome crimp. If there's more than a ¾-inch overhang, trim away the excess.

LINING THE PIE PLATE

Once the dough is slightly larger than your pie plate, you'll want to pick it up and lay it in.

1. Position your plate so it's right behind your rolled-out crust. Fold your dough in half [A], gently pick it up from the folded side (being careful not to squish the two sides together), and, supporting it with your hands, center it over your pie plate [B].

2. Unfold your dough and gently press it into the bottom and up the sides of the dish [C]. There will be about ¾ inch of overhang along the side of the plate; if there's more than that, trim the excess evenly [D].

3. If you're making a single-crust pie, fold the overhang under along the edge of the pie plate and crimp it (see page 19). For a double-crust pie, simply leave the

Liner Notes

If your crust decides to stick to the counter or tear while you are transferring it to the plate, you can always reshape it into a flat disk and start again. The nature of pie crust dough allows for just one extra reroll. Any more than that and your dough will begin to get tough and you'll be left with a chewy crust. So, if at first you don't succeed, try just once more.

overhang (trimming it if necessary to make it even) until you've filled your pie and placed the second crust on top (see page 22). Then tuck both overhanging crusts under along the edge and crimp to seal in the insides.

CRIMPING THE CRUST

The crimp of a pie is the decorative edge along its perimeter. There are a million different ways to crimp a crust . . . well maybe not a million, but it seems to me that everyone I've met in the pie world has his or her own way of doing it. Some people like a thick crimp, for that extra bite of crumbly crust at the end of a slice; some people crimp for speed; and some people have a crimp so complicated even I've had trouble getting the hang of it.

Following are a couple of options, including my favorite, the V crimp. If you have some time on your hands, you can Google "how to crimp a pie crust" and delve into a few of those million different techniques. Who knows, you may find your signature crimp.

THE V CRIMP

1. Form a small V with your thumb and pointer finger [A].

2. Using the pointer finger of your other hand, push the dough into the other two fingers, letting that natural V shape the dough [B].

3. Repeat, working your way around the edge of the crust [C].

Crimp Tip

Fork-crimped crusts tend to darken really quickly, so watch them carefully when baking.

THE FORK CRIMP

1. Press the tines of a fork into the tucked-under edge of crust, pressing hard enough to leave an indentation [A].

2. Repeat, working your way around the edge of the crust and lining up the tines beside each of the previous indentations [B].

THE CARE AND HANDLING OF TEENY PIES

Rolling out and lining Teeny Pies—my little 5-inch favorites—is basically the same as rolling out a regular 9-inch pie; there are just more pies and they are smaller. The recipe in this book for whole wheat crust is ideal for Teeny Pies, because the nuttiness of the flour adds an entirely new level of flavor to these tiny desserts. A batch of Whole Wheat Crust dough (page 28) makes enough for four Teeny Pies with top and bottom crusts, or eight Teeny Pies with bottoms only; the Savory Pie Crust (page 32) makes six Teeny Pies with double crusts.

I separate my chilled dough into equal-size balls before I start rolling out, so there's no moment of panic when I realize I've run out of dough and I'm a pie crust short. I also like to put each finished crust-lined plate back into the fridge while I roll out the next one, so the dough stays nice and chilled. If I'm making Teeny Pies that require a top and a bottom crust, the order in which I do things is as follows:

1. Roll out a bottom crust into a circle roughly 6 inches in diameter. Use it to line a pie plate and put it directly into the fridge. Repeat with the remaining bottom crusts.

2. Roll out all the top crusts into roughly 6-inch circles, stack them on a plate, separated by small sheets of wax paper or plastic wrap, and put them in the fridge.

3. Remove the lined pie plates from the refrigerator and divide the filling among them.

4. Place the top crusts on the pies, crimp to seal the edges, and bake as directed (noted in Make 'Em Teeny Pies throughout).

LAYING ON A TOP CRUST

1. Roll out your top crust the same way you rolled out the bottom crust (see page 17), making a circle that's about 11 inches in diameter [A]. Gently fold the circle of dough in half, pick it up from the fold, and supporting it with your hand, center it directly over the filling and bottom crust [B].

2. Carefully unfold the crust and make any slight adjustments to center the top crust over the pie [C].

3. As with the bottom crust, you want a ¾-inch overhang around the edge; trim off any excess dough with a paring knife [D]. Tuck the overhanging top crust under the overhanging bottom crust [E] and crimp all the way around to seal in the filling [F].

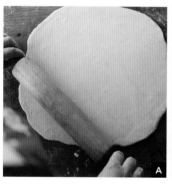

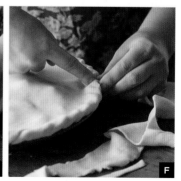

VENTING A TOP CRUST

A double-crust pie requires a way for steam to escape while baking, so you can either cut a few simple 1- to 2-inch slits in the top [A] or use a cute pie bird, which acts as a chimney for the steam.

To use a pie bird, place it in the middle of your pie so it's resting on the bottom crust, amid the filling [B]. Cut out a small circle in the center of your rolled-out top crust, making sure it's large enough to accommodate the top of the pie bird. Carefully place the top crust on top of the filling, being sure to position the circle you cut earlier around the bird [C]. Trim and crimp the crust as you would any other double-crust pie.

DECORATING A TOP CRUST

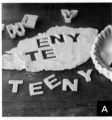

I like to get creative with my top crusts by cutting out creative steam vents with small cookie cutters. Cut out the different shapes from the rolled-out top crust before you place it on top of the pie. You can also cut additional shapes from scraps of rolled-out dough and use them to decorate the pie [A]. To affix the shapes, brush the bottom of each shape with a bit of egg wash (see Golden Glow, page 25) and gently stick it to the surface of the top crust [B].

MAKING A LATTICE

Using a lattice in place of a top crust is probably one of the prettiest ways to perk up a pie. Lattices are especially lovely with berry pies, where they allow the vibrant color of the fruit to peek through. Here's how to make one:

1. Roll out the top crust into a rough 11-inch circle [A] (for Teeny Pies, roll out the crusts into rough 6-inch circles). Using a pastry wheel or butter knife, cut the dough into 1- to 1½-inch strips [B] (½-inch strips for Teeny Pies).

2. Begin your lattice: Lay half of the strips horizontally over the filling, spacing them ½ inch to ¾ inch apart [C]. I like the look of a fairly tight lattice, but you can space them as close or as far apart as you like, as long as the strips are evenly spaced all the way across.

3. Pull back every other strip to reveal the filling [D], and lay your first strip beneath

them perpendicularly, placing it near the edge of the pie.

4. Unfold the pulled-back strips so they rest on top of the new strip [E].

5. Weave in the remaining dough strips in this fashion [F], alternating which strips you pull back, until the top of the pie is covered. Tuck the ends of the strips (if necessary, trim them down to about ¾ inch) under the bottom crust overhang [G] and crimp to seal the two together [H].

CRUST COOKIES

Don't toss those dough scraps! If you have a few left over once the pie is assembled, you might consider another use for them. When I was little, my mom would press the scraps into tiny tins and sprinkle them with cinnamon sugar. She'd bake them alongside the big pie, setting a separate timer for 10 minutes and pulling them out when they were golden brown.

I like to use cookie cutters to cut shapes out of dough. I place the baked cookies atop single-crust pies, or sprinkle them with cinnamon sugar before baking, and give them away with my pies.

GOLDEN GLOW

I've never been one to bother with egg washes in general, usually preferring a more rustic look, but if you're interested in giving your top crust a bright sheen, then an egg wash is the way to go. Once you've assembled your pie, whisk together 1 egg and 1 tablespoon of milk. Using a pastry brush, spread the mixture over the entire top crust, making sure to get all of the valleys and hills, and then sprinkle with sugar before baking (omit the sugar for savory pies). Your pie will come out with a shiny golden glow.

PREBAKING A PIE SHELL

If you're making a cream, custard, or curd pie and the recipe calls for a prebaked crust, your rolling and lining techniques are going to be the same as for fruit pies. However, there are a few additional steps to ensure that your crust won't slouch or shrink when you put it into a hot oven unfilled.

Once you've placed the dough in the pie plate, prick the bottom and sides with the tines of a fork. This step, called docking, will prevent a certain amount of blistering. Put the crust-lined dish in the freezer for twenty minutes or so until the dough is hard

(I've found that freezing dough is one of the most successful ways to prevent shrinkage). Meanwhile, preheat your oven to 350°F; you should always take care to put your frozen crust into a preheated oven, otherwise your crimp will slouch or fall out completely.

Remove the frozen dough from the freezer and line it with parchment paper or aluminum foil, taking care to press it up along the sides. Fill the paper or foil with pie beads or dried beans or peas. Bake the crust until it's set, about 15 minutes, then lift out the weighted parchment or foil and let the crust bake until it's golden brown, an additional 10 minutes or so. Let the crust cool on a wire rack on the countertop, then fill it as you wish!

FREEZING PIE

You never know when a pie emergency might strike; it's always nice to have on hand a few pies or the makings thereof just in case. Over the past few years I've had to be away from home fairly frequently—such is the life of a vagabond pie baker—and Aaron is always superappreciative when I manage to leave a few crimped crusts and ziplock bags of fillings in the freezer along with individual baking instructions. It guarantees that he'll never be without breakfast pie whether or not I'm home to bake it for him.

If you're on a crust-making kick, throw together a few extra batches and put them in the freezer. Wrapped separately in plastic wrap and bagged in a freezer baggie, each batch of dough should last for up to three months. When you're ready to use the dough just leave it out on the counter for a few hours or in the refrigerator overnight until it's thawed enough to roll out.

If you're looking to make a pie and bake it at a later date, freezing may be the way to go. Although I wouldn't recommend it for the cream, curd, French silk, or brownie pies (because those pies require cooking the filling separately on the stovetop or whisking in the bowl of a mixer, which makes them impossible to freeze and then reuse), it works well with fruit pies and the loose-filling pies, such as chess, pecan, pumpkin, and sweet potato.

TO FREEZE A FRUIT PIE: Wrap the assembled, unbaked pie in plastic wrap (make it a double layer . . . just to be safe) and stick it in the freezer. It'll last up to a week in its frozen state, and you can put it straight from the freezer into the oven. You don't have to adjust the baking time, just be sure you put any frozen pie into a preheated oven! If you put it in the oven before the oven has reached the proper temp, your crimp will fall out and you'll be left with a goofy-looking crust. If your oven doesn't have an indicator light that lets you know when it's preheated, or if yours heats to a lower temp than it should, you might want to consider getting an oven thermometer. They're inexpensive and available at most hardware stores, and will help you gauge when the proper baking temperature has been reached (or how much to turn your dial to get it there).

FOR THE LOOSE-FILLING PIES, you'll want to freeze the crimped crust and the filling separately. The crust you can wrap in a double layer of plastic wrap; the filling can go into a freezer-safe ziplock bag. When you're ready to bake those pies, take the filling out first and let it thaw in the refrigerator overnight or on the counter for a few hours until it's completely defrosted. You can pour the defrosted filling directly into your frozen crust and put it straight into your preheated oven.

Crimped crusts await their fate.

Crust patties ready for rolling

Pie Crusts

Whole Wheat Crust

PREP TIME: 15 MINUTES • **CHILL TIME:** 1 HOUR, IDEALLY OVERNIGHT •
TOTAL TIME: 1 HOUR 15 MINUTES • **MAKES:** ONE 9-INCH DOUBLE CRUST,
FOUR 5-INCH DOUBLE CRUSTS, OR EIGHT 5-INCH SINGLE CRUSTS

INGREDIENTS

1½ cups all-purpose flour

1 cup white whole wheat or whole wheat flour

2 teaspoons salt

2 tablespoons granulated sugar

¾ cup (1½ sticks) cold unsalted butter, cut into small pieces

¼ cup (4 tablespoons) cold vegetable shortening

¼ cup (4 tablespoons) cold vodka

½ cup (8 tablespoons) cold water, plus extra as needed

Whole wheat crust is my go-to for nearly every pie I bake. Whole wheat flour is slightly more challenging to work with because of its low gluten content, but adding vodka to the mix makes for a wonderful, workable dough. I keep my (cheap) vodka in the freezer and the chill of it serves to cool down the rest of my ingredients as I mix the dough together. If you have made pie crust before, you might wonder about the amount of liquid I call for here; I have found that whole wheat flour requires a little more liquid to come together into a ball of dough.

This recipe makes enough dough for a nine-inch top and a bottom crust. If you need only a bottom crust, you can freeze half of this recipe for up to 3 months (see page 26) and save it for later.

1. In a large bowl, stir together the flour, salt, and sugar until everything is thoroughly combined. Add the butter and shortening and cut the mixture together using a pastry cutter until it forms small pea-size crumbs coated in flour.

2. Pour the vodka evenly over the dry ingredients, a few tablespoons at a time, using a rubber spatula to press the dough together. Similarly, add the water, and continue to press the dough together to form a large ball. The dough

should be fairly wet and sticky; if for some reason it seems particularly dry, add a little extra ice water a tablespoon at a time until everything comes together easily. (Be careful to work the dough as little as possible; otherwise the crust may be tough.)

3. Divide the dough into two equal balls, press each into a disk, wrap each in plastic, and refrigerate for at least an hour or up to 2 days before rolling out.

Mom's All-Shortening Crust

PREP TIME: 10 MINUTES • **CHILL TIME:** NONE • **TOTAL TIME:** 10 MINUTES •
MAKES: ONE 9-INCH DOUBLE CRUST OR THREE 5-INCH DOUBLE CRUSTS

This is the crust recipe that I grew up with. Aside from all of the nostalgic reasons for loving it, I think it's great because it takes so little time. My mom has never refrigerated her crust dough after making it—in fact the first time I made my crust for her and told her it needed to sit in the fridge for an hour, she looked at me like I was a crazy person. She doesn't refrigerate her shortening, she uses warm water as opposed to ice water, and once she makes a batch of dough she rolls it out immediately, and yet her pies are always perfect. So, if you're in a time crunch or you'd just like a simple, flaky crust, this is the recipe for you. It makes a double crust—if you need only a single, you can freeze the remainder for up to 3 months (see page 26).

If you'd rather make a single whole wheat crust at the outset, simply follow the directions at left using these quantities:

INGREDIENTS

¾ cup all-purpose flour

½ cup white whole wheat or whole wheat flour

1 teaspoon salt

1 tablespoon granulated sugar

6 tablespoons (¾ stick) cold unsalted butter, cut into 1-inch pieces

⅛ cup (2 tablespoons) cold vegetable shortening

⅛ cup (2 tablespoons) cold vodka

¼ cup (4 tablespoons) cold water, plus extra as needed

INGREDIENTS

2 cups all-purpose flour

1½ tablespoons granulated sugar

1 teaspoon salt

⅔ cup vegetable shortening

5 to 6 tablespoons warm water

1. In a large bowl mix together the flour, sugar, and salt until everything is thoroughly combined. Add the shortening and cut it in using a pastry cutter, fork, or your fingers until each piece of shortening is the size of a small pea and coated in flour.

2. Add the warm water a tablespoon at a time and using your hands or a rubber spatula, press the dough together to form a large ball. (Be careful to handle the dough as little as possible, otherwise the crust may be tough.)

3. Divide the dough into two equal balls, press each into a 1-inch disk, and you're ready to roll out your crusts.

Buttery All-Purpose Crust

INGREDIENTS

2½ cups all-purpose flour

2 teaspoons salt

2 tablespoons granulated sugar

¾ cup (1½ sticks) cold unsalted butter, cut into 1-inch pieces

¼ cup (4 tablespoons) cold vegetable shortening

¼ cup (4 tablespoons) cold vodka

6 tablespoons cold water, plus extra as needed

PREP TIME: 15 MINUTES • **CHILL TIME:** 1 HOUR • **TOTAL TIME:** 1 HOUR 15 MINUTES • **MAKES:** ONE 9-INCH DOUBLE CRUST OR FOUR 5-INCH DOUBLE CRUSTS

Sometimes I'm just not in the mood for a whole wheat crust. Either I think it's going to compete with the flavors that I'm using in the filling, or I'm just feeling slightly less nutty (ha!) and want a crust made with only all-purpose flour. I decided to develop my own all-purpose-flour recipe because as much as I like my mom's recipe (page 29), I love the richness that butter adds. My mom's recipe is wonderfully flaky, whereas this recipe is slightly more decadent because of the butter. It's fairly similar to my recipe for Whole Wheat Crust; it simply calls for less liquid.

I find that whole wheat flour needs a little more moisture than all-purpose in order to come together nicely, so I've adjusted this recipe accordingly. This recipe yields a double crust; if you want to make only enough dough for a single crust, simply halve the recipe (or make the whole batch and freeze half; see page 26).

1. In a large bowl mix together the flour, salt, and sugar until everything is thoroughly combined. Add the butter and shortening and cut the mixture together using a pastry cutter until it forms small pea-size crumbs coated in flour.

2. Pour the vodka over the dry ingredients a few tablespoons at a time while using a rubber spatula to press the dough together. Similarly, add the water, and continue to press the dough together to form a large ball. The dough should be fairly wet and sticky; if for some reason it seems particularly dry, add a little extra ice water a tablespoon at a time until everything comes together easily. (Be careful to work the dough as little as possible, otherwise the crust may be tough.)

3. Divide the dough into two equal balls, press each into a 1-inch disk, wrap each in plastic, and refrigerate for at least 1 hour or up to 2 days before rolling out.

Savory Pie Crust

PREP TIME: 15 MINUTES • **CHILL TIME:** 1 HOUR • **TOTAL TIME:** 1 HOUR 15 MINUTES • **MAKES:** SIX 5-INCH DOUBLE CRUSTS OR THREE 9-INCH SINGLE CRUSTS

INGREDIENTS

2 cups all-purpose flour

1¼ cups whole wheat flour

3 teaspoons salt

2 teaspoons ground black pepper

1 cup (2 sticks) plus 2 tablespoons cold unsalted butter, cut into 1-inch pieces

6 tablespoons cold vegetable shortening

6 tablespoons cold vodka

¾ cup (12 tablespoons) cold water, plus extra as needed

Savory pie crusts can provide a fun canvas for experimenting with different spices and seasonings. I like mine with cracked black pepper, but I've also tried ones with poultry seasoning, lemon pepper, red pepper flakes . . . anything that complements the flavor of the filling is fair game. I'm also a firm believer in individual-size savory pies. Maybe it's because I grew up eating store-bought individual chicken potpies, and the most thrilling part of the meal was always dumping the pie upside down on my plate so I could eat it from the bottom up. Or maybe it's because you want to eat a potpie while it's warm and steamy, which is the exact moment it's hardest to slice and serve a large pie without it falling to pieces. Whatever the reason, this recipe makes enough dough for six 5-inch double-crust (Teeny) pies though you can use it to make 9-inch crusts, too.

1. In a large bowl mix together the flour, salt, and pepper until everything is thoroughly combined. Add the butter and shortening and cut the mixture together using a pastry cutter until it forms small pea-size crumbs coated in flour.

2. Add the vodka and, using a rubber spatula, press the dough together. Add the water, and again using the rubber spatula, press the dough together to form a large ball. The dough should be fairly wet and sticky; if for some reason it seems

particularly dry, add a little extra ice water a tablespoon at a time until everything comes together easily. (Be careful to work the dough as little as possible, otherwise the crust may be tough.)

3. Divide the dough into three equal balls, press each into a 1-inch disk, wrap each in plastic, and refrigerate for at least 1 hour or up to 2 days before rolling out.

Gluten-Free Crust

PREP TIME: 15 MINUTES • **CHILL TIME:** 1 HOUR • **TOTAL TIME:** 1 HOUR 15 MINUTES • **MAKES:** ONE 9-INCH SINGLE CRUST OR THREE 5-INCH SINGLE TEENY CRUSTS

I don't claim to be an expert when it comes to gluten-free pie crust, but having a few friends who live gluten free for one reason or another, I happen to think that nobody should be denied pie just because they have an "abnormal immune reaction to partially digested gliadin." (Thanks, Wikipedia!) After trying a few different recipes early on with disastrous results, I finally developed one that came closest to traditional crust in behavior and taste.

This recipe works with most gluten-free all-purpose flour mixes, but I'm partial to Gluten Free Pantry's multipurpose flour (available at natural foods supermarkets like Whole Foods), because I don't have to spend time mixing assorted gluten-free flours and it bakes the most similarly to a regular crust. The egg works to hold everything together nicely and I am able to roll the crust fairly easily once it's rested in the refrigerator.

INGREDIENTS

1¼ cups gluten-free all-purpose flour

1 tablespoon granulated sugar

1 teaspoon salt

6 tablespoons (¾ stick) cold unsalted butter, cut into 1-inch pieces

1 large egg

¼ cup (4 tablespoons) ice water, plus extra as needed

I always roll out gluten-free crusts between two pieces of parchment (or aluminum foil) because it makes transferring the crust to the pie plate much easier and also cuts down on any potential for cross-contamination. Once the crust is rolled out, I peel off the top piece of parchment slowly and use the second piece to help maneuver the crust "parchment-free" side down into the pie plate. Then I peel away the second piece of parchment and tuck and crimp the edge as usual. Pie for all and all for pie.

1. In a large bowl mix together the flour, sugar, and salt until everything is thoroughly combined. Add the butter and cut it in with a pastry cutter until the mixture forms small pea-size crumbs coated in flour.

2. In a small bowl lightly whisk together the egg and the ¼ cup ice water.

3. Pour the egg mixture over the flour mixture, and lightly mix the dough with a rubber spatula or your hands until everything starts to come together. Gently press the dough into a large ball, using the dough to gather any small crumbs from the bottom of the bowl. This is a fairly malleable dough, with a consistency closer to mashed potatoes rather than a typical pie dough, so if it feels dry and there are a lot of small crumbs on the bottom that won't stick together, add a little more ice water, a tablespoon at a time, until the dough forms.

4. Press the dough into a 1-inch disk, wrap it in plastic, and refrigerate for at least 1 hour or up to 2 days before rolling it out between two pieces of parchment paper. (Don't be alarmed

if the crust cracks or falls apart; just patch it together with your fingers.)

Graham Cracker Crust

PREP TIME: 10 MINUTES • **BAKE TIME:** 5 TO 7 MINUTES • **TOTAL TIME:** 20 MINUTES • **MAKES:** ONE 9-INCH SINGLE CRUST OR FOUR 5-INCH SINGLE CRUSTS

There are some pies that traditionally require a graham cracker crumb crust, like Key lime and French silk. For a long time when a recipe called for a graham cracker crust, I just followed the recipe on the side of the box of graham crackers. But I've come to realize that with a little more graham and a little more butter, I'm able to make a slightly thicker crust that not only gives each slice a sturdier base but also makes for a delightful crunch.

To make the graham cracker crumbs, pulse the crackers in a food processor until they form very fine crumbs, or seal them in a large ziplock bag and crush them with a rolling pin or the palm of your hand.

1. Preheat the oven to 350°F with a rack in the middle position.

2. Whisk together the graham cracker crumbs and the sugar in a medium bowl to combine. Pour the melted butter over the crumbs and mix with a spoon or a rubber spatula until the butter is evenly distributed. The graham mixture will be slightly darker and should clump easily when pressed together.

INGREDIENTS

- 1½ cups graham cracker crumbs (from 8 to 9 graham cracker sheets)
- 2 tablespoons granulated sugar
- 6 tablespoons (¾ stick) unsalted butter, melted

3. Spoon three quarters of the mixture into a 9-inch pie plate and, using your fingers, press the mixture up along the side of the plate until you have a ¼-inch-thick shell all the way around. Spoon the rest of the mixture into the center of the plate and press it to form the bottom of the shell, making sure the bottom and sides are joined.

4. Bake until the shell is slightly browned, 5 to 7 minutes. Remove it from the oven and let it cool on a rack before filling.

Pretzel Crust

PREP TIME: 15 MINUTES • **BAKE TIME:** 5 TO 7 MINUTES • **TOTAL TIME:** 20 MINUTES • **MAKES:** ONE 9-INCH SINGLE CRUST OR FOUR 5-INCH SINGLE CRUSTS

INGREDIENTS

1¼ cups pretzel crumbs (from about 2 cups pretzels)

½ cup (1 stick) unsalted butter, melted

I don't have a huge sweet tooth, so I often try to temper my sweet offerings with a touch of salt. I originally came up with this pretzel crumb crust to go with my peanut butter brownie pie, but it also complements the French Silk Pie (page 134) and Chocolate Cream Pie (page 131) quite nicely.

To make the pretzel crumbs, I grind up pretzels in a food processor until they resemble coarse sand. If you don't have a food processor, you can always put the pretzels in a ziplock baggie and crush them with your rolling pin.

1. Preheat the oven to 350°F with a rack in the middle position.

2. Place the pretzel crumbs in a medium bowl. Pour the melted butter over them and mix with a spoon or a rubber spatula until they are coated evenly and clump readily when pressed together.

3. Spoon three quarters of the mixture into a 9-inch pie plate and, using your fingers, press the mixture up along the side of the plate until you have a ¼-inch-thick shell all the way around. Spoon the rest of the mixture into the center of the plate and press it to form the bottom of the shell, making sure the bottom and sides are joined.

4. Bake until the shell is slightly browned, 5 to 7 minutes. Remove it from the oven and let it cool on a rack, then transfer it to the refrigerator to chill for at least 30 minutes before filling.

Sugar Cookie Crust

PREP TIME: 55 MINUTES • **BAKE TIME:** 25 MINUTES • **TOTAL TIME:** 1 HOUR 20 MINUTES • **MAKES:** ONE 9-INCH SINGLE CRUST

I originally developed a sugar cookie crust because I knew I wanted to pair it with the Earl Grey Cream Pie (page 147) and have the end result taste like tea and cookies, which it does! But this crust also goes so well with any of the cream pies, especially the Chai Cream Pie (page 150), and it adds a little extra sweetness to the Grapefruit and Pomegranate Pie (page 123) as well.

INGREDIENTS

½ cup (1 stick) unsalted butter, at room temperature

½ cup granulated sugar

¼ teaspoon salt

1 large egg

1½ cups all-purpose flour

This crust can be made in advance and stored, wrapped in plastic, in the refrigerator for up to two days before filling.

1. In the bowl of a stand mixer fitted with the paddle attachment, or in a large bowl using a handheld electric mixer, beat together the butter, sugar, and salt on medium speed until the mixture is light and fluffy, about 3 minutes.

2. Scrape down the side of the bowl with a rubber spatula and add the egg. Mix on medium speed until the egg is fully incorporated, about 2 minutes.

3. Scrape down the side of the bowl again and add the flour, ¼ cup at a time, mixing after each addition until everything just comes together. Form the dough into a large ball, wrap it in plastic, and refrigerate it for at least 30 minutes or up to 1 hour.

4. Press the dough into a 9-inch pie plate, making sure to press it evenly so it's ¼ inch thick all the way around and up the side. Prick the bottom and side with a fork and chill, unwrapped, in the freezer until it is frozen through, at least 20 minutes.

5. Meanwhile, preheat the oven to 325°F with a rack in the middle position.

6. Take the crust directly from the freezer, line it with parchment paper or aluminum foil, and fill it with pie weights. Bake until the side is golden brown, 15 to 20 minutes. Remove the pie weights and the liner and bake until the bottom is golden brown, an additional 5 minutes, covering the crimp with aluminum foil or a crust cover if it is overbrowning. Let cool before filling.

WHEN GOOD CRUSTS GO BAD

Crust dough can be frustratingly temperamental and uncooperative. This handy-dandy chart is here to help you diagnose and, hopefully, treat your particular batch.

THE DOUGH IS TOO DRY

Symptoms: Lots of crumbs at the bottom of the bowl that simply won't come together in a nice and reasonable ball.

Treatment: Drizzle ice water, one tablespoon at a time, into the bottom of the bowl and use your hands to pick up all the little dry crumbs and gently press everything together. Shape the dough into a ball, press it into a disk, wrap it, and let it chill for at least an hour before rolling it out.

THE DOUGH IS TOO WET

Symptoms: Your dough seems wet and sticky and clings to the bottom of the bowl rather than forming a ball.

Treatment: Don't worry, it's savable! Sprinkle about a tablespoon of all-purpose flour on top of your dough and use a spatula to scrape it away from the sides of the bowl. Sprinkle another tablespoonful on the countertop and plop your wet dough onto it, gently rolling it around in the flour until the outside is thinly coated and no longer sticky to the touch. Press the dough into a disk, wrap it in plastic wrap, and let it rest for an hour and a half in the refrigerator, so it gets really cold and firm. When you roll out the dough later, be extra generous with your flour sprinkling and flip and rotate the dough often to prevent sticking.

Note: I've noticed that weather and location can really affect my pie crust dough. If it's particularly humid or warm in my kitchen, I tend to use one to two tablespoons less liquid than I do under normal circumstances. To maker sure you don't overwater your dough, I suggest adding a couple of tablespoons less than the recipe calls for and if the dough seems dry when mixed together, then add the rest.

THE DOUGH IS TOO MELTY

Symptoms: Your pie crust dough should be relatively elastic when you roll it out and press it into your pie plate. If it splits easily or has the consistency of soft cookie dough when you try to roll it out, you may have added too much fat. (About a year ago I was trying to make a pie from memory and ended up accidentally adding four extra tablespoons of shortening. The crust was strangely thick and unpliable as I rolled it out, and it split before I could get it into the pie plate. I realized much too late that I had a shortening issue and ended up tossing the whole batch of dough and starting over.)

Treatment: Yup, you guessed it. Unfortunately, if you try to cut in more flour, your crust will become tough and overworked. It's best to throw it away, take a deep breath, and start again.

THE DOUGH IS GLUEY

Symptoms: If your dough is the consistency of gluey mashed potatoes, it's been overworked after the water was added and will, again, be impossible to roll out. You most likely won't experience this if you're using a pastry cutter and your hands; I've noticed it happens most often when I'm using a food processor. (It's just so easy to get carried away with the pulsing.)

Treatment: Sorry, but you have to toss it and start over. Next time you use a food processor or a mixer, I recommend using the machine to incorporate your fats until they are the prerequisite pea size, then transferring the mixture to a bowl and slowly adding the water and forming the dough by hand so you don't end up with gooey, gluey dough.

THE DOUGH HAS AWKWARD SHRINKAGE

Symptoms: In general, pie dough is good for a single reroll. If you try to reroll it more than once, it becomes very tight and seems to pull in on itself.

Treatment: It's tough to roll overworked dough to the proper size, and when you bake it, it tends to shrink asymetrically. Rather than trying to force the dough into submission, consider using it to make crust cookies instead (see page 125) and making a whole new batch of dough for your pie. In the future, avoid rerolling the dough so you don't end up bringing a goofy shrunken pie to your dinner party or picnic.

Crumbles & Creams

Crumbles are an amazing combination of sugar (or in the case of savory pies, perhaps salt), spices, and butter with a little flour thrown in for structure. They are a pretty spectacular and indulgent way to add a little flavor and texture to any fruit pie.

Homemade whipped cream is perhaps one of my favorite ways to top a pie, and it's surprisingly easy to make. A small rich dollop is the perfect finish for a fall pumpkin pie or a springtime cream.

Cinnamon Crumble

PREP TIME: 15 MINUTES • **TOTAL TIME:** 15 MINUTES • **MAKES:** ABOUT 2 CUPS

INGREDIENTS

1 cup all-purpose flour

½ cup packed light brown sugar

½ cup granulated sugar

1 teaspoon ground cinnamon

7 tablespoons unsalted butter, melted

I used to think that if I were short on butter or flour I could just throw together a quick crumble instead of making enough dough for a top crust, but the truth is if you want a good crumble, there's no skimping on the ingredients (especially the butter). You'll notice I haven't held back here—I hope you'll try this toothsome cinnamony topping on any of the fruit pies as an occasional substitute for a top crust.

1. In a large bowl mix together the flour, sugars, and cinnamon with a whisk or a fork.

2. Pour the melted butter over the flour mixture and stir together with a rubber spatula or your hands until everything is combined. The mixture will be darker in color and should stick together easily if pressed in your hand.

3. Sprinkle three quarters of the crumble over the top of the fruit pie of your choice, a handful at a time to coat. Squeeze together the remaining crumble mixture to make some larger pieces, and gently scatter them over the top.

4. Bake the pie as directed. The crumble should be golden brown—if it starts to brown faster than the crust, cover the pie with a sheet of aluminum foil, then uncover it during the last 10 minutes of baking to toast.

Oat-and-Nut Crumble

PREP TIME: 15 MINUTES • **TOTAL TIME:** 15 MINUTES • **MAKES:** ABOUT 2½ CUPS

This recipe calls for almonds because they happen to be my favorite nut to add to a crumble; they are light and slightly sweet without being overwhelmingly nutty. If almonds aren't your favorite feel free to use a quarter cup of your nut of choice; both pecans and walnuts are tasty options. If you're allergic to nuts, leave 'em out completely and add an extra quarter cup of oats.

1. In a large bowl mix together the flour, oats, almonds, brown sugar, cinnamon, and salt with a fork or your hands until combined.

2. Pour the melted butter over the mixture and stir with a rubber spatula or your hands until everything is thoroughly combined. The crumble mixture should clump easily when pressed together in your hand.

INGREDIENTS

1 cup all-purpose flour

½ cup old-fashioned rolled oats

¼ cup sliced almonds

1 cup packed light brown sugar (dark is fine, too)

1 teaspoon ground cinnamon

½ teaspoon salt

7 tablespoons unsalted butter, melted

3. Sprinkle three quarters of the crumble over the top of the fruit pie of your choice, a handful at a time to coat. Squeeze together the remaining crumble mixture to make some larger pieces, and gently scatter them over the top.

4. Bake the pie as directed. The crumble should be golden brown—if it starts to brown faster than the crust, cover the pie with a sheet of aluminum foil, then uncover it during the last 10 minutes of baking to toast.

Stuffing Crumble

PREP TIME: 10 MINUTES • **TOTAL TIME:** 10 MINUTES • **MAKES:** ABOUT 2 CUPS

INGREDIENTS

4 tablespoons (½ stick) unsalted butter

1 box (6 ounces) turkey, chicken or vegetable stuffing mix (about 2¾ cups dry)

I'm going to let you in on a little secret. I'm a sucker for boxed stuffing. I've always been so enamored of the taste of the boxed version and usually so put off by other people's homemade versions that I've never spent any time trying to make my own. I just get a box of Stove Top or occasionally splurge on Pepperidge Farm, mix in the water and butter as directed, and plop it atop my pies. I don't even add celery, onion, or sausage like my mom likes to do; I'm a straight-up Stove Top turkey kind of gal. If you have a stuffing recipe that you love, feel free to swap it in place of the boxed stuff. This crumble is essential for the Thanksgiving Dinner Pies (page 153) but is also stellar on top of Aaron's Chicken Potpies with Kale and Cannellinis (page 97).

1. Bring 1½ cups water to a boil in a large skillet. Add the butter, stirring occasionally until it's melted.

2. Add the stuffing mix and stir until all of it is slightly moistened. Remove the skillet from the heat and set it aside to cool.

3. Once the stuffing is cool, gently press it onto the top of the savory pie of your choice, one handful at a time, until the pie is covered.

4. Bake as directed. The crumble should be crispy and lightly browned; if it's browning too quickly, cover the pie with aluminum foil, then uncover it during the last 10 minutes of the baking to toast.

Variation: If you'd like to add a little extra flavor and texture to the stuffing, sauté ¼ cup combined diced celery and onion in the skillet until they become tender and slightly translucent, 7 to 10 minutes, before adding the water and bringing it to a boil.

Homemade Whipped Cream

PREP TIME: 5 TO 10 MINUTES • TOTAL TIME: 5 TO 10 MINUTES • MAKES: ABOUT 2 CUPS

Homemade whipped cream is one of those things that is so much better than the stuff you get in a can or a tub that I can't really imagine why we ever stopped making it. If I'm left alone in the kitchen with a bowlful of whipped cream, more of it will end up in my belly than on top of a pie. Once I dig in, I can't stop. And don't even get me started on all of the different flavors you can add to it with extract or zest. I'm convinced that

INGREDIENTS

1 cup heavy (whipping) cream

3 tablespoons confectioners' sugar

1 teaspoon pure vanilla extract

it's perfect with any pie, and once you've made your own, you'll never go back to that silly can again. Plus, if you're alone in the kitchen, you can eat it by the large spoonful . . . no one will ever know.

I've given you directions for whipping cream with an electric mixer, but if you don't have one, two old-school methods—both involving good old elbow grease—follow. Whipped cream should be made right before you use it because it has a tendency to fall flat if it sits for too long. If you have to make it ahead of time, cover it and store in the refrigerator. You may have to re-whip it a bit to perk it up before topping the pie.

Electric-Mixer Method: In the bowl of a stand mixer fitted with the whisk attachment, or in a large bowl using a handheld electric mixer, beat together the cream, sugar, and vanilla on high speed until the mixture has doubled in size and become stiff enough to stick to the whisk, about 3 minutes. (If you whisk it for too long it will begin to turn into butter, which is never a pretty sight—unless that's your intention!—so just keep an eye on it and stop whisking when it reaches the consistency that you like.)

Old-School Method #1: Combine all of the ingredients in a large bowl and whisk them together with a wire whisk until your arm feels like it will fall off and your cream has doubled in size and soft peaks begin to form.

Homemade Whipped Cream will keep for 1 to 2 days when stored, covered, in the refrigerator.

Old-School Method #2: Combine all of the ingredients in a large jar, screw on the lid tightly, and shake, shake, shake until you have whipped cream.

Variations on a Whipped-Cream Theme

This may be unbelievably nerdy, but I love coming up with interesting whipped cream flavors. Incorporating just a hint of zest or aromatics is a really wonderful way to add something exciting to your pie. Here are a few of my favorite combinations:

Lemon Zested Whipped Cream

(YUM WITH PUMPKIN PIE, PAGE 71)

The credit for this delightful combination lies solely in the hands of my dear friend R. B., and you should definitely try it! I promise you won't be disappointed. Add 1 to 2 teaspoons freshly grated lemon zest along with the vanilla.

Peppermint Whipped Cream

(SERVE WITH FRENCH SILK PIE, PAGE 134)

Turn a regular French silk pie into a holiday treat: Add peppermint whipped cream and sprinkle a few crushed candy canes on top for decoration. Add 1 teaspoon peppermint extract in place of the vanilla.

Orange Zested Whipped Cream

(PERFECT ATOP CHOCOLATE CREAM PIE, PAGE 131)

The Chocolate Cream Pie in this book is incredibly decadent, and I like to cut the sweetness with a touch of citrus. Add 1 to 2 teaspoons freshly grated orange zest along with the vanilla.

Rosewater Whipped Cream

(GREAT WITH SWEET AND SIMPLE APPLE PIE, PAGE 53)

Add 2 tablespoons rosewater in place of the vanilla.

Espresso Whipped Cream

(AMAZING WITH CHAI CREAM PIE, PAGE 150)

One of my favorite drinks in the wintertime is a dirty chai tea latte, which is a chai tea latte with a shot of espresso for a little pick-me-up. If you want to turn your Chai Cream Pie into a dirty chai, simply add espresso to your whipped cream. Add 2 tablespoons cooled, freshly pulled espresso along with the vanilla.

CHAPTER 3

Fall

Pies to Frolic With

Fall is my favorite season. The air gets cold enough to warrant wearing light sweaters that help chase away the chill and my trusty Converse All Stars make a reappearance after I tuck away my summertime TOMS. The days begin to shorten and the leaves on the trees begin their spectacular fall transformations. The cooler it gets outside the more I relish being in the kitchen, enveloped in the toasty, fragrant warmth of baking pies.

Converses in Cambridge

Finding fall with Aaron

As a certain crispness starts to permeate the air, fresh berries and pitted fruits become scarce and expensive at the grocery stores and disappear altogether from the farmers' markets. Large squash and plump pumpkins take their place, and the pies that I bake undergo a similar change. I savor the last of the berries, plucked while they are plump and juicy; a few cups go toward those final pies and the rest get squirreled away in the freezer (see page 26), waiting to make a reappearance when times get tough in the winter. Sweet potatoes and pumpkins begin to make their grand entrance and I delight in pairing them with copious amounts of cream, cinnamon, and sugar.

My Tour of Pie was scheduled to start in September 2011, and the weeks leading up to it were full of anticipation. I felt as though I had joined the ranks of kids who were saying good-bye to the dwindling days of summer and getting ready to go back to school. I was filled with "first-day nerves" as I set to work packing my backpack, which, rather than being filled with freshly sharpened pencils and colorful folders, held my trusty rolling pin wrapped in my favorite apron, and a spare pastry cutter, just in case.

Fall biking

My two fall stops were meticulously planned down to the last detail. Seattle was first, where I'd hoped to catch the tail end of the Washington berry season at High 5 Pie. I was looking forward to visiting the famed Pike Place Market, biking a few of the city's most popular trails, and going on at least one ferry ride on Puget Sound. From there I would travel across the country to upstate New York, where I would spend October working with some close friends at Emmy's Organics, apple-picking and pie-baking my way through an Ithaca fall. With my favorite season fast approaching, I began my vagabond baking life.

I arrived in Seattle the first week of September. When I originally approached Dani Cone about going to work with her at High 5 Pie, she had been selling her pies wholesale for two years and had been in the midst of making her then-eight-month-old shop a success. She is by no means new to owning a business. Fuel Coffee is also hers, and I imagine the success of that business was one of the reasons she felt so comfortable diving into pie—that, and she had a soft spot for her grandmother's all-butter crust.

Any apprehension I may have had before beginning the tour evaporated when I met Dani. She was pixie-like, and wore all of her hair piled on top of her head and tied up in a bright scarf. Constantly in motion, she had boundless energy that invigorated the whole shop. I slowly felt my tension ease as she introduced me to the people I would be working with over the next four weeks. Not only was Dani eager to play host, she was enthusiastic about my project and

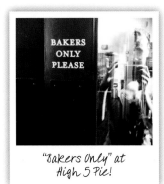

"Bakers Only" at High 5 Pie!

seemed enthralled with the idea of the apprenticing tour (I also have a feeling that she was as excited as I was to meet another pie baker with big pie plans). For the first time in a very long while, I felt that I was in the right place, doing exactly what I was supposed to be doing. A month earlier I had told myself I was going to be a professional pie baker, and as Anna, High 5 Pie's head baker, settled me in among the other bakers, handing me one of the kitchen's aprons and a rolling pin, I became one.

September flew by in a flurry of marionberries and bike rides, and the end of the month meant it was time to say good-bye to High 5 Pie and fly cross-country to say hello to Emmy's Organics. I had spent four years in Ithaca as an undergrad at Ithaca College, and now I was particularly excited about spending some time in the small town as an unofficial "townie" rather than as a student. October was the perfect time to be in Ithaca: It was "gorges," there was an

Fall in Ithaca means apple cider in a Mason jar.

overwhelmingly large and wonderful supply of local produce, and, most important, there were friends who understood the desire to follow a dream and were ready to help in any way they could.

Fall turned out to be the perfect time to start a grand adventure.

Sweet and Simple Apple Pie

PREP TIME: 30 MINUTES • **BAKE TIME:** 50 TO 60 MINUTES • **TOTAL TIME:** 1 HOUR 30 MINUTES • **MAKES:** ONE 9-INCH DOUBLE-CRUST PIE (6 TO 8 SLICES) OR FOUR 5-INCH DOUBLE-CRUST TEENY PIES

On average, a pie in our apartment lasts four or five days, as Aaron happily eats a slice every morning for breakfast and I have a slice or two during the week as an afternoon snack . . . that is, every pie except for apple. An apple pie in our apartment used to sit on our kitchen counter, half eaten, until I got tired enough of looking at it to finally throw it away. It was simply not our favorite pie. Until the fall of 2012. With our move to D.C., we had signed ourselves up for a Community Supported Agriculture (CSA) share through Norman's Farmer's Market, where not only did we get a big basket of veggies once a week, we also got a smaller basket of whatever fruit was in season. Given that we started the share in September, that meant a lot of apples. So, I went back to the drawing board on my standard apple pie recipe and took out a few extraneous spices like allspice and ginger, leaving only a dash of cinnamon and a pinch of nutmeg. These two, when paired with the crisp and tangy apples Maryland had to offer, were perfect. Aaron and I have finished every apple pie since.

If you're opting to make Teeny Pies with this recipe, I recommend dicing the peeled apples into 1-inch cubes rather than slices, because they fit so much more easily into the 5-inch tins.

INGREDIENTS

1 cup granulated sugar

2 teaspoons ground cinnamon

¼ teaspoon salt

1 teaspoon ground nutmeg

6 tablespoons all-purpose flour, plus up to ¼ cup extra for rolling out the crust

About 8 apples, peeled, cored, and cut into ½-inch-thick slices (7 cups) or 1-inch cubes for Teeny Pies

2 tablespoons unsalted butter

2 disks dough from Whole Wheat Crust (page 28)

A handful of
what's fresh at the
farmers' market
in the fall*

blackberries
blueberries
apples
sweet potatoes
pumpkins
squash
kale
beets
pears

*Note that the length of
growing seasons varies
from region to region.
The produce in these lists
may not be available for
long in your area (or you
may have a glut of some
items), so please consider
these lists a heads-up on
what should be available
at some point during the
season.

1. Preheat the oven to 400°F with a rack in the middle position.

2. Whisk together the sugar, cinnamon, salt, nutmeg, and flour in a small bowl until combined.

3. Place the apples in a separate large bowl and sprinkle them with the sugar mixture. Toss the apples gently with your fingers or a spoon until they are evenly coated with sugar and spice, and set aside (the apples will begin to juice; cover the bowl with plastic wrap to prevent them from browning).

4. Prepare the bottom crust: Place one disk of dough on a floured work surface and with a floured rolling pin roll it into a rough 11-inch circle about ⅛ inch thick. Lay the crust into a 9-inch pie dish, gently press it in, and trim any excess dough from the edge with a paring knife, being sure to leave a ¾-inch overhang.

5. Give the apples one last stir, making sure they are evenly coated, then layer them into the bottom crust. Continue to layer in the apples to form a slight dome. The apples will be an inch or two higher than the rim of the pie dish.

6. Cut the butter into ¼-inch squares and dot them over the apples.

7. Prepare the top crust: On a floured work surface with a floured rolling pin, roll out the remaining dough disk into a rough 12-inch circle about ⅛ inch. Carefully lay the crust on top of the filling, and trim any excess dough from the edge, leaving a ¾-inch overhang. Tuck the overhanging dough under the underhanging edge of the bottom crust, and crimp

the two crusts together, taking special care to press firmly to seal (apples get very juicy). Cut a few small slits in the top crust with a sharp knife.

8. Set the pie on a rimmed baking sheet and bake until the filling is thickly bubbling and the crust is golden brown (cover the crimp with foil if it begins to brown too quickly), 50 to 60 minutes. Let cool to room temperature before serving.

 MAKE 'EM TEENY PIES

In step 4, divide one disk of the dough into four equal balls and roll out each into a rough 6-inch-wide, ⅛-inch-thick circle. Lay each into a 5-inch pie tin, and trim any excess dough from the edge, being sure to leave a ½-inch overhang.

Give the filling one final stir and spoon an equal amount into each crust-lined teeny tin (roughly 1¾ cups each).

In step 7, divide the remaining dough into four equal balls and roll out each into a rough 7½-inch-wide, ⅛-inch-thick circle. Carefully lay the crusts over the filling, and trim any excess dough from the edge, leaving a ½-inch overhang. Tuck the overhanging dough under the bottom crust and crimp the two crusts together, pressing to seal. Cut a ½-inch slit in the top of each to allow steam to escape.

Bake the Teeny Pies until the filling is thickly bubbling and the crusts are golden brown, 45 to 55 minutes.

Sweet and Simple Apple Pie will keep for about 3 days, covered, on the countertop.

Green Chile Apple Pie with Cheddar Cheese Crust

PREP TIME: 45 MINUTES • **BAKE TIME:** 50 TO 60 MINUTES • **TOTAL TIME:** 1 HOUR 45 MINUTES • **MAKES:** ONE 9-INCH DOUBLE CRUST PIE (6 TO 8 SLICES)

INGREDIENTS

About 8 apples, peeled, cored, and cut into ½-inch-thick slices (7 cups)

½ cup chopped canned green chiles (from about 3 chiles, see headnote)

1 cup granulated sugar

2 teaspoons ground cinnamon

¼ teaspoon salt

1 teaspoon ground nutmeg

½ teaspoon ground cloves

¼ teaspoon ground black pepper

4 tablespoons all-purpose flour, plus up to ¼ cup extra for rolling out the crust

Cheddar Cheese Crust (recipe follows)

2 tablespoons unsalted butter

Apparently, green chile apple pie is a regional favorite out in New Mexico, or so says my new D.C. food friend Jeremy, who is from Albuquerque and was willing to bring back some local chiles for the betterment of pie.

When I was growing up I was never really a fan of spice, but now that my taste buds have matured I think a little heat here and there is not only tasty but exciting. The spice in this pie is especially intriguing because it's paired with something sweet, and the Cheddar crust helps soothe the initial bite. I've been a longtime apples-and-cheese snacker, so I think a cheesy crust paired with this chile-studded apple filling (or traditional apple pie filling) is pretty spectacular. To me it tastes exactly like a Cheez-It cracker, which is always a win in my book!

I was lucky enough to make this pie with local New Mexico chiles, but if you don't have a friend from New Mexico who just happens to be going back home for his mom's birthday and can smuggle you some in his suitcase, then you'll have to go with the next best thing. Hatch chiles—so named because they're grown in the town of Hatch, New Mexico—are the thing to look for; they are sold at natural supermarkets like Whole Foods (if you can't find them, poblanos work too). I recommend buying whole canned chiles and chopping them up yourself (2 to 4 chiles should do the trick). If you're using fresh chiles, stem and seed them before you chop them. Either way, be careful to wash up thoroughly after handling the chiles, because any contact with the oils will trigger a slow (painful) burn. This pie will certainly add a little zip to your fall!

1. Preheat the oven to 400°F with a rack in the middle position.

2. Place the apples in a large bowl, add the chiles, and toss to combine. Set aside.

3. In a separate small bowl whisk together the sugar, cinnamon, salt, nutmeg, cloves, black pepper, and flour until combined. Sprinkle the sugar mixture over the apples, toss gently with your fingers or a spoon to coat evenly, and set aside (the apples will begin to juice; cover the bowl with plastic wrap to prevent them from browning).

4. Prepare the bottom crust: Place one disk of the dough on a floured work surface and with a floured rolling pin roll it into a rough 11-inch circle about ⅛ inch thick. Lay the crust into a 9-inch pie dish, gently press it in, and trim any excess dough from the edge with a paring knife, being sure to leave a ¾-inch overhang.

5. Give the apples one last stir, making sure they are evenly coated, then layer them into the bottom crust. Continue to

layer in the apples until they form a slight dome. The apples will be an inch or two higher than the rim of the pie dish.

6. Cut the butter into ¼-inch squares and dot them on top of the apples.

7. Prepare the top crust: On a floured work surface with a floured rolling pin, roll out the remaining dough disk into a rough 12-inch circle about ⅛ inch thick. Carefully lay the crust on top of the filling, and trim any excess dough from the edge, leaving a ¾-inch overhang. Tuck the overhanging dough under the overhanging edge of the bottom crust, and crimp the two crusts together, taking special care to press firmly to seal (apples get very juicy). Cut a few small slits in the top crust with a sharp knife.

8. Set the pie on a rimmed baking sheet and bake until the filling is thickly bubbling and the crust is golden brown (cover the crimp if it begins to brown too quickly), 50 to 60 minutes. Let cool to room temperature before serving.

Green Chile Apple Pie with Cheddar Cheese Crust will keep for 3 or 4 days, covered, in the refrigerator.

Cheddar Cheese Crust

PREP TIME: 15 MINUTES • **CHILL TIME:** 1 HOUR, PREFERABLY OVERNIGHT •
TOTAL TIME: 1 HOUR 15 MINUTES • **MAKES:** ONE 9-INCH DOUBLE CRUST

1. Stir together the flour, salt, sugar, and cheese in a large bowl until everything is thoroughly combined. Add the butter and shortening and cut the mixture together using a pastry cutter until it forms small pea-size crumbs coated in flour.

2. Add the vodka and, using a rubber spatula, press the dough together. Add the water, and again using the rubber spatula, press the dough together to form a large ball. The dough should be fairly wet and sticky; if for some reason it seems particularly dry, add a little extra ice water a tablespoon at a time until everything comes together easily into a ball. (Be careful to work the dough as little as possible when forming the ball, otherwise the crust may be tough.)

3. Separate the dough into two balls, gently press each into a disk, wrap each in plastic, and refrigerate for at least an hour or up to 2 days before rolling out.

INGREDIENTS

1½ cups all-purpose flour, plus up to ¼ cup extra for rolling out the crust

1 cup white whole wheat or whole wheat flour

2 teaspoons salt

2 tablespoons granulated sugar

1 cup (4 ounces) shredded sharp Cheddar cheese

¾ cup (1½ sticks) cold unsalted butter, cut into 1-inch pieces

¼ cup (4 tablespoons) cold vegetable shortening

¼ cup (4 tablespoons) cold vodka

6 tablespoons ice water

Rosemary Caramel Apple Pie

PREP TIME: 2 HOURS • BAKE TIME: 50 TO 60 MINUTES • TOTAL TIME: 3 HOURS •
MAKES: ONE 9-INCH DOUBLE-CRUST PIE (6 TO 8 SLICES)

°°°

There is something absolutely wonderful about being encouraged to dream in pie. Some pies, like the Thanksgiving Dinner Pies (page 153) and the Earl Grey Cream Pie in a Sugar Cookie Crust (page 147), came into existence after I thought long and hard about very specific flavors. Other pies, like Bourbon Bacon Pecan Pie (page 81) and this rosemary-infused caramel apple pie, came about because I wanted to add something surprising and wonderful to an old favorite. I tried a lot of different caramel apple combinations, and while most of them were good, none of them were exciting enough to warrant the title "dream pie." But something magical happened when I infused sweet buttery caramel with the earthy flavor of rosemary and paired that with tart green Granny Smiths. I simply fell in love with this pie. How wondrous to dream up a pie and have it work so well that even *I* went back for seconds.

1. To make the caramel, place ¼ cup water in a medium saucepan, add the sugar, and cook over low heat, stirring constantly with a heatproof spatula, until the sugar dissolves,

INGREDIENTS

1 cup granulated sugar

½ cup (1 stick) unsalted butter

1 sprig fresh rosemary

½ cup heavy (whipping) cream

About 8 Granny Smith apples, peeled, cored, and cut into ½-inch-thick slices (7 cups)

¼ cup all-purpose flour, plus up to ¼ cup extra for rolling out the crust

2 disks dough from Whole Wheat Crust (page 28)

about 5 minutes. Add the sprig of rosemary, turn up the heat to medium, and let the mixture come to a simmer, about 5 minutes.

2. Let the caramel cook slowly, without stirring, until it turns a warm amber color, 8 to 15 minutes, carefully removing the rosemary sprig with a fork about halfway through. It's very easy to burn caramel, so keep a close eye on the pot; if it seems to be browning too quickly, turn down the heat a bit and let it cook more slowly (it will take longer to reach the proper temperature and color). If the mixture begins to smoke or turns black, the caramel is past the point of no return and you should rinse out your pot and begin again (sorry).

3. As soon as the caramel reaches the right color, remove the pot from the heat and immediately whisk in the heavy cream. (The cream is much colder than the caramel, so it will bubble and steam pretty intensely; I like to use a large whisk so I have more distance between my hand and the pot of boiling sugar.) Quickly whisk everything together until the caramel has settled. Stir in the butter until it melts; the caramel will be a light tan color and should be smooth. If it's not smooth, put it back on the stovetop over very low heat and whisk until any lumps of crystallized sugar disappear. Transfer the caramel to a heat-proof bowl or large measuring cup and put it into the fridge to cool.

4. Place the apples in a large bowl, add the flour, and toss to coat. Set aside.

5. Preheat the oven to 400°F with a rack in the middle position.

6. Prepare the bottom crust: Place one disk of the dough on a floured work surface and with a floured rolling pin roll it into a rough 11-inch circle about ⅛ inch thick. Lay the crust into a 9-inch pie dish, gently press it in, and trim any excess dough from the edge with a paring knife, being sure to leave a ¾-inch overhang.

7. Layer half of the sliced apples into the bottom crust and drizzle evenly with about half of the cooled caramel sauce. Layer the remaining apples over the caramel and pour the rest of the sauce over the top (alternatively, set aside ¼ cup of the sauce to drizzle over the top of the baked pie).

8. Prepare the top crust: On a floured work surface with a floured rolling pin, roll out the remaining dough disk into a rough 12-inch circle about ⅛ inch thick. Carefully lay the crust on top of the filling, and trim any excess dough from the edge, leaving a ¾-inch overhang. Tuck the overhanging dough under the edge of the bottom crust, and crimp the two crusts together, pressing firmly to seal (apples get very juicy). Cut a few small slits in the top crust with a sharp knife.

9. Set the pie on a rimmed baking sheet and bake until the filling is thickly bubbling and the crust is golden brown (cover the crimp with foil if it begins to brown too quickly), 50 to 60 minutes Let cool to room temperature before serving.

Rosemary Caramel Apple Pie will keep for about 2 days, covered, on the countertop.

High 5 Pie
Seattle, WA

At High 5 Pie our place was in the back, behind the double doors with the gentle reminder, BAKERS ONLY PLEASE, posted in the middle. There was such a sense of community as each of us rolled out crusts, mixed fillings, and boxed up wholesale orders, our love of pie permeating the kitchen.

In the afternoons, easy conversation flowed over the wooden counters as we raced against the sunlight slanting over our crusts and threatening to make our

dough too warm to work with. I was delighted when I began using pounds of butter rather than sticks, and started making batches of pie filling that filled buckets rather than bowls.

I'd gone from coaxing two or three pies a week from my tiny kitchen oven to turning out two or three dozen each shift. Each day at High 5 Pie brought me closer to making the transition from a home baker, who made pies on a lark, to being a real-deal pie-baking professional.

Every morning, owner and pie maven Dani Cone was in the shop for the first few hours, helping to make pies and then hastening off to take care of other business in the early afternoon. Anna, High 5's head baker, would often have me roll out crusts in the early hours of my shift, and then teach me how to make one pie or another in the afternoon. I fell into a routine so soon after starting that my shifts became comfortable and easy far more quickly than I had imagined they would. I felt so at ease that it seemed silly to remember how terrified I had been just a week earlier.

On occasion Dani took a few hours out of her day to talk to me about the business side of things, like licensing and the first steps I could take toward owning my own business once I was settled. She infused each conversation with such excitement and confidence that by the end of our talks I was practically ready to throw caution to the wind and start a shop right then and there. Through her enthusiasm I was also able to recognize this trip for what it was: a journey that I needed to see through to completion.

My year of pie had only just begun, and while it felt really wonderful to have found such a strong connection on my very first stop, there were still plenty of shops to visit and further experiences to be had. One of the great things about finding friends in pie was that once they were found I could carry their passion and energy with me throughout the rest of my adventure. Dani inspired a hefty dose of confidence, readied me for whatever my next apprenticeship might offer, and then gently pushed me out of her shop and into the wide world of pie.

1400 12th Avenue
Seattle, WA 98122
206-695-2284
high5pie.com

Next Stop: Ithaca, NY (page 90)

High 5 Pie's Marionberry Pie

PREP TIME: 30 MINUTES • **BAKE TIME:** 45 TO 50 MINUTES • **TOTAL TIME:** 1 HOUR 20 MINUTES •
MAKES: ONE 9-INCH SINGLE-CRUST PIE (6 TO 8 SLICES)

Marionberries are a cross between blackberries and loganberries, cultivated in Marion County, Oregon, and a favorite at High 5 Pie. They taste like the perfect mix between blackberries and raspberries, so if you can't find marionberries in your area, substitute two cups of blackberries and two cups of raspberries in the filling.

The following dough recipe makes enough for a top and a bottom crust, but High 5 Pie traditionally serves their marionberry pie with a crumble, so I recommend trying that your first time around. (The leftover dough can be saved for another pie; simply wrap it in plastic and freeze for up to two months.) If you'd rather have a top crust, skip the crumble and go ahead and roll out both disks of dough, placing the top crust over the filling as directed on page 22.

FOR THE CRUST

2½ cups all-purpose flour, plus up to
¼ cup extra for rolling out the crust

1 teaspoon salt

1 teaspoon granulated sugar

1 cup (2 sticks) cold unsalted butter,
cut into 1-inch dice

¾ cup ice water

FOR THE CRUMBLE

½ cup all-purpose flour

3 tablespoons granulated sugar

⅓ cup packed light brown sugar

1 teaspoon salt

1 tablespoon ground cinnamon

½ cup (1 stick) cold unsalted
butter, cut into ½-inch pieces

¼ cup old-fashioned (rolled) oats

FOR THE FILLING

⅓ cup granulated sugar

¼ cup packed light brown sugar

4 tablespoons cornstarch

½ teaspoon ground cinnamon

¼ teaspoon ground allspice

4 cups fresh marionberries

1. Make the crust: Combine the 2½ cups flour, the salt, and the sugar in a large bowl and mix well.

2. Add the butter to the flour mixture and mix gently with a pastry cutter, until the butter is roughly pea-size. The goal is to lightly incorporate the butter into the dry ingredients, being careful not to mix too much. The butter pieces should be well coated with the dry mixture.

3. Gradually add the water, 1 tablespoon at a time, and continue mixing the dough until it comes together and forms pea-size crumbs; you want to add no more than ¾ cup water. The dough should look like coarse, individual crumbs, not smooth and beaten together like cookie dough.

4. With your hands, gather the dough crumbs and press them lightly together to form two 1-inch-thick disks, being careful not to overwork the dough. Wrap each disk in plastic wrap and chill for at least 2 hours before use. (You can also freeze the dough for up to 2 months.)

5. Meanwhile, prepare the crumble: Combine the flour, granulated sugar, brown sugar, salt, and cinnamon in a large bowl and stir to mix well.

6. Add the butter to the flour mixture and cut it in with a pastry cutter, a fork, or your hands until the texture is like small peas.

7. Add the oats and mix to create a crumbly consistency. Set the crumble aside.

8. Make the filling: Stir together the granulated sugar, brown sugar, cornstarch, cinnamon, and allspice in a separate large bowl. Add the marionberries and toss well until the berries are thoroughly coated. Set aside.

9. Preheat the oven to 350°F with a rack in the middle position. Remove one dough disk from the refrigerator and let it sit on the countertop to soften slightly, about 5 minutes.

10. Prepare the crust: Place one disk of the dough on a floured work surface and with a floured rolling pin roll it into a rough 11-inch circle about ⅛ inch thick. Lay the crust into a 9-inch pie dish, gently press it in, and trim any excess dough from the edge with a paring knife, being sure to leave a ¾-inch overhang. Tuck the overhanging dough under itself and crimp.

11. Give the marionberries one final stir, making sure that all of the sugar and juice evenly coat the fruit, and spoon the mixture into the unbaked pie crust.

12. Sprinkle on the crumble, one handful at a time, until the entire top of the pie is covered. Set the pie on a rimmed baking sheet and bake until the crust and crumble are golden brown, 45 to 50 minutes. Let cool before serving.

High 5 Pie's Marionberry Pie will keep for 3 to 4 days covered, on the countertop.

BIKING FOR BLACKBERRIES

When Seattle became the first stop on the Tour of Pie, my friend Kristen offered up her parents' basement as my month-long home. The Magees were warm and welcoming and had a freezer full of handpicked blackberries just begging to be made into pies. Not only did they offer me my own room and bathroom and free rein in the kitchen, they also loaned me a bike for the duration of my stay.

Because this was my first stop on the tour, I wanted everything to be perfect. I decided to bike to the shop the day before I was due to work, just so I would know exactly where it was and how long it would take me to get there. I didn't want to chance getting lost or being late for my first date with professional pie baking. I had a vague notion of where the shop was in relation to where I was staying, having picked up a map from the local bike shop and Googled biking directions on my phone, so I strapped on my helmet and took off. The weather was ideal, the city skyline was picturesque, and each Seattle hill I encountered, while bigger than anything I'd ever biked up before, was surmountable.

Google had estimated that my trip would take forty minutes, give or take, so after forty-five minutes of confused biking and countless backtracking along the Burke-Gilman Trail I was tired, unbelievably sweaty, and cursing the fact that I hadn't thought to bring a water bottle. In trying desperately to follow increasingly confusing directions I had somehow managed to get myself forty-five minutes farther away from my final destination. Not only did I have to bike back to where I had begun, but it would still be another half hour to the pie shop. I nearly gave up right there.

Maybe the whole trip had been a mistake. Not just the biking portion of my day, but being in Seattle in the first place, chasing after an unlikely dream. I was lost and completely terrified of having made a mess of my life. I dejectedly took off my helmet and wheeled my bike to the edge of the trail. As I sat there feeling sorry for myself I noticed that the bushes lining the trail were overflowing with fresh wild blackberries, ripe and ready to be picked. I plucked one off a bush, popped it into my mouth, and was instantly transported to a memory of picking berries in my grandmother's backyard.

I thought of my brother and me rushing and reaching around thorns to pick as many of the tangy sweet berries as our stomachs could hold. Filling bowls and buckets, the telltale berry stains on our lips proving that we had eaten more than we ever put aside. I remembered my grandmother teaching me how to roll the juicy berries in sugar and bake them into the tiniest of tarts, to be served at our frequent teddy bear picnics. I remembered standing among my aunts and my mother in our unbearably hot kitchen, watching them effortlessly make homemade blackberry jam. I would steal a berry every now and again as they split each batch of jam into their endless supply of Mason jars and set them into the boiling water on the stovetop, waiting for the faint pop that would signify a good seal. I had a history with blackberries, just like I had a history with baking. I figured that to give up before I had even started would be a disappointment not only to me but also to several generations of strong baking ladies.

Those roadside blackberries cleared my head and calmed my spirits. Any city that allowed blackberries to grow wild for the enjoyment of those living there could not have been a mistake to visit. After I'd eaten my fill, I climbed back on my bike and made my way, slowly yet surely, to High 5 Pie.

Pumpkin Pie

PREP TIME: 1 HOUR 30 MINUTES • **BAKE TIME:** 45 TO 55 MINUTES • **TOTAL TIME:**
2 HOURS 30 MINUTES • **MAKES:** ONE 9-INCH SINGLE-CRUST PIE (6 TO 8 SLICES)
OR SIX 5-INCH SINGLE-CRUST TEENY PIES

You could say that this whole Tour of Pie vagabond baker journey began with a pumpkin pie. The fall of 2010 found Aaron and me peeking into our CSA box to discover the cutest of pie pumpkins nestled among the rest of our vibrant veggies, which of course sparked the question, "Do you know how to make pie?" I did, in fact, know how to make pie, and while I know a whole lot more now, it's awfully nice to think back to the little pumpkin that unwittingly changed the rest of my life, and remember the simplicity with which this whole crazy adventure started.

This recipe is based on the one provided by our CSA. For a long time I kept trying to add a few more "Thanksgiving-ish" spices, but Aaron refused to enjoy it as much as he enjoys this simply spiced version, which truly lets the pumpkin shine. This recipe yields just over three and a half cups of filling, so if you're making the Teeny Pie version, it's best to use two disks of the dough because it will line six 5-inch pans(you'll have a bit of crust left over).

No matter which size you go with, I highly recommend serving this pie with the Lemon Zested Whipped Cream on page 47. The bright lemon flavor of the cream is a wonderful foil for the warm, spice-infused pumpkin filling. Yum.

INGREDIENTS

1 small pie pumpkin
(1½ to 2 pounds)

½ teaspoon ground
cinnamon

½ teaspoon salt

½ teaspoon ground ginger

4 large eggs

1 cup honey (local if you
have it)

½ cup heavy (whipping)
cream

1 disk dough from Whole
Wheat Crust (page 28)

Up to 3 tablespoons
all-purpose flour, for
rolling out the crust

1. Preheat the oven to 350°F with a rack in the middle position.

2. Break the stem off the pumpkin and, using a large, sharp chef's knife, cut it in half through the stem end. Scoop out the seeds with a metal spoon (save them for toasting, see page 75), lightly oil the cut surface, and place the halves cut side down on a rimmed baking sheet. Bake the pumpkin until it's tender and a fork pierces the flesh easily, 45 minutes to 1 hour. Remove the pumpkin from the oven and let it cool for 15 minutes. Turn the oven up to 375°F.

3. Using your fingers, remove the pumpkin peel, which will have pulled away from the flesh and should be very easy to take off. Place the flesh in a food processor, and puree until smooth.

4. Place 2 cups of the pumpkin puree in a large bowl, add the cinnamon, salt, and ginger, and stir until everything is combined.

5. Whisk together the eggs in a separate small bowl. Add the eggs to the pumpkin mixture along with the honey and heavy cream, and stir with a spoon until smooth. Set aside.

6. Prepare the crust: Place the dough disk on a floured work surface and with a floured rolling pin roll it into a rough 11-inch circle about ⅛ inch thick. Lay the crust into a 9-inch pie dish, gently press it in, and trim any excess dough from the edge with a paring knife, being sure to leave a ¾-inch overhang. Tuck the overhanging dough under itself and crimp.

7. Set the crust on a rimmed baking sheet before giving the filling one final stir and pouring it into the crust. Bake until a knife inserted 1 inch from the edge comes out clean, 45 to 55 minutes. Let cool at room temperature for at least 30 minutes before serving.

Pumpkin Pie will keep for 4 to 5 days, covered, on the countertop.

 ## MAKE 'EM TEENY PIES

In step 6, divide the dough (remember, you'll want to use both dough disks) into six equal balls. Roll out each into a rough 6-inch circle about ⅛-inch thick. Lay each circle into a 5-inch pie tin, and trim any excess dough from the edge, being sure to leave a ½-inch overhang. Tuck the excess dough under itself and crimp. Set the crust-lined pie plates on a rimmed baking sheet.

Give the filling one final stir and spoon an equal amount into each crust-lined plate.

Bake the Teeny Pies until a knife inserted 1 inch from the edge comes out clean, 40 to 50 minutes. Let cool for 30 minutes before serving.

SNACK ATTACK: TOASTED PUMPKIN SEEDS

Be sure to save the seeds from your scooped-out pumpkin goop! Clean off any bits of flesh, place them in a colander, give them a good rinse, and pat them dry with paper towels. Then simply toss them with oil and a couple of teaspoons of cinnamon sugar or a combination of lemon pepper and salt, spread them on a rimmed baking sheet, and toast them in the oven while the pumpkin bakes. Now you've got a tasty treat to snack on while you wait for your pie to finish baking.

I usually pull a cup and a half to two cups of seeds from my pie pumpkins, but if you pull more than that, you can easily add a little more seasoning; it's pretty hard to mess up. Here's another of my favorite combos:

INGREDIENTS

1½ to 2 cups raw pumpkin seeds, rinsed and dried

½ tablespoon olive oil

1 teaspoon salt

1 teaspoon curry powder

Place the seeds in a large bowl, drizzle them with the olive oil, and toss to coat. Mix together the salt and curry powder in a small bowl and sprinkle over the seeds. Toss until the seeds are evenly coated, then spread the seeds in a single layer on a rimmed baking sheet and bake along with your pumpkin (at 350°F) until crispy, 10 to 12 minutes.

Lady Bakership Lesson #1
A PROPER HAIRDO IS ESSENTIAL

When working with food of any kind, it's pretty essential to keep your hair out of it, and I quickly realized at my first pie shop that bandanas were the cute and colorful baker's choice for making that happen. Luckily, being a biker in Chicago, where bandanas and baby wipes are summer essentials, I was ready to rock my favorite colors with the best of them. I decided to wear my hair in two high buns, like Mickey Mouse ears, with my baby-blue bandana tied in front to catch any flyaways. First shop and I certainly looked the part at least!

Sweet Potato Pie

PREP TIME: 1 HOUR 30 MINUTES • **BAKE TIME:** 45 TO 55 MINUTES •
TOTAL TIME: 2 HOURS 30 MINUTES • **MAKES:** ONE 9-INCH SINGLE-
CRUST PIE (6 TO 8 SLICES) OR SIX 5-INCH SINGLE-CRUST TEENY PIES

I started making this pie after buying a whole case of sweet potatoes while apprenticing in Ithaca, New York, never imagining just how many pies I would have to make before reaching the bottom of the box. Thankfully, after the first few pies Aaron realized it was one of his favorites; paired with a cup of strong black coffee, sweet potato pie is one of the best breakfast pies around. When I began recipe testing for this book, pie after pie of every imaginable flavor popped up on the counter for Aaron to eat his way through. He accepted his pie-tasting duty with enthusiasm, but he was always happiest when I managed to add Sweet Potato Pie to the rotation . . . they provided a monthly cleansing of the pie palate.

Since baking the potatoes takes a bit of time, you can always prebake your taters and make the filling later on. Simply remove the skins from the baked sweet potatoes and store them naked in a sealed container or ziplock bag in the refrigerator for up to a week.

Like the pumpkin pie on page 71, this recipe yields just over three and a half cups of filling, so if you're making Teeny Pies, you'll want to use two disks of the dough because it will give you enough crust for six Teeny Pies.

INGREDIENTS

2 medium-large sweet potatoes

1½ teaspoons ground cinnamon

½ teaspoon salt

1 teaspoon ground ginger

3 large eggs

¾ cup honey (local if you have it)

½ cup heavy (whipping) cream

1 disk dough from Whole Wheat Crust (page 28)

Up to 3 tablespoons all-purpose flour, for rolling out the crust

1. Preheat the oven to 350°F with a rack in the middle position. Line a rimmed baking sheet with aluminum foil.

2. Cut the potatoes in half lengthwise, lightly oil the cut surfaces, and place cut side down on the prepared baking sheet. Bake the potatoes until they are tender and a fork pierces the flesh easily, 45 minutes to 1 hour. Remove the potatoes from the oven and let them cool for 15 minutes. Turn the oven up to 375°F.

3. Scoop the sweet potato from the skins and into a large bowl (discard the skins—or eat them!). Mash the potatoes with a potato masher or fork until as smooth as possible. (If you like a completely smooth sweet potato pie, you can puree the potatoes in the food processor.)

4. Transfer 2 cups of the mashed sweet potatoes to a large bowl, add the cinnamon, salt, and ginger, and stir together until the spices are fully incorporated.

5. Whisk together the eggs in a small bowl. Add them to the sweet potato mixture along with the honey and heavy cream and stir with a spoon until combined. Set aside.

6. Prepare the crust: Place the dough on a floured work surface and with a floured rolling pin roll it into a rough 11-inch circle about ⅛ inch thick. Lay the crust into a 9-inch pie plate, gently press it in, and trim any excess dough from the edge with a paring knife, being sure to leave a ¾-inch overhang. Tuck the overhanging dough under itself and crimp.

7. Place the unfilled crust on a rimmed baking sheet before giving the filling one final stir and pouring it into the crust (this makes it easier to transfer the filled crust to the oven without spilling). Bake until a knife inserted 1 inch from the edge comes out clean, 45 to 55 minutes. Let cool at room temperature for 30 minutes before serving.

Sweet Potato Pie will keep for 4 to 5 days, covered, on the countertop.

 MAKE 'EM TEENY PIES

In step 6, divide the dough (remember, you'll want to use both dough disks) into six equal balls. Roll out each into a rough 6-inch circle about ⅛ inch thick. Lay each circle into a 5-inch pie tin, and trim any excess dough from the edge, being sure to leave a ½-inch overhang. Tuck the overhanging dough under itself and crimp.

Give the filling one final stir and spoon an equal amount into each crust-lined tin.

Bake the Teeny Pies until a knife inserted 1 inch from the edge comes out clean, 40 to 50 minutes. Let cool at room temperature for 30 minutes before serving.

Bourbon Bacon Pecan Pie

PREP TIME: 30 MINUTES • **BAKE TIME:** 50 TO 60 MINUTES • **TOTAL TIME:** 1 HOUR
30 MINUTES • **MAKES:** ONE 9-INCH SINGLE-CRUST PIE (6 TO 8 SLICES) OR FOUR
5-INCH SINGLE-CRUST PIES

Pecan pie has never been my favorite. More often than not it's too sugary and too heavy and the lovely nutty, salty goodness of the pecans is often smashed out of existence by the cloying sweetness of the corn syrup. Every Thanksgiving I barely make it through half a slice before waving the white flag of surrender. Somewhere in the wake of half-eaten, disappointing slices I realized that, as a pie baker, I could make a change. I had the ability to reimagine pecan pie in a way that made it palatable to my sugar-sensitive taste buds.

I started by experimenting with different types of sugar and the quantity in which I used them. The amount of corn syrup I used needed to stay the same because any less and the filling became crumbly as opposed to custardy under the quintessential candied sugar layer. So I tested and tinkered with various sugars—white, dark brown and light—until I hit upon a winner. By the time I was finished I felt like the Goldilocks of pecan pie; light brown sugar was just right.

At that point I had a pretty stellar but altogether traditional pecan pie recipe. A few somethings were missing; I just didn't know what those somethings were yet. While I was looking at a million different recipes to get the proportions right, Google kept mentioning that people often put bourbon into their pecan

INGREDIENTS

6 tablespoons (¾ stick)
  unsalted butter,
  at room temperature

1 cup packed light
  brown sugar

3 large eggs

½ teaspoon salt

1 teaspoon pure vanilla
  extract

¾ cup dark corn syrup

2 tablespoons bourbon

4 strips bacon, well cooked
  and roughly chopped

1½ cups chopped pecans

1 disk dough from
  Whole Wheat Crust
  (page 28)

Up to 3 tablespoons
  all-purpose flour,
  for rolling out the crust

pies. Having grown up in the company of fairly conservative, "by the Betty Crocker book" bakers, I'd never heard of liquor in a pie. As an adult, however, I'd developed a pretty serious crush on bourbon; I was certainly willing to give it a try. Unsurprisingly, I loved it. The hint of bourbon played nicely with the pecans, and the first few bites had me smiling with delight . . . but the "sweet" was still too emphatic. I realized, at this point, I was on the lookout for something salty.

That's when my bacon wheels started turning. One day I crumbled a few strips into my filling, and the result was out of this world. Bourbon Bacon Pecan Pie is good. It's slap-you-in-the-face-and-then-eat-a-second-slice good. It's the coming together of diverse but delicious ingredients to create the ultimate super-tasty pie.

There are people who have questioned this union, confused and cautious, having already formed a strong opinion about whether or not bacon belongs in a pie. They are easily won over. Others recognize right away the greatness of combining bourbon, bacon, and pecans. They are usually on their second slice by the time the doubters realize how much they like what they are eating. Between the two, Bourbon Bacon Pecan Pie rarely lasts longer than an evening. Slowly but surely I've won people over, and Bourbon Bacon Pecan Pie has become one of my signature recipes.

1. Preheat the oven to 350°F with a rack in the middle position.

2. Whisk together the butter and sugar with a wire whisk in a large mixing bowl until the mixture is light and fluffy.

Add the eggs, one at a time, mixing after each addition. Add the salt, vanilla, corn syrup, and bourbon and whisk until everything is fully incorporated. Stir in the bacon and 1 cup of the chopped pecans. Set aside.

3. Prepare the crust: Place the dough on a floured work surface and with a floured rolling pin roll it into a rough 11-inch circle about ⅛ inch thick. Lay the crust into a 9-inch pie dish, gently press it in, and trim any excess dough from the edge with a paring knife, being sure to leave a ¾-inch overhang. Tuck the overhanging dough under itself and crimp. Place the lined pie dish on a rimmed baking sheet.

4. Arrange the remaining ½ cup of pecans in a layer on the bottom of the pie shell. Give the filling one last stir, in case anything has settled to the bottom. Pour the filling over the pecans and bake until the crust and the pecans are golden brown and the middle of the pie no longer wobbles, 50 to 60 minutes. Let cool at room temperature until the filling is set, at least 45 minutes, before serving.

Bourbon Bacon Pecan Pie will keep for 4 to 5 days, covered, on the countertop.

In step 3, divide the dough into four equal balls. Roll out each into a rough 6-inch circle about ⅛ inch thick. Lay each circle into a 5-inch pie tin, and trim any excess dough from the edge, being sure to leave a ½-inch overhang. Tuck the overhanging dough under itself and crimp.

Divide the ½ cup pecans among the crusts as directed. Give the filling one final stir and pour an equal amount into each crust (about ¾ cup each).

Bake the Teeny Pies until the crust and pecans are browned and the middle of the pies no longer wobbles, 45 to 55 minutes. Let cool at room temperature until the filling has set, at least 45 minutes, before serving.

Browned Butter Pecan Pie

PREP TIME: 30 MINUTES • **BAKE TIME:** 50 TO 60 MINUTES • **TOTAL TIME:** 1 HOUR 30 MINUTES • **MAKES:** ONE 9-INCH SINGLE-CRUST PIE (6 TO 8 SLICES) OR FOUR 5-INCH SINGLE-CRUST TEENY PIES

If, for some crazy, out-of-control, very silly reason, you can't make a Bourbon Bacon Pecan Pie (perhaps you're taking pie to a vegan potluck, and as the only meat-eating friend in the bunch, you don't want to offend) here's a non-bacon-filled, still stellar pecan pie recipe. The idea to brown the butter came from a Greensboro, Alabama, local I met while working at PieLab whose mom's brown butter pecan pie had won awards. The browned butter adds a wonderful flavor . . . and can almost compete with bacon. Almost.

1. Preheat the oven to 375°F with a rack in the middle position.

2. To brown the butter, place it in a small saucepan or shallow skillet over medium-low heat and cook, whisking, until it melts and begins to bubble, 4 to 5 minutes. Continue to cook, whisking constantly, until the butter darkens and turns a nutty tan color and small dark specks begin to form on the bottom of the pan, 2 to 3 minutes more. Immediately remove it from the heat, continuing to whisk it for 30 seconds. Set it aside to cool.

INGREDIENTS

6 tablespoons (¾ stick) unsalted butter

¾ cup dark corn syrup

1 cup packed light brown sugar

½ teaspoon salt

3 large eggs

1 teaspoon pure vanilla extract

1½ cups chopped pecans

1 disk dough from Whole Wheat Crust (page 28)

Up to 3 tablespoons all-purpose flour, for rolling out the crust

3. Whisk together the corn syrup, brown sugar, and salt in a large bowl until fully combined and smooth.

4. Slowly whisk in the cooled browned butter, taking care to leave behind most of the sediment that has settled into the bottom of the pan (a little is just fine!). Continue whisking until the mixture is smooth and the butter is fully incorporated.

5. Whisk together the eggs and vanilla in a separate small bowl. Add them to the corn syrup mixture along with half the chopped pecans, and whisk until they are fully incorporated as well. Set aside.

6. Prepare the crust: Place the dough on a floured work surface and with a floured rolling pin roll it into a rough 11-inch circle about ⅛ inch thick. Lay the crust into a 9-inch pie dish, gently press it in, and trim any excess dough from the edge with a paring knife, being sure to leave a ¾-inch overhang. Tuck the overhanging dough under itself and crimp.

7. Set the unfilled crust on a rimmed baking sheet. Sprinkle the remaining half of the chopped pecans onto the bottom of the crust. Give the filling a final stir, in case anything has settled to the bottom, and pour it over the pecans.

8. Bake until the crust and pecans are browned and the middle of the pie no longer wobbles, 50 to 60 minutes. Let cool at room temperature until the filling has set, at least 45 minutes, before serving.

Browned Butter Pecan Pie will keep for 4 to 5 days, covered, on the countertop.

 **MAKE 'EM TEENY PIES**

In step 6, divide the dough into four equal balls. Roll out each into a rough 6-inch circle about ⅛ inch thick. Lay each circle into a 5-inch pie tin, and trim any excess dough from the edge, being sure to leave a ½-inch overhang. Tuck the overhanging dough under itself and crimp.

Divide the ½ cup pecans among the crusts. Give the filling one final stir and pour an equal amount into each crust (about ¾ cup each).

Bake the Teeny Pies until the crust and pecans are browned and the middle of the pies no longer wobbles, 45 to 55 minutes. Let cool until the filling has set, at least 45 minutes, before serving.

Lady Bakership Lesson #2
MASTER SOMETHING NEW

At High 5 Pie they use a French rolling pin rather than a roller rolling pin, which meant I had to learn an entirely new way of rolling out dough. They hand-roll all of their crusts at High 5, and the combination of the French rolling pin and the very cold, very hard, all-butter dough left the palms of my hands aching by the end of the day. By the end of the first week, however, I was a master of the French rolling pin, with some newfound baker muscles and an overwhelming desire to answer *"oui"* to every question.

Honey Ginger Pie

PREP TIME: 30 MINUTES • **CHILL TIME:** 2 TO 4 HOURS • **TOTAL TIME:**
4 HOURS 30 MINUTES • **MAKES:** ONE 9-INCH SINGLE-CRUST PIE (6 TO 8 SLICES)

INGREDIENTS

2 cups whole milk

⅓ cup honey (local if
    you have it)

3 tablespoons cornstarch

3 large egg yolks

2 teaspoons freshly
    grated peeled ginger
    (from about a 2-inch
    piece of ginger;
    see Note)

3 tablespoons unsalted
    butter

1 prebaked 9-inch Buttery
    All-Purpose Crust
    (page 30)

Homemade Whipped
    Cream (page 45),
    for serving

I recently started using honey in place of sugar for a few different pies and have been particularly besotted with the results. I think honey is especially nice in fall and winter pies because it adds a sweetness that isn't overwhelming. It's a warm sort of sweet, rather than a shocking, toothache-inducing sweet.

When I was little I went through a phase where I would put honey in my milk while my brother doused his with Hershey's chocolate syrup. When trying to think of new and exciting flavors for age-old cream pies I was reminded of this childhood habit and decided to see if I could make a milk-and-honey pie; the fantastic end result was this recipe. I particularly like the small bite of flavor that fresh grated ginger provides.

This pie calls for a single flaky, prebaked crust; for prebaking instructions, see page 25. And don't skimp on the whipped cream—you'll be glad I reminded you!

1. Whisk together 1¾ cups of the milk with the honey in a medium saucepan until the honey has dissolved and the mixture is smooth.

2. Whisk together the remaining milk, the cornstarch, and egg yolks in a separate small bowl until smooth. Add this mixture to the milk and honey in the saucepan.

3. Cook the milk mixture over medium heat, whisking constantly, until it comes to a boil, 10 to 15 minutes. Let it boil, still whisking constantly and being sure to scrape the bottom of the pan to prevent it from scorching, until the mixture is smooth and thick enough to scoop up, but still pourable, about 2 minutes more. Immediately remove it from the heat.

4. Add the ginger and butter and whisk until the butter has melted completely and the mixture is smooth. Pour the hot filling into the pie crust and cover, while still hot, with plastic wrap before putting it in the refrigerator to prevent a film from forming on the top.

5. Let the pie chill until it is set, at least 2 hours. Remove the plastic wrap, top with the whipped cream, and serve cold.

NOTE: I like to use a very fine grater to grate my ginger so there are no large chunks in the smooth filling; Microplane is my favorite brand. Make sure to peel the ginger's tough outer skin (easily done with a teaspoon) before grating.

Honey Ginger Pie will keep for 2 to 3 days, covered, in the refrigerator.

Sam and Ian, owners of Emmy's Organics

Emmy's Organics

Ithaca, NY

Emmy's Organics is owned and operated by my good friends Samantha Abrams and Ian Gaffney. All of their products are vegan and gluten free, and, rather than baking their incredibly wonderful macaroons, granola, and fudge, they use the process of dehydrating.

I was determined to have Emmy's Organics as a stop on the Tour of Pie because Samantha and Ian are rock-star business partners who exude an energy and a business savvy that I hope to emulate someday. They began making raw and gluten-free macaroons in 2008, and their business has grown by leaps and bounds since then.

I loved spending time in their kitchen, dancing along to whatever music was playing (usually something with a pretty impressive beat that kept us awake and lively) and spreading granola onto dehydrating trays or packaging macaroons in their eco-friendly bags. The kitchen itself was large and open, with several long tables delineating different

workstations. Rows of tall dehydrators lined the far wall of the space and were constantly filled with rotating trays of macaroons, granola, and Sunnies (Emmy's flavored sunflower seeds). There's something remarkable about making something with your hands; it's such a tangible thing, seeing and handling the product from start to finish. Sam and Ian managed to fill their kitchen with like-minded, passionate people, and the love they have for their food and the lifestyle it promotes is wonderfully clear on their faces. It made them a joy to work with, and to learn from. Their dedication to sustaining and growing their business made it clear just how much time and effort it takes to be successful, and how important it is to have an unwavering belief in yourself and your product.

Not only did I get to experience the pace of the Emmy's Organics kitchen while I was apprenticing, but Samantha and Ian spent a considerable amount of time helping me understand the ins and outs of owning a small business. Their advice was invaluable (I still find myself saving all of my receipts and weighing my ingredients . . .) but one of the things that really stuck with me was the notion of buying in bulk as often as possible, from people I could develop a personal relationship with. While I was in town I bought my very first commercial-size bag of whole wheat flour from Farmer Ground Flour, which is milled right in Trumansburg, New York. It made me incredibly happy to buy flour from a small local business, knowing that while I was supporting their endeavors they, in turn, with their high-quality product, would be supporting mine. With a little extra time on my hands and a lot of extra flour to use before the end of the month, I thought about trying to sell my pies locally. And after a lot of nudging from Sam and Ian, I found myself sitting at a high table in the back of Felicia's Atomic Lounge, listening to the Saturday lineup of musicians rock out, selling a slew of Teeny Pies on the busiest night of the week.

It was one of my first forays into selling my own pies and while I should have been intimidated I was remarkably calm and collected. Sam and Ian had helped me see that by using ingredients I had sourced locally, I was ensuring not only that they would taste delicious but that the community would, in turn, rise up to support me. Greeted with new and familiar faces each week, I began to establish a place for myself as the "pie lady" within the walls of that tiny bar. My dozen pies sold out one Saturday after the next. Once a week, the tiniest of sweet potato and apple pies would share the cocktail napkins of strangers, who turned into customers and, in some wonderful instances, into friends. It was a small but important start of something as I came to love being part of the community I was peddling pie to.

202 Taughannock
Boulevard
Ithaca, NY 14850
607-319-5113
emmysorganics.com

Next Stop: Somerville, MA (page 116)

Emmy's Berry Cobbler

PREP TIME: 20 TO 30 MINUTES • **CHILL TIME:** 30 MINUTES • **TOTAL TIME:** 1 HOUR
SERVES: 6 TO 8

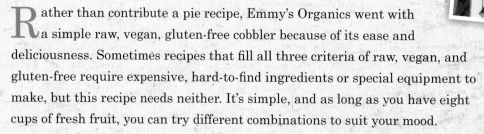

Rather than contribute a pie recipe, Emmy's Organics went with a simple raw, vegan, gluten-free cobbler because of its ease and deliciousness. Sometimes recipes that fill all three criteria of raw, vegan, and gluten-free require expensive, hard-to-find ingredients or special equipment to make, but this recipe needs neither. It's simple, and as long as you have eight cups of fresh fruit, you can try different combinations to suit your mood.

The dates in the crust and topping provide some sweetness and a chewy texture. To save on prep time, soak them while you pull together the other ingredients.

FOR THE CRUST-TOPPING

2 ounces pitted dates (10 to 12 dates; see Note)

3 cups chopped walnuts

¼ teaspoon ground cinnamon

¼ teaspoon ground nutmeg

¼ teaspoon pure vanilla extract (alcohol-free is best)

⅛ teaspoon salt (preferably Himalayan)

1 tablespoon coconut oil

FOR THE FILLING

4 cups fresh raspberries

4 cups fresh blueberries

½ teaspoon freshly grated lemon zest

2 tablespoons freshly squeezed lemon juice

2 tablespoons agave nectar or maple syrup

1 tablespoon pure vanilla extract (alcohol-free is best)

⅛ teaspoon salt

1. Place the dates in a small bowl, add water to cover, and let them sit until softened, about 30 minutes. Drain.

2. Place the dates and the remaining crust ingredients (except for the coconut oil) in a food processor and pulse until everything is combined and the walnuts are still a little chunky.

3. Lightly grease the sides and bottom of a 9-inch square pan with the coconut oil. Lightly press half of the crust mixture into the bottom of the pan to form the crust. Set aside the remaining mixture.

4. Set aside a combined ¼ cup of the berries for garnish and place the rest of the filling ingredients in a large bowl and toss to combine well. Spread evenly over the bottom crust.

5. Sprinkle the remaining crust mixture on top of the filling, one handful at a time, until the filling is covered.

6. Place the cobbler in the refrigerator to set, about 30 minutes. Garnish with the reserved berries and serve cold.

NOTE: If you can't find pitted dates, feel free to buy whole dates and remove the pits yourself: Simply slice the date lengthwise with a paring knife or small serrated knife until you hit the pit, then grasp the pit with your fingertips and pull it out.

Emmy's Berry Cobbler will keep, covered, in the refrigerator for 1 to 2 days.

Sweet Roasted Almond Pie

PREP TIME: 30 MINUTES • **BAKE TIME:** 50 TO 60 MINUTES • **TOTAL TIME:**
1 HOUR 30 MINUTES • **MAKES:** ONE 9-INCH SINGLE-CRUST PIE (6 TO 8 SLICES)

INGREDIENTS

Vegetable oil, for greasing
the baking sheet

1½ cups sliced almonds

5½ tablespoons unsalted
butter

¾ cup packed light
brown sugar

1 teaspoon ground
cinnamon

½ teaspoon salt

3 large eggs

¾ cup light corn syrup

1 disk dough from
Whole Wheat Crust
(page 28)

Up to 3 tablespoons
all-purpose flour,
for rolling out the crust

When I was growing up, my mom always had raw almonds in the house. Along with the usual canisters of flour, sugar, and coffee, she also kept a little jar with raw almonds in it. Maybe it was so that when my brother and I got the urge to snack we had something healthy nearby, or maybe it's just because my mom really likes almonds. Whatever the reason, I learned to love almonds at an early age and never really stopped. While I don't keep my own jar of raw almonds on the counter now, I definitely wanted a pie in my cookbook to feature my favorite nut. What I love about this recipe is that the end result tastes just like the sweet-and-cinnamony nuts that are offered by any roasted-nut vendor in New York City: the perfect snack for a chilly fall day.

1. Preheat the oven to 375°F with a rack in the middle position. Lightly grease a rimmed baking sheet with the vegetable oil.

2. Spread the sliced almonds on the prepared baking sheet and bake until they begin to turn golden brown, 5 to 7 minutes. Set them aside to cool.

3. Place the butter in a small saucepan or shallow skillet over medium-low heat and cook, whisking, until it melts and

begins to bubble, 4 to 5 minutes. Continue to cook, whisking constantly, until the butter darkens and turns a nutty tan color and small dark specks begin to form on the bottom of the pan, 2 to 3 minutes more. Immediately remove it from the heat, continuing to whisk it for 30 seconds. Set it aside to cool.

4. Stir together the brown sugar, cinnamon, and salt in a small bowl.

5. Whisk together the eggs and corn syrup in a large bowl to combine thoroughly. Add the brown sugar mixture and the reserved browned butter and whisk until everything is incorporated and the mixture is smooth. Set aside.

6. Prepare the crust: Place the dough on a floured work surface and with a floured rolling pin roll it into a rough 11-inch circle about ⅛ inch thick. Lay the crust into a 9-inch pie plate, gently press it in, and trim any excess dough from the edge, being sure to leave a ¾-inch overhang. Tuck the overhanging dough under itself and crimp. Place the unfilled crust on a rimmed baking sheet.

7. Stir the toasted almonds into the filling mixture and pour it into the crust-lined plate.

8. Bake until the crust is golden brown and the middle of the pie no longer wiggles when you shake it, 50 to 60 minutes. Let cool at room temperature until set, at least 45 minutes, before serving.

Sweet Roasted Almond Pie will keep for 4 to 5 days, covered, on the countertop.

ALWAYS BUY IN BULK

While I was on the road I had an increasingly tight budget, and I soon realized that a huge chunk of my savings was going toward pie ingredients. While in upstate New York, at Sam and Ian's urging, I bought my very first twenty-five-pound bag of flour and ten-pound case of sweet potatoes. Buying in bulk is key to keeping costs low and production high. Not only did it give me more bang for my buck, but having massive quantities of ingredients on hand provided a constant incentive to make pie. Faced with the possibility of being the proud owner of a case full of rotten potatoes, those sweet potato pies were flying out my oven and into the hands of anyone and everyone I knew.

Aaron's Chicken Potpies with Kale and Cannellinis

PREP TIME: 1 HOUR 30 MINUTES • **BAKE TIME:** 40 TO 50 MINUTES •
TOTAL TIME: 2 HOURS 30 MINUTES • **MAKES:** SIX 5-INCH
DOUBLE-CRUST TEENY PIES

One of the advantages of living with Aaron is that everything has the potential to become a pie. If he likes a certain drink or has a favorite sandwich, he's willing to imagine it as a pie. While that doesn't always work out (I think he's still shuddering at my BLT pie attempt, which, to be fair, was kind of terrible), it's a pretty wonderful way to live. It's fun to have a partner in pie dreaming.

This recipe is a perfect example of Aaron's unparalleled skills in inventing pies. In the fall of 2012, as we were settling into our new apartment in Washington, D.C., Aaron made a kale and chicken soup that became an instant favorite. The third or fourth time he made it we discussed, between delicious steaming mouthfuls, how it would make the perfect chicken potpie. The chicken, potatoes, and carrots usher in the traditional chicken potpie flavors, while kale and cannellini beans add a little updated twist. Aaron went to town and turned that amazing soup into an even better pie.

I always make these—and other savory pies—as 5-inch Teeny Pies because they are much easier to serve. If you'd rather make one large pie, simply use a 9-inch pie plate and two disks of dough from the recipe for Savory Pie Crust on page 32.

INGREDIENTS

FOR THE CHICKEN AND POTATOES

2 boneless, skinless chicken breasts

4 tablespoons olive oil

Salt

1 teaspoon ground black pepper

½ teaspoon red pepper flakes

4 medium potatoes (I like red), cut into 1- to 2-inch chunks

1 teaspoon fresh thyme leaves

FOR THE CRUSTS AND FILLING

3 disks dough from Savory Pie Crust (page 32)

About ¼ cup all-purpose flour, for rolling out the crusts

2 tablespoons olive oil

1 medium onion, peeled and diced

2 carrots, peeled and diced

5 tablespoons all-purpose flour

4 cups chicken stock (canned or boxed is fine)

2 tablespoons finely grated Parmesan cheese

Salt and ground black pepper

4 cups chopped fresh kale

1 can (15 ounces) cannellini beans, drained

1. Preheat the oven to 350°F with a rack in the middle position. Line a rimmed baking sheet with aluminum foil.

2. Prepare the chicken and potatoes: Rub the chicken breasts on both sides with 2 tablespoons of the olive oil and lay them on the prepared baking sheet. Season the chicken with 1 teaspoon salt and the black pepper and red pepper flakes.

3. Place the potatoes in a large bowl, add the remaining olive oil, the fresh thyme, and a few sprinkles of salt, and toss to coat. Spread the potatoes around the chicken on the baking sheet and roast everything together until the chicken is cooked through and the potatoes are tender, 35 to 40 minutes. (If using smaller chicken breasts, check for doneness after 20 minutes; if they are cooked through, remove them from the oven and set them aside while the potatoes continue to roast.) Set aside to cool while you roll out the crusts. Turn the oven temperature up to 375°F.

4. Prepare the crusts: Divide the dough into 12 equal balls and return 6, wrapped in plastic, to the refrigerator. (Six will be used for the bottom crusts and the other 6 for the tops.) Place the 6 dough balls on a floured work surface and with a floured rolling pin roll each into a rough 6-inch circle about ⅛ inch thick. Lay each crust into a 5-inch pie dish, gently press it in, and trim any excess dough from the edge with a paring knife, being sure to leave a ½-inch overhang (do not crimp!). Place the crust-lined tins in the refrigerator.

5. Dust the work surface and rolling pin with flour again, if needed, and remove the remaining dough balls from the

refrigerator. Roll out each into a rough 6-inch circle about ⅛ inch thick. Stack the dough circles on a plate, separated by plastic wrap, and return them to the refrigerator.

6. Prepare the filling: Using two forks, shred the cooled chicken into bite-size pieces; set aside.

7. Heat the olive oil in a large skillet over medium heat. Add the onion and sauté until it is tender and becoming translucent, about 5 minutes. Add the carrots and cook, stirring occasionally, until tender, about 15 minutes.

8. Add the flour to the skillet, stir to coat the vegetables, and cook for 1 minute. Add the chicken stock and simmer, using a wooden spoon to scrape any of the flour bits from the bottom of the pan.

9. Add the shredded chicken, potatoes, and Parmesan cheese and season to taste with salt and black pepper. Bring to a simmer and cook, stirring occasionally, until the liquid is reduced by half, about 15 minutes.

10. Stir in the kale and cannellini beans, and remove from the heat. Transfer everything to a large heatproof bowl and let cool to room temperature. (If you wish to reduce the cooling time, refrigerate the filling for 15 to 20 minutes, stirring occasionally to let the heat escape. But resist the temptation to put hot filling into cold crusts: It will melt the butter in the crusts and they won't hold a crimp!)

11. Remove the crusts from the fridge. Fill each bottom crust with about 1 cup of the filling. Lay a top crust on each, and

trim any excess dough from the edge, being sure to leave a ½-inch overhang. Tuck the overhanging dough under itself, and crimp all the way around to seal.

12. Using a paring knife, cut a small steam vent, roughly ½ inch long, in the top of each pie.

13. Transfer the potpies to a rimmed baking sheet and bake until the crust is golden brown, 40 to 50 minutes. Serve immediately.

Aaron's Chicken Potpies with Kale and Cannellinis will keep for 2 to 3 days, covered, in the refrigerator.

WHEN CRUST WAS JUST ANOTHER NAME FOR LUNCH BOX

Savory pies happen to be some of my favorite kinds; tasty fillings surrounded by a warm, flaky crust make for the perfect meal. But there was a time when it would have seemed strange to consume the pies' bready exterior. When meat pies were introduced to medieval Europe the crust wasn't considered an edible component and was instead treated as more of a lunch box. Savory meats and stews were baked inside a rather inedible crust, usually two to three inches thick, and the crust was tossed after the filling was eaten.

Thank goodness for butter, lard, and shortening, which finally made their way into the pie picture. These fats transformed crusts from doomed-to-be-discarded carrying cases into light, flaky dough pockets meant to enhance their rich fillings.

Apple and Pork Potpies

PREP TIME: 1 HOUR 15 MINUTES • **BAKE TIME:** 45 TO 55 MINUTES • **TOTAL TIME:** 2 HOURS 10 MINUTES • **MAKES:** SIX 5-INCH DOUBLE-CRUST TEENY PIES

INGREDIENTS

1½ pounds ground pork

2 medium onions, peeled and diced

2 cloves garlic, minced

1 teaspoon salt

1 teaspoon ground black pepper

½ to 1 teaspoon red pepper flakes

2 tablespoons chopped fresh sage leaves

2 cups peeled, cored, and roughly chopped apples (from about 2 apples)

2 tablespoons cornstarch

3 disks dough from Savory Pie Crust (page 32)

Up to ¼ cup all-purpose flour, for rolling out the crusts

One of my favorite meals growing up was pork chops with my mom's homemade applesauce. She made the type of applesauce that was minimally spiced, which helped the flavor of the apples shine through, and had large chunks of fruit in every bite. I've always been big on creating the perfect bite, so during those meals I measured everything out just so, making sure I had a little bit of applesauce on my fork for every bite of pork I took. This potpie is a slightly more complex version of that meal; the large chunks of apple temper the spice of the pork, and the sage ties everything together nicely.

I like to use Fuji apples for this recipe, because they are a little tart and firm enough to hold up during baking. Braeburn, Granny Smith, or Pink Lady apples would also be a good choice.

1. Preheat the oven to 375°F with a rack in the middle position.

2. Brown the ground pork in a large skillet over medium heat until it's nearly cooked through and only faintly pink, 7 to 10 minutes. Drain the grease from the pan and return the meat in the skillet to the heat.

3. Add the onions, garlic, salt, black pepper, and red pepper flakes and continue to cook, stirring occasionally, until the

onions are translucent, 5 to 7 minutes. Stir in the sage and apples and cook until the apples just start to soften, 5 to 10 minutes more. Remove the skillet from the heat, drain any juices into a small saucepan, and set them aside; transfer the pork mixture to a large bowl and set it aside.

4. Place the cornstarch in a small bowl, add 3 tablespoons water, and whisk together until the mixture is smooth. Add the cornstarch slurry to the small saucepan with the pan juices and cook over medium heat, whisking constantly, until the mixture begins to boil and thicken, 5 to 7 minutes. Remove from the heat and pour the gravy over the pork mixture, stirring until everything is incorporated. Set aside to cool to room temperature. (To reduce the cooling time, you can refrigerate the filling for 15 to 20 minutes, stirring occasionally to let the heat escape. But be sure not to put hot filling into cold crusts, which will melt the butter in the crimp!)

5. Prepare the crusts: Divide the dough into 12 equal balls and return 6, wrapped in plastic, to the refrigerator. (Six will be used for the bottom crusts and the other 6 for the tops.) Place the 6 dough balls on a floured work surface and with a floured rolling pin roll each into a rough 6-inch circle about ⅛ inch thick. Lay each crust into a 5-inch pie dish, gently press it in, and trim any excess dough from the edge with a paring knife, being sure to leave a ½-inch overhang (do not crimp!). Place the crust-lined tins in the refrigerator.

6. Dust the work surface and rolling pin with flour again, if needed, and remove the remaining balls of dough from the refrigerator. Roll out each into a rough 6-inch circle about ⅛ inch thick. Stack the dough circles on a plate, separated by plastic wrap, and return them to the refrigerator.

7. Once the filling is cool, remove the crusts from the fridge. Give the filling one final stir and scoop an equal amount into each bottom crust. Lay a top crust on each and trim any excess dough from the edge, being sure to leave a ½-inch overhang. Tuck the overhanging dough under itself and crimp all the way around to seal.

8. Using a paring knife, cut a small steam vent, roughly ½ inch long, in the top of each pie.

9. Transfer the potpies to a rimmed baking sheet and bake until the crust is golden brown, 45 to 55 minutes. Serve warm.

Apple and Pork Potpies will keep for 2 to 3 days, covered, in the refrigerator.

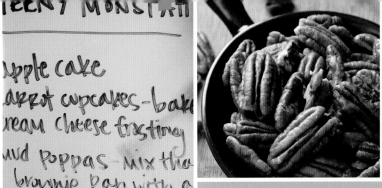

TEENY MONSTAH

apple cake
carrot cupcakes—bake
cream cheese frosting
mud poppas—mix tha
brownie pan with a
ganache, roll into a
meatball & roll in
crumbs (with melted
a bit of salt)
lemon blueberry bar
coffee cake
cookies— whatever

CHAPTER 4

Winter

Pies to Hibernate By

Winter is the season when I go into hibernation mode. I like to cozy up on the couch and read for hours, bundle up from head to toe when I'm forced to go outside, and counteract the chill with pies filled to the brim with bourbon-splashed pecans or melted chocolate. It's the perfect time for baking as my kitchen becomes a sanctuary for anyone seeking to ward off the cold. The promise of warm pie accompanied by a piping-hot toddy is usually enough to tempt friends to come over, even in the dreariest of weather.

Tipsy Pecans

Along with winter comes a certain amount of indulgence. I've found that sharing thick slices of chocolate cream or browned butter pecan pie while playing round after round of dominoes (which can get surprisingly raucous the more sugar we consume) is my ideal way of whiling away those long frigid evenings. Winter fruits like grapefruit, oranges, and pomegranates add a certain zip of flavor, strong enough to wake up slumbering taste buds, and the earthy aroma of rosemary caramel helps to temper the tartness of winter apples.

By October my joyful fall apprenticeships were drawing to a close. I was looking forward to continuing the adventure at a third pie shop, but I became more than slightly worried as the end of the month neared and I was still scrambling to find one. Stop number four, beginning in January, was taken care of: I'd be returning to the city I'd called home for the past five years to take up an apprenticeship at Sweet Sensations Pastry on the north side of Chicago. In the meantime, though, I needed a place to spend my first pie-packed Thanksgiving.

I began my search in Boston, because I knew as long as Aaron was at Harvard, I had a place to stay. Petsi Pies, then in its eighth year of successful business, soon became my top contender. I called the bakery every afternoon, trying to schedule a phone interview with the owner, Renee McLeod. Renee, being the owner of two Boston-area pie shops—one in Cambridge and one in Somerville—and a restaurant in Cambridge's Inman Square, was a hard lady to get hold of. But eventually my persistence paid off, and after a quick explanation of the Tour of Pie and what I could offer for the upcoming months, Renee said yes without hesitation! It was agreed that I would join the team at Petsi Pies for November and part of December.

I arrived in the small city of Somerville the first week of November. The end of fall was around the corner. The last of the bright orange pumpkins lined the sidewalks in front of every store and the distinct smell of approaching colder weather was in the air. Any nervous energy I may have had my first day at the shop lasted all of ten minutes. I was swept up in the general

Winter Teeny Pie offerings

happy exhaustion that permeated the place; Thanksgiving was on its way, and it was time to jump in and get my hands floury.

Pie pumpkins awaiting their fate

The typical Thanksgiving pies, including pumpkin, apple, and sweet potato, were all spoken for before they ever reached the shelves. Pies like Mississippi mud and apple pear cranberry, which were new to me, seemed equally beloved and sought after by the Boston population, all looking to bear the perfect pie to their family festivities.

The pace of the holidays never slowed and before I knew it the end of December had arrived and it was time for me to move on. I rather tearfully said good-bye to my new baking family in Boston and packed my bags for Chicago. I arrived in the city, breathed in the bitter Midwest winter air, and felt as though I'd come home. I spent the first few days reacquainting myself with the city, hopping on and off of the "L" with practiced ease and stopping by friends' apartments bearing pie. After a lovely, friend-filled New Year's I made my way to Sweet Sensations, to meet owner and head baker Sharin Nathan and to check out the bakery where I would be spending the next month.

Bakeries are notoriously slow during January. I think it has something to do with general holiday overindulgence; people are determined to stick to their New Year's resolutions—at least for a little while—and that keeps the pastry lovers away from their favorite bakeries. Despite knowing this, Sharin was happy to host an apprentice, and we got right to work. Depending on the week, I spent two or three days in her small but sweet bakery, passing the hours with a plethora of browned butter, cute cupcakes, and the occasional pie. My focus, during my stay at Sweet Sensations, shifted from being centered entirely around pie and broadened to encompass other essential baking and kitchen techniques. Sharin is a very measured and specific baker, and over the course of my month there I learned to slow down in the kitchen and hone my natural skills into something more professional. She helped me understand that baking is a craft that requires constant practice and attention.

Between Petsi and Sweet Sensations, I was lucky enough to spend the long winter months cozied up in new kitchens, making friends alongside pies.

A handful of what's fresh at the farmers' market in the winter

pumpkins
pears
apples
sweet potatoes
oranges
grapefruit
pomegranates
lemons
limes
squash
kale
beets

Pear and Goat Cheese Tart

PREP TIME: 20 MINUTES • **BAKE TIME:** 30 TO 40 MINUTES • **TOTAL TIME:**
1 HOUR • **MAKES:** 2 TARTS (SERVES 4 TO 6 EACH)

I love how simple yet flavorful this tart is. If you're short on time, it's incredibly easy to put together, and in no time you have an awesome sweet-savory appetizer or a quick dessert.

I recently had a pie party and we started with this tart. The goat cheese got a little toasty and the simple spices made the pear flavor pop. The flavors stayed in my mind the entire evening, and it ended up being my favorite "pie" of the night. It's one of the easiest recipes in the book, so be sure to take advantage of that and bake it all the time.

When placing the crust dough rounds on the baking sheet, don't worry if the circles overlap. You'll fill and form the tarts one at a time, and once the first tart's edge is folded up, you can adjust the spacing on the baking sheet, then fill and form the second tart.

1. Preheat the oven to 400°F with a rack in the middle position. Line a large baking sheet with aluminum foil.

2. Stir together the sugar, cinnamon, and cornstarch in a small bowl until combined.

3. Place the pears in a large bowl and pour the sugar mixture over them. With your hands or a large spoon, gently toss the fruit to coat evenly. Set aside.

INGREDIENTS

¼ cup granulated sugar

½ teaspoon ground cinnamon

2 tablespoons cornstarch

2 to 3 pears, preferably Bartlett, peeled, cored, and roughly chopped (equal to 2 cups; see Note)

2 ounces fresh goat cheese

1 disk dough from Whole Wheat Crust (page 28)

Up to 3 tablespoons all-purpose flour, for rolling out the crust

4. Roll out the crusts: Divide the dough into two equal pieces and form each into a 1-inch-thick disk. On a lightly floured surface with a lightly floured rolling pin, roll one piece of dough into a rough 12-inch circle about ⅛ inch thick. Transfer the dough circle to the baking sheet. Repeat with the remaining dough disk, placing it next to the first dough circle on the baking sheet.

5. Give the pear mixture one final stir and arrange 1 cup of pears in the center of the first dough circle, leaving a 1-inch edge all around (if your pears are very juicy, you may wish to strain off half of the liquid first). Crumble half of the goat cheese evenly over the fruit filling.

6. Starting on one side, fold the edge of the crust up and over the edge of the filling. Make your way around the circle, folding up the extra crust and pleating it as you go. The crust should not meet in the center; the edges just have to be tucked up toward it. The look you're going for by the end is a very rustic tart.

7. Repeat the filling, topping, and folding with the remaining pears, goat cheese, and dough circle.

8. Bake until the crusts are golden brown and the cheese has browned on top, 30 to 40 minutes. Serve warm.

NOTE: If you prefer your pears skin-on, you can skip the peeling and cut them into roughly ¼-inch slices.

Pear and Goat Cheese Tart will keep for up to 3 days, covered, in the refrigerator.

Poached Pear Pie with Cinnamon Crumble

PREP TIME: 12 HOURS (MOST OF IT INACTIVE!) • BAKE TIME: 45 TO 55 MINUTES **TOTAL TIME**: 13 HOURS • **MAKES**: ONE 9-INCH SINGLE-CRUST PIE (6 TO 8 SLICES) OR FOUR 5-INCH SINGLE-CRUST TEENY PIES

INGREDIENTS

1¼ cups plus 1 tablespoon honey (local if you have it)

6 to 7 pears, preferably Bartlett, peeled, cored, and cut into ½-inch thick slices (to equal 6 cups)

2 cinnamon sticks

½ teaspoon ground cinnamon

2 tablespoons cornstarch

1 disk dough from Whole Wheat Crust (page 28)

1 batch Cinnamon Crumble (page 42)

Up to 3 tablespoons all-purpose flour, for rolling out the crust

When I was growing up, my mom and aunts always did a lot of canning late in the summer to stock up on fruit and veggies for the cold Colorado winters. They would make their own applesauce, pickle their own sweet-and-sour pickles, and poach peaches and pears in a sweet syrup. Dessert during the fall was often just sweet pear slices with a dash of cinnamon alongside warm, buttered toast drizzled with honey. It's those simple and homey flavors that I wanted to capture with this pie, as a little nod to my childhood.

Similar to the apple pie on page 53, if you'd like to make Teeny Poached Pear Pies, you'll want to dice the pears into 1-inch cubes rather than slicing them.

1. To poach the pears, bring 4 cups of water and 1¼ cups of the honey to a simmer in a large pot over medium-high heat, stirring often to dissolve the honey, 10 to 15 minutes.

2. Add the pears and cinnamon sticks, cover the pot, and let everything simmer together until the pears are tender and can be pierced with a fork, 20 to 25 minutes.

3. Remove the pot from the heat and let cool to room temperature. For the best flavor, place the covered pot in the fridge overnight. If you don't have time to set the pears aside overnight, a few hours will suffice; the flavor simply won't be as strong.

4. When ready to bake, preheat the oven to 400°F with a rack in the middle position.

5. Spoon the chilled pears into a large bowl, reserving ¾ cup of the steeping liquid in a small saucepan (remove and discard the cinnamon sticks).

6. Add the ground cinnamon, cornstarch, and remaining 1 tablespoon of honey to the reserved steeping liquid and whisk until fully incorporated. Cook over medium heat, whisking constantly, until it begins to simmer and thicken, 5 to 7 minutes. Remove from the heat and let cool for a few minutes.

7. Pour the thickened honey sauce over the pears and stir to coat well. Set aside to cool completely while you prepare the crust.

8. Place the dough on a floured work surface and with a floured rolling pin, roll it into a rough 11-inch circle about ⅛-inch thick. Lay the crust into a 9-inch pie dish, gently press it in, and trim any excess dough from the edge with a paring knife, being sure to leave a ¾-inch overhang. Tuck the overhanging dough under itself and crimp.

Pear Picking

When picking your pears they should be ripe but still firm, with minimal bruising. I like to use Bartlett pears, because they have a sweet flavor and hold up nicely during the poaching process. If you can't find them, Boscs are a good alternative.

9. Spoon the cooled pear filling into the crust and sprinkle the cinnamon crumble over the top, one handful at a time, until the pie is covered.

10. Set the pie on a rimmed baking sheet and bake until the crust and crumble are golden brown, 45 to 55 minutes, covering the crust with foil if it browns too quickly. Let cool for 45 minutes before serving.

Poached Pear Pie with Cinnamon Crumble will keep for up to 3 days, covered, on the countertop.

 ## MAKE 'EM TEENY PIES

In step 8, divide the dough into four equal balls. Roll out each into a rough 6-inch circle about ⅛-inch thick. Lay each circle into a 5-inch pie plate, and trim any excess dough from the edge, being sure to leave a ½-inch overhang. Tuck the overhanging dough under itself and crimp.

Give the filling one final stir and divide it among the crusts (roughly 1½ cups each). Sprinkle the cinnamon crumble over each pie as directed.

Set the Teeny Pies on a rimmed baking sheet and bake until the crust and crumble of each is golden brown, 40 to 50 minutes.

Lady Bakership Lesson #4

YOU MEAN I CAN'T JUST CRUMPLE MY RECEIPTS?

I'd always been told to keep my receipts and file them in an orderly fashion once I'd accumulated enough of them, but until I started the Tour of Pie, I never actually did. I was a huge perpetrator of the "crumple and throw away before even leaving the store" filing system, never understanding why I would need a record of what I'd bought at the grocery store or CVS. But as it turns out, when you're self-employed, it's imperative to understand where your money is going in order to create a comprehensive and reasonable budget . . . not to mention being able to fill out those pesky 1040 tax forms at the end of the year without going into a blind panic trying to figure out how much you spent on granulated sugar.

I now file my receipts away like a lady. One folder for ingredients, one folder for equipment, and one folder for miscellaneous. That way, if anyone tries to dispute just how much I was able to spend on butter in a year, I have plenty of receipts to prove it.

Full-fledged Petsi Pies employee

Petsi Pies

Somerville, MA

I arrived in Somerville, a suburb of Boston, a week before my Petsi Pies apprenticeship began. Six days later I showed up at the shop early and eager: Having had two successful stops on the tour already, I was ready to jump into the third. Renee McLeod, the owner, beamed as she introduced me to the other bakers, the managers, and the baristas on our tour of the tiny kitchen.

This Thanksgiving was Petsi Pies' eighth, so they were old hands at the craziness I was about to experience for the first time. They had just over two thousand pies to make and bake over the span of five days. Two thousand pies. Five. Days. Late-night and earliest-of-early-morning shifts were being scheduled, hundreds and hundreds of pie shells were waiting to be pressed and stored in the walk-in, vast batches of fillings were being made, and Petsi's staff understood that the ovens would be on and piping hot 24/7 until the last pie was baked. The few days before Thanksgiving passed in a blur as I alternated between making buckets of apple mix, whisking together the deliriously pungent pumpkin pie spices, and sheeting top crusts with the best of them, all to the eclectic mix of music emanating from the communal iPod. The front-of-house staff diligently answered the continuously ringing phone and boxed pie after endless pie. When the café no longer resembled a café but instead looked like a packing and shipping plant and there were boxes of pies covering every available surface, we knew we were close.

There was something special about being a part of that holiday bake-off. Everyone was overworked and exhausted by the time they left every day, but no one ever seemed to be upset about it. There were a lot of former employees who came back just to help out with the holidays, each person picking up seamlessly from where the last person left off. Even when cheerfulness seemed impossible, someone was always dancing or joking their way around the kitchen, and the mood stayed light. We depended on one another, laughed, probably felt like crying at some point or another because we were all so tired, but we got through it and, at the end of it all, we managed to make, bake, and box our way to a spectacular Thanksgiving.

In the weeks following Thanksgiving I found my footing as a baker in the Petsi Pies kitchen. I began to feel settled in a way that can come only with time. I finally knew where everything was and as a result I found myself moving around the kitchen with ease. It was the first time since that fateful pie pumpkin that I felt like a professional baker. My presence was taken in such stride that I simply became one of the girls and learned the ins and outs by watching and listening.

Apple pies in mid-assembly

I would arrive each day to my very own list of to-do's that I would need to finish before I left. Cracking eggs, whisking batters, and crafting everything from rich brioche to Mississippi mud pie became easier and easier.

Of course, I still had a few mistakes to make before I moved on to the next stop. I forgot to put sugar in an apple cake, left the eggs out of the blueberry muffins, and one dramatic day managed to smash my finger in the sheeter. A sheeter, you may not know, is a machine consisting of two adjustable rollers, whose only purpose is to flatten dough. People use it to make all sorts of things, like pasta sheets, croissant dough, and, of course, pie dough. Petsi Pies uses the sheeter to roll out their top crusts, effectively saving time and the staff's shoulders by drastically cutting down on the amount of hand-rolling required. There are a million warnings about not placing your hands or fingers anywhere near the two rollers, but due to a brief lapse

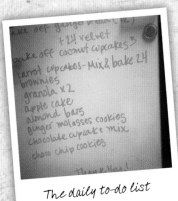

The daily to-do list

Ready for the oven!

of attention, I managed to catch the very tip of my finger in between them. I immediately turned off the machine and took my bruised, rather flattened fingertip to the back to show the other girls and ask what on earth I should do next.

They gathered around like little clucking hens, made me put my head between my knees because I had turned a strange sort of greenish white, and regaled me with their own stories of stupidity to make me feel a little less idiotic. Feeling slightly less mortified, I took a break, ate a slice of pie, and returned to face my newfound fear. Luckily, since then I've not sheeted any part of myself, and that singular experience made me feel like I was one of the gang: In a professional kitchen, burns, cuts, and sheeted fingers are commonplace and the scars are something to be proud of.

Everyone who worked at Petsi Pies was his or her own type of awesome. Bakers, baristas, and managers alike were quirky and hilarious and each of them brought something to the bakery that was entirely and unapologetically *them*. Their personalities helped make the place feel cozy, not cramped, warmly bustling rather than overwhelmingly busy. Because of the people who worked at Petsi, it became my favorite place to be on any given day in Boston. Renee had done a phenomenal job in bringing together an unlikely but altogether wonderful group of people who were much less like employees and much more like family. The atmosphere that I found there gave me something to aspire to as I began to imagine what a pie shop of my own might someday look like.

285 Beacon Street
Somerville, MA 02143
617-661-7437
petsipies.com

Next Stop: Chicago, IL (page 142)

Petsi Pies' Sweet Potato Pie

PREP TIME: 30 MINUTES • **BAKE TIME:** 1 HOUR • **TOTAL TIME:** 1 HOUR 30 MINUTES
MAKES: ONE 9-INCH SINGLE-CRUST PIE (6 TO 8 SLICES)

This was one of my favorite pies to make while I was at Petsi Pies because it meant roasting tray after tray of sweet potatoes in the large commercial ovens. The tubers' sweet, earthy smell filled the small space as they baked, and they were especially fun to peel and plop into large plastic containers, where they sat before being mashed and combined with different spices and poured into the waiting pie shells.

The crust recipe below makes enough dough for three 9-inch pies, so you can use one dough disk right now and refrigerate or freeze the other two for later. The dough will last up to two days in the refrigerator and up to two weeks in the freezer.

FOR THE CRUST

3 cups all-purpose flour, plus up to 3 tablespoons extra for rolling out the crust

¾ cup cold shortening

¾ cup (1½ sticks) cold unsalted butter

1 large egg

5 tablespoons cold water

1 tablespoon white vinegar

1 teaspoon salt

FOR THE FILLING

2 cups peeled, mashed cooked sweet potatoes (from about 2 large potatoes; see Note)

2 large eggs

1¼ cups evaporated milk

½ cup granulated sugar

½ cup packed light brown sugar

½ teaspoon salt

½ teaspoon ground cinnamon

½ teaspoon ground nutmeg

½ teaspoon ground ginger

2 tablespoons pure vanilla extract

¼ cup (½ stick) unsalted butter, melted

1. Make the crust: Place the 3 cups flour, shortening, and butter in a large bowl and gradually work it together with a pastry cutter until it resembles a coarse meal, 3 to 4 minutes.

2. Beat the egg with a fork in a small bowl. Pour it into the flour mixture. Add the cold water, vinegar, and salt and stir together gently until all of the ingredients are incorporated.

3. Separate the dough into 3 equal balls and place each into a large plastic bag or wrap tightly in plastic wrap. Flatten the balls into disks about ½ inch thick. Seal the bags or plastic wrap and refrigerate for at least 1 hour (or longer—see headnote). (If you will be using the dough immediately, you can put it in the freezer for 15 to 20 minutes to chill, instead.)

4. Meanwhile, preheat the oven to 375°F with a rack in the middle position.

5. Make the filling: In the bowl of a food processor or a stand mixer fitted with the paddle attachment, combine the sweet potatoes, eggs, evaporated milk, sugars, salt, cinnamon, nutmeg, ginger, vanilla, and butter and blend on medium speed until smooth. Set aside while you roll out the crust.

6. Remove one disk of dough from the refrigerator or freezer and allow it to thaw until it's still cold but malleable. On a floured surface roll the dough, starting at the center and working your way out. (Sprinkle some flour over the top of the dough if it's a bit too moist.) If the dough is sticking, use a metal spatula and carefully scrape it up and flip it over and continue rolling until it's about ½ inch larger in diameter than your pie pan and ⅛ inch thick.

7. With the plastic scraper or spatula, lift the dough carefully from the surface of the counter into the pie pan. Gently press the dough into the pie pan and crimp the edges. Set the lined pie pan on a rimmed baking sheet.

8. Give the sweet potato filling one final stir and pour it into the unbaked pie shell. Bake for 10 minutes at 375°F, then reduce the heat to 300°F and bake until the filling is firm and a knife inserted 1 inch from the edge comes out clean, 50 minutes more. Let cool for 10 to 20 minutes, until the pie firms up a bit and won't be hot to the touch, before serving.

NOTE: To bake the sweet potatoes, scrub them, prick the skins all over with the tines of a fork, and place them in a 375°F oven until they are soft when pierced with a fork, about 1 hour.

Petsi Pies' Sweet Potato Pie will keep for 3 to 4 days, covered, on the countertop.

Grapefruit and Pomegranate Pie

PREP TIME: 30 MINUTES • **CHILL TIME:** 1 HOUR • **TOTAL TIME:** 1 HOUR 30 MINUTES
MAKES: ONE 9-INCH SINGLE-CRUST PIE (6 TO 8 SLICES)

Grapefruit has always been my favorite winter citrus fruit. In college I would have eaten a grapefruit with every meal if it weren't quite so acidic, so I had to resign myself to one a day, as a mid-afternoon snack. I would peel the grapefruit like an orange and strip it of its particularly sour pith before biting off the surprisingly sweet and flavorful segments. It was a messy affair, requiring several paper towels, and it always took at least twenty minutes to finish the whole thing. Only recently did I discover that Aaron's favorite winter fruit is a pomegranate, and that his process of eating one is startlingly similar to my aforementioned grapefruit process. This pie is the combination of both of those fresh flavors; the tart grapefruit curd envelops the sweet pops of pomegranate, making for a wonderful winter pie.

The fresh grapefruit juice called for here is definitely worth the effort. You want grapefruit with thin skin that will depress slightly when pressed. Before cutting them in half, roll them on the counter, applying pressure with the heel of your hand; you will get more juice out of each grapefruit. And don't worry about straining the pulp out of the juice. I usually use three or four grapefruit per pie, and I spend the rest of the day enjoying the

INGREDIENTS

1¼ cups granulated sugar

4 tablespoons packed cornstarch

2 cups freshly squeezed grapefruit juice (from 3 to 4 grapefruits)

3 large egg yolks

2 tablespoons unsalted butter

½ teaspoon lemon extract

1¼ cups pomegranate seeds (see Note)

1 prebaked 9-inch Sugar Cookie Crust (page 37) or Whole Wheat Crust (page 28)

Homemade Whipped Cream (page 45), for topping

citrus smell that lingers on my palms.

Save any leftover curd and use it as you would marmalade. It will keep for up to 1 week, covered, in the refrigerator.

1. Whisk together the sugar and cornstarch in a medium saucepan until combined. In a small bowl whisk together the egg yolks with ¾ cup water. Stir in the grapefruit juice, and pour into the saucepan. Whisk everything together until the mixture is smooth and a little frothy; the sugar and cornstarch should be fully incorporated.

2. Cook the grapefruit mixture over medium heat, whisking constantly, until it begins to simmer slightly, about 8 minutes.

3. Continue to cook, still whisking constantly, over medium heat until the mixture comes to a full boil, about 1 minute. Let boil for 1 minute, again whisking constantly and scraping the bottom of the pan so the mixture doesn't scorch. Immediately remove from the heat. The mixture should easily coat the back of a spoon and look smooth and glassy.

4. Add the butter and the lemon extract to the grapefruit curd and whisk until smooth. Fold in 1 cup of the pomegranate seeds with a rubber spatula until they are evenly distributed.

5. Pour the hot grapefruit curd into the pie shell and let sit, uncovered, at room temperature to set and cool completely, at least 1 hour.

6. Spread the whipped cream over the cooled pie, scatter with the remaining pomegranate seeds, and serve.

Grapefruit and Pomegranate Pie will keep for 1 to 2 days, covered, in the refrigerator.

NOTE: Getting pomegranate seeds out of the actual pomegranate can be a little tricky, so I like to cut the pomegranate in half lengthwise (through the stem end) and then into quarters. Then I take each segment and bend the rind outward to expose the seeds. Most of the seeds will easily come away from the outer skin and then all you have to do is peel away the thin white membrane between each layer of seeds. If you don't have time to peel the pomegranate yourself, you can buy the seeds at a natural foods supermarket like Whole Foods . . . but only when they are in season!

A LITTLE HELP FROM MY FRIENDS

Two months into the Tour of Pie I was faced with an unwelcome reality: Despite my careful budgeting, I wouldn't last more than six months on the tour unless I raised some money. Which is when I turned to Indiegogo. Indiegogo, similar to Kickstarter, is an online crowd-funding website filled to the brim with new and exciting projects from all over the world. Hoping I had a project that would garner the attention of friends and strangers alike, I put together a video outlining my pie-funding plea and peppered it with mouthwatering photos of tiny blackberry pies and Mason jars masquerading as sweet apple pies. I uploaded it onto the website and waited to see if luck and love were on my side. The results were staggering. Never had I felt more supported and encouraged to follow my dreams. Friends, family, and a slew of strangers all rallied around my vagabond pie ideas and donated to the project. While I didn't make my ultimate goal, I certainly had enough to continue the journey. Feeling awed and grateful, I did just that.

Orange Cream Pie

PREP TIME: 30 MINUTES • **CHILL TIME:** 4 HOURS • **TOTAL TIME:** 4 HOURS 30 MINUTES • **MAKES:** ONE 9-INCH SINGLE-CRUST PIE (6 TO 8 SLICES) OR FOUR 5-INCH SINGLE-CRUST TEENY PIES

INGREDIENTS

½ cup granulated sugar

½ teaspoon salt

¼ cup packed cornstarch

2 cups whole milk

4 large egg yolks

2 tablespoons unsalted butter

2 teaspoons freshly grated orange zest

½ cup freshly squeezed orange juice, strained through a fine-mesh sieve

2 to 3 teaspoons orange extract (optional)

1 prebaked 9-inch Buttery All-Purpose Crust (page 30)

Homemade Whipped Cream (page 45), for topping

When I was young, I lived for orange Creamsicles in the summertime. That rich vanilla and tart orange ice cream bar was the best way to cool down after a long bike ride or several hours running around the park. While the makers of my sugary summer treat probably didn't care much about cooking in season, they did understand that oranges and cream are a stellar combination. And since citrus is in season during the dreary winter months, what better way to celebrate fresh flavors than by squeezing your own ripe oranges, bursting with flavor, and whisking them into a dreamy orange cream pie? The inspiration for this pie might suggest that it's frozen, but in fact, it's not . . . it's just a little salute to childhood summers gone by.

1. Whisk together the sugar, salt, and cornstarch in a medium saucepan. Add the milk and egg yolks and whisk together until there are no lumps.

2. Place the saucepan over medium heat and cook, whisking constantly, until the mixture comes to a low simmer and begins to thicken, about 8 minutes. Continue cooking, whisking constantly and being sure to scrape the bottom of

the pan to prevent scorching, until the mixture begins to boil, about 1 minute more. Still whisking constantly, let it boil for a full minute, then immediately remove it from the heat.

3. Add the butter, orange zest, and orange juice and whisk until the butter is melted and everything is fully incorporated. If the orange flavor isn't quite strong enough, stir in 2 teaspoons of the orange extract, adding more if necessary. The mixture should be creamy, thick, and smooth.

4. Pour the orange cream into the pie shell and, while hot, cover it with plastic wrap to prevent a film from forming on the top. Refrigerate the pie until the filling has set, at least 4 hours. Remove the plastic wrap and top with the whipped cream before serving.

Orange Cream Pie will keep for 2 to 3 days, covered, in the refrigerator.

 ## MAKE 'EM TEENY PIES

Prepare and prebake the crust in four 5-inch teeny tins as directed. In step 4, divide the filling among the crusts and proceed with the recipe as directed.

WINTER WANDERINGS AT WALDEN POND

In early December my time in Massachusetts was coming to an end, and I was trying to see more of the place that was fast becoming one of my favorites. Just before bidding farewell to Boston, Aaron and I took a last-minute trip to Walden Pond. I had baked several Teeny Pies earlier in the week, with the express purpose of taking pictures of them about town, and Walden seemed perfectly picturesque. Fall had made its chilly transition and the brisk air left the pond nearly empty. Aaron and I wandered our way around the winter water, occasionally saying hello to the few other people who seemed to find as much joy as we did in a place deserted, our tiny pastries bringing bemused smiles to the faces of our fellow Walden walkers. When we happened upon the statue of Henry David Thoreau himself, we were in for a delightful surprise. It was as though this bronze-cast Thoreau had been waiting decades to cradle a pie in his outstretched hand. Once we placed our offering in his grasp, his quizzical gaze fell adoringly on the tiny pie, as if he couldn't imagine how this lovely bit of dessert, brimming with tart, crisp apples, had come to rest in his palm, or how he had lived so long without it. I like to imagine that if he'd had the opportunity to eat a Teeny Pie while on his sojourn away from society, the title of his book may have varied ever so slightly. *Walden Pie*, perhaps.

Thoreau gazing lovingly at his Teeny Pie.

Peanut Butter Brownie Pie with a Pretzel Crust

PREP TIME: 40 MINUTES • **BAKE TIME:** 35 TO 40 MINUTES • **TOTAL TIME:**
1 HOUR 20 MINUTES • **MAKES:** ONE 9-INCH SINGLE-CRUST PIE (6 TO 8 SLICES)

After Aaron sent me an article featuring mouthwatering pretzel-crusted brownies, I began daydreaming about a brownie pretzel pie topped with decadent swirls of creamy peanut butter. I went searching far and wide to find the perfect brownie recipe for this pie and eventually turned to my blog followers for help. Many of them sent in their favorite family recipes, for which I was incredibly grateful. After some happy experimenting, I devised a recipe for a chewy, rich chocolate brownie, the bulk of which came from Rebecca, a fan of my Teeny Pies blog, who had answered the brownie plea. To that I added the peanut butter twist and the pretzel crust, which, with its salty crunch, is perhaps my favorite part.

If you have any leftover brownie batter and peanut butter swirl when you make this pie, bake them off as individual brownies alongside the pie. Simply pour the brownie batter into Teeny Pie (or muffin) tins, swirl the peanut butter through it as directed, and pull them from the oven about ten minutes earlier than the big pie (or when a knife inserted in the middle comes out clean).

INGREDIENTS

6 tablespoons (¾ stick) unsalted butter

6 ounces semisweet chocolate (I use individually wrapped 1-ounce pieces)

½ cup creamy commercial peanut butter, such as Skippy

¼ cup unsweetened cocoa powder

2 large eggs

1 cup granulated sugar

2 teaspoons pure vanilla extract

¾ cup all-purpose flour

¼ teaspoon baking powder

¼ teaspoon salt

1 prebaked 9-inch Pretzel Crust (page 36)

1. Preheat the oven to 350°F with a rack in the middle position.

2. Fill a medium saucepan with water, leaving a space of 2 to 3 inches at the top, and bring to a boil over medium-high heat.

3. Place the butter, chocolate, and ¼ cup of the peanut butter in a large heatproof bowl (it should be big enough to sit on top of the saucepan without touching the water). Set the bowl on the saucepan and heat, stirring occasionally, until the butter, chocolate, and peanut butter have melted. Remove the bowl from the heat and whisk in the cocoa powder until smooth. Set the bowl aside to cool.

4. Place the remaining ¼ cup peanut butter in a small saucepan over low heat and cook, stirringly occasionally, until it's thinner and almost runny, 5 to 7 minutes. Remove from the heat and set aside.

5. Whisk together the eggs, sugar, and vanilla in a large bowl. Slowly pour the cooled chocolate mixture into the egg mixture and whisk briskly until smooth.

6. Stir together the flour, baking powder, and salt in a small bowl. Add to the brownie batter and stir until smooth.

7. Pour the brownie batter into the pretzel crust, filling it to just below the very top. Spoon three or four small dollops of the melted peanut butter on top of the brownie batter and gently swirl it into the batter with a table knife or a toothpick.

8. Bake until a knife inserted 2 inches from the edge of the crust comes out clean, 35 to 40 minutes. Let cool before serving.

Peanut Butter Brownie Pie with a Pretzel Crust will keep for 2 to 3 days, covered, on the countertop.

Chocolate Cream Pie

PREP TIME: 30 MINUTES • CHILL TIME: 4 HOURS • TOTAL TIME: 4 HOURS
30 MINUTES • MAKES: ONE 9-INCH SINGLE-CRUST PIE (6 TO 8 SLICES) OR
FOUR 5-INCH SINGLE-CRUST TEENY PIES

One of my favorite Chicago coffee shops offers the most decadent chocolate pudding on its menu. I'm not often predisposed to order dessert anywhere, but while I was in Chicago for the Tour of Pie I was in the mood for a homey, sweet treat to accompany my coffee, and on a whim I ordered the pudding. I could eat only a few bites because it was so rich, but it got me thinking about the perfect chocolate cream pie. I imagined that a rich chocolate pudding would taste divine in a buttery, flaky crust and that a thin slice topped with airy whipped cream would be the perfect, decadent serving size. It was only after sharing this pie with friends that we collectively came to the conclusion that a little Orange Zested Whipped Cream was the perfect finishing touch; the bright citrus cut into the deep cocoa taste, adding a breath of fresh flavor to this rich chocolate pie.

1. Whisk together the sugar, cocoa powder, cornstarch, and salt in a large saucepan until well combined.

2. Whisk together the milk, cream, and egg yolks in a separate small bowl until smooth. Pour the milk mixture into the saucepan and whisk until everything comes together and the mixture looks like frothy chocolate milk.

INGREDIENTS

¾ cup granulated sugar

¼ cup unsweetened cocoa powder

3 tablespoons packed cornstarch

¼ teaspoon salt

1½ cups whole milk

½ cup heavy (whipping) cream

4 large egg yolks

1 cup semisweet chocolate chips

1 prebaked 9-inch Buttery All-Purpose Crust (page 30)

Orange Zested Whipped Cream (page 48), for topping

3. Place the saucepan over medium heat and cook, whisking constantly, until the mixture comes to a low simmer and begins to thicken, about 8 minutes. Continue cooking, whisking constantly and being sure to scrape the bottom of the pan to prevent scorching, until the mixture begins to boil, about 5 minutes more. Still whisking constantly, let it boil for a full minute, then immediately remove it from the heat.

4. Add the chocolate chips to the thickened chocolate cream and whisk until they melt completely and the mixture is smooth.

5. Pour the chocolate filling into the pie crust and, while still hot, cover it with plastic wrap to prevent a film from forming on the top. Refrigerate the pie until it's set, at least 4 hours.

6. Before serving, remove the plastic and top with the whipped cream. Serve cold.

Chocolate Cream Pie will keep for 2 to 3 days, covered, in the refrigerator.

MAKE 'EM TEENY PIES

Prepare and prebake the crusts in four 5-inch teeny tins as directed. In step 5, divide the filling among the crusts and proceed with the recipe as directed.

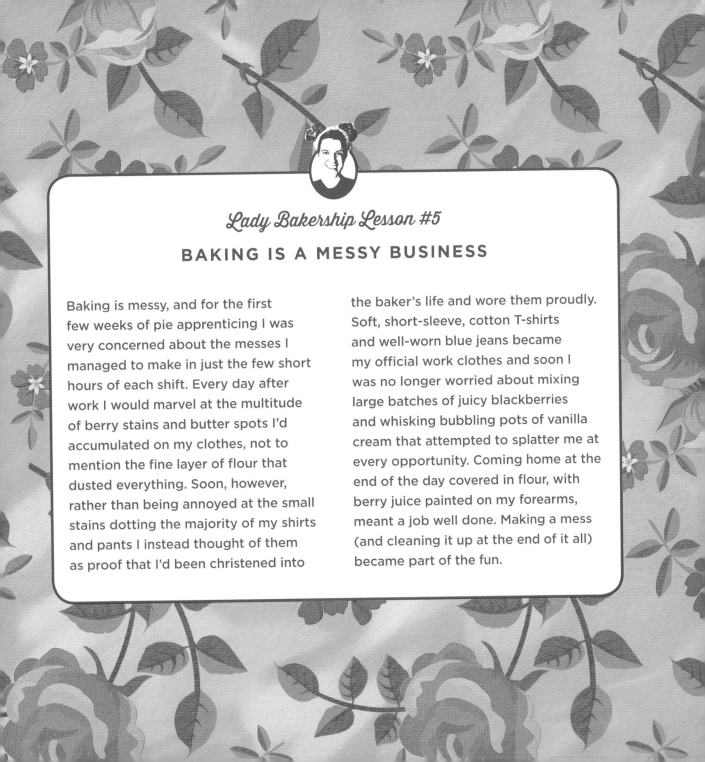

BAKING IS A MESSY BUSINESS

Baking is messy, and for the first few weeks of pie apprenticing I was very concerned about the messes I managed to make in just the few short hours of each shift. Every day after work I would marvel at the multitude of berry stains and butter spots I'd accumulated on my clothes, not to mention the fine layer of flour that dusted everything. Soon, however, rather than being annoyed at the small stains dotting the majority of my shirts and pants I instead thought of them as proof that I'd been christened into the baker's life and wore them proudly. Soft, short-sleeve, cotton T-shirts and well-worn blue jeans became my official work clothes and soon I was no longer worried about mixing large batches of juicy blackberries and whisking bubbling pots of vanilla cream that attempted to splatter me at every opportunity. Coming home at the end of the day covered in flour, with berry juice painted on my forearms, meant a job well done. Making a mess (and cleaning it up at the end of it all) became part of the fun.

French Silk Pie

PREP TIME: 25 MINUTES • **CHILL TIME:** 4 HOURS • **TOTAL TIME:** 4 HOURS 25 MINUTES • **MAKES:** ONE 9-INCH SINGLE-CRUST PIE (6 TO 8 SLICES) OR FOUR 5-INCH SINGLE-CRUST TEENY PIES

INGREDIENTS

¾ cup (1½ sticks) unsalted butter, at room temperature

1 cup granulated sugar

3 ounces unsweetened chocolate, melted and cooled (see headnote)

1½ teaspoons pure vanilla extract

3 pasteurized large eggs (see Note)

1 prebaked 9-inch Graham Cracker Crust (page 35)

Homemade Whipped Cream (page 45), for topping

When I decided to try my hand at making a French silk pie for the first time I was very intimidated. (I mean, it was FRENCH . . . it had to be hard to do, right?!) I very quickly realized it was one of the easiest pies to make, and it's now one of those standbys that I "just whip up" to impress people's pants off. It's kind of like watching a magic show: The speed of the electric mixer (required for this recipe, I'm afraid) and the slow addition of each egg turn a few simple ingredients into a silky, fluffy mass of the most decadent chocolate filling.

To melt the chocolate, I simply heat it in a double boiler over low heat, stirring constantly, for about 5 minutes, or microwave it in a small heat-proof bowl on high power for 1 to 2 minutes, pausing after 1 minute to stir it.

As the spring fruit starts to sneak its way back into the market you can consider layering sliced strawberries or mashed raspberries underneath the filling. My friend Duncan loves to create a starburst-shaped layer of sliced strawberries on top of the graham cracker crust before piling it high with the whipped chocolate; it's like a pretty little secret hiding just below the surface.

1. In the bowl of a stand mixer fitted with the paddle attachment, or in a large bowl using a handheld electric mixer, beat together the butter and sugar on medium-high speed until it is light and fluffy, about 4 minutes.

2. Add the melted chocolate and the vanilla, and beat until smooth. Turn off the mixer and scrape down the side of the bowl to ensure that all of the ingredients are combined.

3. With the mixer running on medium speed, add the eggs one at a time, beating for 3 minutes after each addition. After the third egg is beaten in, the mixture should be lighter in color and smoother and silkier in texture.

4. Spoon the filling into the cooled graham cracker crust, smooth the top with a spatula, and refrigerate, uncovered, for at least 4 hours. Before serving, top with the whipped cream. Serve cold.

NOTE: This recipe calls for raw eggs, so please make sure you use pasteurized—they are available at most supermarkets.

French Silk Pie will keep for 2 to 3 days, covered, in the refrigerator.

 **MAKE 'EM TEENY PIES**

Prepare and prebake the crust in four 5-inch teeny tins as directed. In step 4, spoon an equal amount of filling into each of the crusts (about ½ cup each), smooth the top of each pie with a spatula, and refrigerate for at least 2 hours or up to 4 hours. Before serving, top each with the whipped cream. Serve cold.

Espresso French Silk Pie with Blackberry Compote

PREP TIME: 25 MINUTES • **CHILL TIME:** 4 HOURS • **TOTAL TIME:** 4 HOURS 25 MINUTES
MAKES: ONE 9-INCH SINGLE CRUST PIE (6 TO 8 SLICES) OR FOUR 5-INCH SINGLE-CRUST TEENY PIES

When I was little I would beg my mom to put a few spoonfuls of her coffee into my hot chocolate so I could be a lady and drink a "mocha." This pie reminds me of that, the way the light and fluffy chocolate is piled high and topped with whipped cream with just a hint of espresso to surprise your taste buds. (Since I don't have an espresso maker, I go to my local coffee shop and ask for a shot of espresso to go.)

This pie is similar to the more traditional French silk on page 134 (and also requires a stand mixer or handheld electric mixer to make), but here the espresso and blackberries lend some unexpected twists. In a manner similar to layering strawberries into the bottom of a traditional French silk pie, I like to spoon a sweet blackberry compote over the slices of this one when serving. It reminds me of my time in Seattle, where I was surrounded by coffee and blackberries at every turn.

1. Cream together the butter and sugar in the bowl of a stand mixer fitted with the paddle attachment, or in a large bowl using a handheld electric mixer, on medium-high speed until it is light and fluffy, about 4 minutes.

INGREDIENTS

¾ cup (1½ sticks) unsalted butter, at room temperature

1 cup granulated sugar

3 ounces unsweetened chocolate, melted and cooled (see headnote, page 134)

3 tablespoons freshly brewed espresso, at room temperature

½ teaspoon pure vanilla extract

3 pasteurized large eggs (see Note)

1 prebaked 9-inch Graham Cracker Crust (page 35)

Homemade Whipped Cream (page 45), for topping

Blackberry Compote (page 140), for serving

2. Scrape down the side of the bowl with a rubber spatula and add the melted chocolate. Mix on high until the mixture is very fluffy, 5 minutes. While the mixer is still running add the espresso and vanilla and continue to mix for another minute.

3. Turn the speed down to medium and add the eggs, one at a time, beating for 3 minutes after each addition. After the addition of the third egg the mixture should be lighter in color and smoother and silkier in texture.

4. Spoon the filling into the cooled graham cracker crust, smooth the top with a spatula, and refrigerate, uncovered, for at least 4 hours. Before serving, top with the whipped cream and serve cold with the blackberry compote on top or alongside.

NOTE: This recipe calls for raw eggs. Unpasteurized eggs may contain harmful bacteria, so please make sure you use pasteurized eggs. They are available at most supermarkets.

espresso French Silk Pie will keep for 3 to 4 days, covered, in the refrigerator.

🥧 MAKE 'EM TEENY PIES

Prepare and prebake the crusts in four 5-inch teeny tins as directed. In step 4, spoon an equal amount of filling into each of the crusts (about ½ cup each), smooth the top of each pie with a spatula, and refrigerate for at least 2 hours or up to 4 hours. Before serving, top each with the whipped cream. Serve cold with the blackberry compote if you like.

Blackberry Compote

MAKES: ABOUT 2 CUPS

INGREDIENTS

¼ cup granulated sugar

Pinch of ground cinnamon

2 tablespoons cornstarch

About 1 teaspoon brewed espresso, at room temperature (optional)

1½ cups fresh or frozen blackberries

When I found myself hopelessly lost in Seattle (see page 69) I comforted myself with wild blackberries, and soon after that I realized I wanted to add them to everything. Their tantalizing tart yet sweet flavor is a perfect match for the subtle espresso notes featured in this light-as-air chocolate pie.

1. Whisk together the sugar, cinnamon, and cornstarch in a small bowl. Add ½ cup water and the espresso, if using, and whisk until smooth.

2. Place the blackberries in a medium saucepan, add the sugar mixture, and cook over medium-low heat, stirring often to prevent scorching, until the berries thicken enough to coat the back of a spoon, 7 to 10 minutes. Let the mixture come to a boil and cook, stirring occasionally, for 1 minute, then remove the pan from the heat.

3. Let the compote cool completely before using it to top the individual slices of pie.

Blackberry Compote will keep for 1 week, covered, in the refrigerator.

FROM BLOG TO BOOK

At first the Teeny Pies blog was just a way to keep in touch with my friends, but after a few months I realized it might help garner some publicity for my educational pie endeavor. I started shopping my story around to a bunch of different sites that I was interested in and keeping my fingers crossed for a positive response. Most of them thought I was a robot spammer, which is ridiculous because 1) robots can't bake pies and take pictures of them, and 2) my grammar, compared to that of a robot, is impeccable.

Despite being mistaken for a robot, I had a few successes, namely with The Hairpin and The Huffington Post, which is how I found myself on the receiving end of an email from my now-editor at Workman Publishing asking if I'd ever thought about writing a cookbook. I grew up having more books than friends, and while I'd never considered the possibility that I'd become an author someday, the idea made more sense than I thought it would. I'd been blogging twice a week, I was unabashed in my love for all things pie, and I was slowly discovering how to write about it. Had I consciously thought about writing a cookbook? Nope. Was I thrilled and excited beyond belief to be asked to try? YES! This was a year of being scared witless, of tossing out my expectations of doing "life" in a normal way, and of following my dreams . . . so I wasn't about to say no to writing a book. I bet none of those robot spammers could write a book if their robot lives depended on it.

Sweet Sensations Pastry *Chicago, IL*

Sweet Sensations Pastry isn't a pie-specific bakery, but Sharin Nathan, owner-baker, was open to the idea of having a weekly pie offering during the few weeks of my apprenticeship. Sharin had gone to pastry school, had taken a break from baking professionally to raise her kids, and had recently gotten back into the business in 2010 when she opened Sweet Sensations. Her tiny pink bakery is right off the Montrose stop on the Brown Line "L," and it's a beautiful, open space where customers can peer into the back to watch the baking take place. A long prep table splits the work space in half and large bins of flour and sugar are nestled below. It is just the right size to fit two bakers comfortably, and I soon learned the rhythm of the kitchen. Because Sharin bakes in the back and also serves in the front, she knows most of her regulars by name and greets them warmly when they come in. The bakery is small enough that the smell of baked goods envelops you the moment you walk in the door and any thought you had about not overindulging flies right out of your head.

I arrived a few mornings each week, clutching my hot coffee like a shield against the cold January weather, to find a new recipe perched on the prep table for my perusal. I took my time reading over the recipe and warming up before embarking on the day's baking. Occasionally Sharin would correct a technique or double-check my work, but for the most part she simply helped guide me through each recipe. Just the right number of cupcakes, cookies, and cakes graced the front display case by mid-morning, and the rich smell of cardamom hot chocolate wafted through the bakery.

Sharin bakes with precision and a sense of specificity that I strove to emulate. Whether it was a new bread recipe or an experimental pear pie I was trying to get just right, I learned to slow down in the kitchen and really pay attention to what I was doing. Without the pressure of Thanksgiving looming, I felt as though I finally had the time to explore the idea of baking as a craft. As people's New Year's resolutions kept them clear of bakeries,

I was able to spend the hours needed to perfect a Bundt cake or carefully construct a dozen cupcakes from start to finish. Sharin's adventurous creations—like Boston cream pie cupcakes and peanut butter and jelly bars—inspired me to think about pie flavors in an entirely new way. Because our pie offerings were limited, it was lovely to dream up new pie possibilities one week and then execute them with care the next. Our first pie collaboration, a browned butter pear pie (page 144), ended up being my favorite. A slice of that pie fresh from the oven, with the rich browned butter sauce drizzled over the ripe winter pears, went a long way to keeping me warm on my cold trek home.

1918 West Montrose Ave.
Chicago, IL 60613
773-275-0697
sweetsensationspastry.com

Next Stop: Greensboro, AL (page 174)

Sweet Sensations' Browned Butter Pear Pie

PREP TIME: 45 MINUTES • **BAKE TIME:** 55 TO 65 MINUTES • **TOTAL TIME:** ABOUT 2 HOURS •
MAKES: ONE 9-INCH SINGLE-CRUST PIE (6 TO 8 SLICES)

Warm pears and slightly nutty browned butter made the harsh weather of a Chicago winter much more bearable. Sharin's pie crust (a traditional French pâte brisée) begins as a very workable dough, but it's hard when it first comes out of the refrigerator. I usually let it sit on the counter for five minutes or so to let it warm up before attempting to roll it out. This incredible crumb pie will scare away any winter weariness.

FOR THE CRUST

1½ cups all-purpose flour, plus extra
    for rolling out the crust

½ teaspoon salt

½ cup (1 stick) cold unsalted butter,
    cut into ½-inch cubes

⅛ to ¼ cup ice water

FOR THE STREUSEL

¼ cup granulated sugar

½ cup packed light brown sugar

1 teaspoon ground cinnamon

Pinch of salt

¾ cup all-purpose flour

¾ cup (1½ sticks) unsalted butter,
    melted

FOR THE FILLING

¾ cup (1½ sticks) unsalted butter

3 large eggs

¾ cup granulated sugar

1 teaspoon pure vanilla extract

1 cup all-purpose flour

½ teaspoon salt

7 cups peeled, cored, and thinly
    sliced pears (7 to 8 pears)

1. Make the crust: Stir together the flour and salt in a medium bowl to combine. Add the cold butter and incorporate with a pastry cutter until the mixture resembles coarse meal.

2. Gradually add the ice water, a tablespoon at a time, and stir just until the dough starts to stick together. Press the dough into a ball and gather up any loose crumbs from the bottom of the bowl. Turn the dough out onto a flat, lightly floured surface and, being careful not to overwork it, press it together to form a flat disk, roughly the size of your hand. Wrap the disk in plastic and chill for at least 1 hour (or up to 2 days) while you prepare the streusel and the filling.

3. Make the cinnamon streusel: Place the dry ingredients in a large bowl and stir to combine. Add the melted butter and stir with a fork until the mixture is crumbly. Set aside.

4. Preheat the oven to 400°F with a rack in the middle position.

5. Prepare the filling: Place the butter in a small saucepan or shallow skillet over medium-low heat and whisk it with a wire whisk as it starts to melt. After 2 to 3 minutes the butter will be melted completely and will begin to bubble. Continue to cook, whisking constantly, until the butter turns from light yellow to caramel brown and small dark specks begin to form on the bottom of the pan. Immediately remove the butter from the heat and continue to whisk for 30 seconds. Strain the butter through a small wire-mesh strainer to remove the browned bits (it's fine if a few get through) and set it aside to cool.

6. Take the crust out of the refrigerator and let it sit at room temperature for about 5 minutes while you prepare the rest of the filling.

7. In the bowl of a stand mixer fitted with the paddle attachment, or in a medium bowl using a handheld electric mixer, beat together the eggs and sugar on medium-high speed until light and fluffy. Turn the mixer down to low and add the cooled butter and the vanilla. With the mixer still on low, beat in the flour and salt until everything is incorporated. Set aside.

8. Roll out the crust: On a lightly floured surface with a lightly floured rolling pin, roll out the dough into a rough 11-inch circle about ⅛ inch thick. Lay the crust into a 9-inch pie dish, gently press it in, and trim any excess dough from the edge with a paring knife, being sure to leave a ¾-inch overhang. Tuck the overhanging dough under itself and crimp.

9. Place the pears in a large bowl, pour 1½ cups of the cooled brown butter filling over them, and stir gently to evenly coat. (Any leftover brown butter filling can be refrigerated for up to a week or frozen for up to 2 weeks, and used for other pies or pear cobblers.) Layer the filling into the crust, with the pears coming to a slight dome in the center of the pie. Sprinkle the cinnamon streusel evenly over the top.

10. Set the pie on a rimmed baking sheet and bake for 20 minutes. Then lower the oven temperature to 350°F and bake until the crust and streusel are golden brown, 35 to 45 minutes more. (If the crust begins to get too brown, cover it with aluminum foil.)

Sweet Sensations' Browned Butter Pear Pie will keep for 4 to 5 days, covered, in the refrigerator.

Earl Grey Cream Pie in a Sugar Cookie Crust

PREP TIME: 1 HOUR • **CHILL TIME:** 4 HOURS • **TOTAL TIME:** 5 HOURS •
MAKES: ONE 9-INCH SINGLE-CRUST PIE (6 TO 8 SLICES)

When I was a junior in college I was lucky enough to spend the fall semester abroad in London, where I tromped through the city to see the sights, watched dozens of plays, pulled pints at a local pub, and indulged in my fair share of teatimes. The English drink their black teas with ample milk and sugar and savor biscuits (cookies) alongside. Each winter, when the inclination to hibernate becomes overwhelming, I like to indulge in a warm cup of afternoon tea while I read or bake. This year I became intrigued with the idea of infusing cream pies with various types of tea in order to create different "teatime pies." This one in particular, with its cookie crust, tea-colored filling, and distinctly Bergamot-flavored infusion, is spot on . . . absolutely reminiscent of my London days. Because this is a cream pie, the cookie crust should be prebaked and allowed time to cool in the refrigerator while you assemble the filling (similarly, you can make the whipped cream while the filling sets).

1. Bring the milk to a simmer in a small saucepan over medium heat and cook, stirring constantly so it doesn't stick to the bottom, 10 minutes. Remove the saucepan from the heat and

INGREDIENTS

2½ cups whole milk

3 individual Earl Grey tea bags

4 large egg yolks

½ cup granulated sugar

3 tablespoons packed cornstarch

½ teaspoon salt

2 tablespoons unsalted butter, at room temperature

1 prebaked 9-inch Sugar Cookie Crust (page 37)

Homemade Whipped Cream (page 45), for topping

add the tea bags to the hot milk. Set aside and let the tea steep for 30 minutes.

2. Remove the three tea bags from the milk (which will have cooled) and whisk in the egg yolks. In a medium saucepan whisk together the sugar, cornstarch, and salt.

3. Whisk the milk mixture into the sugar mixture until there are no lumps. Cook over medium heat, whisking constantly, until the mixture comes to a low simmer and begins to thicken, about 8 minutes. Continue cooking, whisking constantly and being sure to scrape the bottom of the pan to prevent scorching, until the mixture begins to boil, about 1 minute. Still whisking constantly, let it boil for a full minute, then immediately remove it from the heat.

4. Add the butter and whisk until it is completely melted and the mixture is smooth.

5. Pour the Earl Grey cream into the prebaked crust and, while still hot, cover it with plastic wrap to prevent a film from forming on the top. Refrigerate the pie until the filling has set, at least 4 hours.

6. Before serving, remove the plastic wrap and top with the whipped cream. Serve cold.

Earl Grey Cream Pie with a Sugar Cookie Crust will keep for 2 to 3 days, covered, in the refrigerator.

Chai Cream Pie

PREP TIME: 30 MINUTES • **CHILL TIME:** 2 TO 4 HOURS • **TOTAL TIME:**
4 HOURS 30 MINUTES • **MAKES:** ONE 9-INCH SINGLE-CRUST PIE
(6 TO 8 SLICES) OR FOUR 5-INCH SINGLE-CRUST TEENY PIES

INGREDIENTS

4 individual chai tea bags

½ teaspoon ground cinnamon

½ teaspoon ground ginger

¼ cup boiling water

½ cup granulated sugar

3 tablespoons packed cornstarch

½ teaspoon salt

2 cups whole milk

4 large egg yolks

2 tablespoons unsalted butter, at room temperature

½ teaspoon pure vanilla extract

1 prebaked 9-inch Buttery All-Purpose Crust (page 30)

Homemade Whipped Cream (page 45), for topping

While I enjoy the occasional cup of tea—especially in wintertime—I'm much more of a "black coffee every morning" kind of lady. But my friend Jenn is a full-fledged tea drinker. She buys her favorite morning tea in bulk, drinks it in the English style with milk and sugar, and without fail whenever we go to get coffee and catch up she orders a chai tea latte. I have heard many a chai tea analysis, for she is an absolute connoisseur; and it was her love of all things tea that inspired this pie.

Instead of steeping the tea in milk for an infusion of flavor, as in the Earl Grey Cream Pie on page 147, in this recipe I steep the chai tea in a small amount of water with other spices so it provides an extra punch of chai goodness.

1. Place the tea bags in a small heatproof bowl and add the cinnamon and ginger. Pour the boiling water over all, stir gently to incorporate the spices, then set aside and let the tea steep until the water is dark brown, 10 to 20 minutes. Discard the tea bags.

2. Meanwhile, whisk together the sugar, cornstarch, and salt in a medium saucepan. Add the milk and egg yolks and whisk

together until there are no lumps. Cook over medium heat, whisking constantly, until the mixture comes to a low simmer and begins to thicken, about 8 minutes. Continue cooking, whisking constantly and being sure to scrape the bottom of the pan to prevent scorching, until the mixture begins to boil, about 1 minute more. Still whisking constantly, let it boil for a full minute, then immediately remove it from heat.

3. Add the butter, vanilla, and brewed chai and whisk until the butter is melted and the mixture is smooth.

4. Pour the chai cream into the prebaked pie crust and, while still hot, cover it with plastic wrap to prevent a film from forming on the top. Refrigerate the pie until the filling is set, at least 2 hours or up to 4 hours.

5. Before serving, remove the plastic wrap and top with the whipped cream. Serve cold.

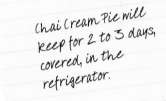

Chai Cream Pie will keep for 2 to 3 days, covered, in the refrigerator.

 **MAKE 'EM TEENY PIES**

Prepare and prebake the crust in four 5-inch teeny tins as directed. In step 4, divide the filling among the crusts and proceed with the recipe as directed.

Lady Bakership Lesson #6

PIE = BRAVERY

I'm not exactly a person who revels in change, so the decision to leave my very comfortable life and become a pie baker was not something that I came to lightly, despite the levity of the subject I was pursuing. I was occasionally homesick and fairly often terrified, but during the course of the year I came to understand that the disappointment and heartache I would feel if I gave up on the adventure trumped any brief misgivings or feelings of fear. As scary as it was, I managed to build a life around a dream I thought was worth pursuing, and it turns out, the possibilities have been almost endless.

Thanksgiving Dinner Pies

PREP TIME: 30 MINUTES • **BAKE TIME:** 10 TO 15 MINUTES • **TOTAL TIME:**
45 MINUTES • **MAKES:** SIX 5-INCH SINGLE-CRUST TEENY PIES

Thanksgiving has always been my favorite holiday. It carries no other expectation than that people meet, eat a rather fantastical abundance and assortment of foods, and enjoy one another's company. It's a holiday when families gather simply because they are a family. Rather than the promise of presents or the allure of individual attention, this celebration offers conversation, raucous laughter, and the chance to revel in our own family's idiosyncrasies. It's a holiday that embraces traditions that are centered on and grounded in giving thanks. Plus there is always a plethora of pies. It is, in fact, *the* pie holiday.

Despite these being called Thanksgiving Dinner Pies, and despite the fact that they're a stellar way to get rid of Thanksgiving leftovers, I find that I rarely make them during Thanksgiving. I tend to get a hankering for them in the middle of February or March because the actual Thanksgiving meal is such a distant memory that I have to re-create it in pie form. Unfortunately, this late-winter hankering means I don't usually have leftovers to use up; when I find myself in that situation I just roast a turkey breast or two and use that instead (see Note). Whether or not you choose to make this pie during the

INGREDIENTS

2 tablespoons unsalted butter

½ medium onion, peeled and diced

2 stalks celery, roughly chopped

2 carrots, peeled and roughly chopped

¼ cup all-purpose flour, plus more if needed for rolling out the crust

3 cups turkey or chicken stock (canned or boxed is fine), plus extra as needed

2 small sweet potatoes, peeled and cut into 1-inch pieces

2 cups shredded cooked turkey (see Note)

2 teaspoons poultry seasoning

½ cup frozen peas, thawed

Salt and ground black pepper

½ cup fresh or dried cranberries (I prefer fresh when they're available)

2 cups prepared Stuffing Crumble (page 44)

6 prebaked 5-inch Savory Pie Crusts (page 32)

holidays—as a way to use up your leftovers, perhaps—it always manages to coax those warm feelings with the familiarity of its flavors.

1. Preheat the oven to 350°F with a rack in the middle position.

2. Melt the butter in a large saucepan over medium heat. Add the onion and cook until tender and translucent, about 10 minutes. Stir in the celery and carrots and cook until they start to soften, about 2 minutes. Add 4 tablespoons of the flour and stir until the veggies are coated and the flour begins to brown, about 2 minutes.

3. Add the 3 cups chicken stock and bring the mixture to a simmer. Add the sweet potatoes and simmer, uncovered, until they are tender, 10 to 15 minutes. Stir in the turkey, poultry seasoning, and peas, and add salt and pepper to taste.

4. At this point the liquid in the pan should have the consistency of gravy. If it's not thick enough, you can mix 2 to 3 tablespoons of the remaining flour with ¼ cup water or stock in a separate small bowl until smooth and stir it into the simmering liquid. Let simmer until the liquid thickens, about 5 minutes. Stir in the cranberries and take the pan off the heat.

5. Set the crusts on a rimmed baking sheet and spoon the filling into them. Sprinkle the Stuffing Crumble evenly over the pies to top them. Bake until the stuffing is lightly browned, 10 to 15 minutes.

NOTE: If you don't have leftover turkey, you can easily cook some for the purpose. Preheat the oven to 350°F, rub one large or two small boneless, skinless turkey breasts (about 1 pound total) with olive oil, salt, and pepper to taste, and bake on a rimmed baking sheet until cooked through and no longer pink inside, 30 to 40 minutes. I let them sit on the countertop while I prepare my crust, and once they are cooled I shred them with my fingers and use 2 cups of turkey in the recipe and keep the rest for sandwiches and general nibbling.

Pickled Beet and Goat Cheese Tarts with Candied Walnuts

PREP TIME: 30 MINUTES TO 4 HOURS • **BAKE TIME:** 30 TO 40 MINUTES
TOTAL TIME: 1 TO 5 HOURS • **MAKES:** 2 TARTS (SERVES 4 TO 6 EACH)

This recipe is adapted from a delicious tart made by my friend Matthew. Matthew is a Chicago friend and a pie connoisseur. He's delighted with all kinds of pie and is always up for a trip to any of the several stellar shops that grace Chicago. He also loves to make pie, and the last time I was in the city we managed to have a tart-baking, *Downton Abbey*–watching party, in which this pickled beet tart, the pear tart on page 109, and numerous *Downton Abbey* episodes were consumed. Since that tart party I've made a few of my own adaptations, but for the most part this is Matthew's tried-and-true recipe.

I like to pickle my own beets for this, but if you don't have a few free hours to let them soak, you can always pick up some jarred pickled beets in the canned vegetables aisle of the supermarket (Nellie's is Matthew's favorite brand).

1. Preheat the oven to 400°F with a rack in the middle position. Line a large rimmed baking sheet with parchment paper or aluminum foil.

INGREDIENTS

¼ cup packed light brown sugar

¼ cup granulated sugar

½ teaspoon salt

1 cup shelled walnuts

1 tablespoon olive oil

1 cup thinly sliced white or yellow onion

2 cups sliced Pickled Beets (recipe follows)

4 ounces goat cheese

1 disk dough from Whole Wheat Crust (page 28)

Up to ¼ cup all-purpose flour, for rolling out the crust

2. Whisk together the sugars and salt in a medium bowl. Add 2 tablespoons water and whisk until smooth. Add the walnuts and stir until they are evenly coated in the sugar. Spread the walnuts on one prepared baking sheet and bake until the sugar begins to caramelize and brown, about 20 minutes. Set aside and let them cool.

3. Meanwhile, heat the olive oil in a medium skillet over medium-high heat. Add the onion and cook, stirring occasionally, until it is caramelized and a deep golden brown, 10 to 12 minutes. Set aside to cool.

4. Prepare the crusts: Dust a second large baking sheet with flour. Divide the dough into two equal pieces and form each into a 1-inch-thick disk. On a floured surface using a floured rolling pin, roll one disk out into a rough 12-inch circle about ⅛ inch thick; place it toward one end of the prepared baking sheet. Roll out the second dough disk in the same fashion and place it next to the first on the baking sheet. (Don't worry if the circles overlap slightly; there will be enough room for both tarts once they are formed.)

5. Arrange 1 cup of the pickled beets in the middle of the first crust circle, leaving a 1-inch edge all around. Scatter half of the caramelized onions over the beets and crumble 2 ounces of the goat cheese on top of the onions.

6. Starting on one side, fold the edge of the crust up and over the edge of the filling. Make your way around the circle, folding up the extra crust and pleating it as you go. The crust should not meet in the center; the edges just have

to be tucked up toward it. The look you're going for by the end is called a galette, or a very rustic tart.

7. Repeat filling, topping, and folding with the remaining beets, onions, goat cheese, and crust.

8. Bake the tarts until the crust is golden brown and the top of the goat cheese has started to brown, 30 to 40 minutes. Top the tarts with the candied walnuts and serve warm.

Pickled Beet and Goat Cheese Tarts will keep for 3 to 4 days, covered, in the refrigerator. Let any chilled tarts come to room temperature before serving.

Pickled Beets

PREP TIME: 40 MINUTES • **PICKLING TIME:** AT LEAST 3 HOURS (IDEALLY OVERNIGHT) • **TOTAL TIME:** 3 HOURS 40 MINUTES • **MAKES:** 2 TO 3 CUPS

INGREDIENTS

4 large beets (2 to 2½ pounds total), scrubbed and greens removed

½ cup white or rice vinegar

¼ cup apple cider vinegar

1 tablespoon granulated sugar

1 teaspoon salt

1. Place the beets in a large saucepan and add water to cover by 1 inch. Bring to a boil over high heat and cook until the beets pierce easily with a knife, 20 to 30 minutes.

2. Meanwhile, whisk together the vinegars, sugar, and salt in a small bowl until the sugar and salt are dissolved.

3. Once the beets are soft, remove them from the heat and run them under cold water to cool. Working under the water, slip the skins off (they should come off very easily). Set the beets on a cutting board to cool to the touch.

4. Cut the beets into ¼- to ½-inch slices and place them in a large bowl. Add the pickling liquid, cover with plastic wrap, and set aside for at least 3 hours, ideally overnight. (The longer the beets sit, the more pickle-y they get.)

Pickled Beets will keep for 1 week, covered, in the refrigerator.

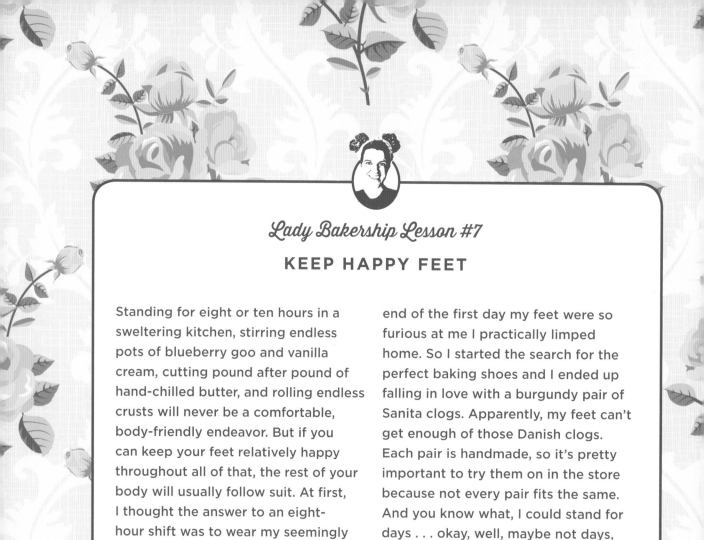

KEEP HAPPY FEET

Standing for eight or ten hours in a sweltering kitchen, stirring endless pots of blueberry goo and vanilla cream, cutting pound after pound of hand-chilled butter, and rolling endless crusts will never be a comfortable, body-friendly endeavor. But if you can keep your feet relatively happy throughout all of that, the rest of your body will usually follow suit. At first, I thought the answer to an eight-hour shift was to wear my seemingly comfortable TOMS shoes, but by the end of the first day my feet were so furious at me I practically limped home. So I started the search for the perfect baking shoes and I ended up falling in love with a burgundy pair of Sanita clogs. Apparently, my feet can't get enough of those Danish clogs. Each pair is handmade, so it's pretty important to try them on in the store because not every pair fits the same. And you know what, I could stand for days . . . okay, well, maybe not days, but a ten-hour shift is a breeze.

CHAPTER 5
Spring
Pies to Chase Away the Chill

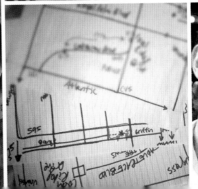

The arrival of spring is always a treat. There are those few awkward weeks when I somehow end up wearing one too many layers because I haven't realized it's not quite as cold outside as I thought it was, but soon enough I manage to get my act together and dress myself appropriately. Perhaps the most exciting part of the season for me is the arrival of new produce. I've squealed audibly with delight when the first of the strawberries make their way to the market, and I tend to take far too many photos

A strawberry basil beauty

of the long stalks of rhubarb once they gather on the grocery store shelves.

First rhubarb of the season

Trips to the nearest farmers' market become a mandatory weekend outing, and the results are a nice mix of fresh cream pies and early spring fruit pies. Lemon meringue and Key lime curd, with their generous helpings of zest and freshly squeezed juice, refresh frost-dulled senses, and winter is successfully banished with the tropical one-two punch of toasted coconut and banana cream. These are the perfect pies to coax even the most stubborn person out of hibernation.

After starting off 2012 with a cold but productive January in Chicago, I'd gone back to Somerville, Massachusetts, to stay with Aaron. It was like going home: There was comfort in the return to familiar surroundings (and Aaron!), and I was able to pick up regular hours at Petsi Pies, which gave me some room to figure out the next few stops on the Tour of Pie. But it took only a couple of months of staying in one place before I was itching to start traveling again. April in Alabama, by way of an apprenticeship at PieLab, was first on my list. After Alabama, I would head to Florida for the month of May, where I would work at the famed Bob Roth's New River Groves to try my hand at perfecting Key lime pie. I was ready for springtime in the South.

Stepping onto the main street in Greensboro, Alabama, feels like stepping back in time, when people moved a little slower and life was a little simpler. Crumbling facades and dilapidated storefronts dot the three blocks of Main Street, and the town itself is home to a mere 2,500 people. It's also home to the increasingly popular PieLab.

PieLab is owned by the umbrella group HERO, the Hale Empowerment and Revitalization Organization, a housing-advocacy nonprofit that also sponsors community-minded local initiatives. Along with running PieLab and other small businesses throughout Greensboro, HERO helps build affordable housing in impoverished areas in the Alabama Black Belt. The idea behind PieLab is an intriguing one, the founder's motto being: pie + conversation = change. Considering one of the original (albeit somewhat tongue-in-cheek) tenets of the Tour of Pie was "saving the world, one pie at a time," PieLab seemed like a perfect fit. Within the first few days I found myself easing nicely into small-town baking life, sharpening my gossiping skills and learning the secrets of Southern pie. My days were made up of nattering away with the neighbors and baking for all of the out-of-towners who frequented the shop. All too soon it was time to leave behind the sweet-tea-sipping, front-porch-sunning lifestyle and scoot on down to Davie, Florida, for some lessons in Key lime.

Bob Roth's New River Groves is the home of Terry's Famous Key Lime Pies. Terry began baking her famous pies from her home kitchen in the early 1970s and the business has grown exponentially ever since. Although Terry passed away from cancer in 2002, her husband, Bob, has maintained her legacy, and her pies remain a cornerstone of this wonderful family business. Their tart treats have been featured on the Cooking Channel and CBS, enjoyed by several big names including Hillary Clinton and Nick Nolte (just to drop a few), and even had a hand in electing Key lime pie as the state pie of Florida. So it was an honor to learn Key lime in the Roths' small but abundantly friendly kitchen.

I adored my time in the South and the people I met there. The warmth and generosity of that part of the country infuses the pies they make and moved me to try my hand at a few sunshine-inspired pies of my own.

Strawberry Basil Pie

PREP TIME: 20 MINUTES • **BAKE TIME:** 40 TO 50 MINUTES • **TOTAL TIME:**
1 HOUR 10 MINUTES • **MAKES:** ONE 9-INCH DOUBLE-CRUST PIE (6 TO
8 SLICES) OR FOUR 5-INCH DOUBLE-CRUST TEENY PIES

INGREDIENTS

About 2 pints strawberries, hulled and cut into ½-inch-thick slices (4 cups)

¼ cup chopped fresh basil

½ cup granulated sugar

¼ cup quick-cooking tapioca, finely ground (see Note)

2 disks dough from Whole Wheat Crust (page 28)

Up to ¼ cup all-purpose flour, for rolling out the crust

If there is one other person in my life who eats more pie than Aaron, it has got to be my goofball friend Carly. I would say that Aaron eats pie because he likes it and more often than not there is at least one pie in his general vicinity. Carly, on the other hand, consumes pie as though it's the only pastry in the entire world that will make her truly happy. Since Carly and I no longer live in the same city (she was a fellow performer and baby wrangler with me in Chicago before moving to Philly to host a show on Sprout), she's been using my recipes to fill her life with pie happiness. Strawberry basil happens to be her favorite, and she fondly refers to it as "strawbs basil." Maybe it's because she comes from a huge Italian family and basil is in her blood, or maybe it's because the earthy herb makes the sweetness of the strawberries really come through. Regardless, it's always a good day when I receive a photo of Carly, the pie phenomenon, proudly holding her fave pie.

1. Preheat the oven to 400°F with a rack in the middle position.

2. Toss together the strawberries and basil in a medium bowl.

3. Stir together the sugar and tapioca in a small bowl to combine. Sprinkle the sugar mixture over the fruit and toss

gently with your hands to coat. Set aside while you roll out the crust; the fruit will begin to juice.

4. Prepare the bottom crust: Place one disk of the dough on a floured work surface and with a floured rolling pin roll it into a rough 11-inch circle about ⅛ inch thick. Lay the crust into a 9-inch pie dish, gently press it in, and trim any excess dough from the edge with a paring knife, being sure to leave a ¾-inch overhang.

5. Give the filling one last stir, making sure everything is evenly coated, then spoon it into the crust.

6. Prepare the top crust: On a floured work surface with a floured rolling pin, roll out the remaining dough disk into a rough 11-inch circle about ⅛ inch thick. Carefully lay the crust on top of the filling, and trim any excess dough from the edge, leaving a ¾-inch overhang. Tuck the overhanging dough under the overhanging edge of the bottom crust, and crimp the two crusts together. Cut a few small slits in the top crust with a sharp knife.

7. Set the pie on a rimmed baking sheet and bake until the filling is thickly bubbling and the crust is golden brown (cover the crimp with foil if it begins to brown too quickly), 50 to 60 minutes. Let cool to room temperature before serving.

NOTE: I've taken to grinding quick-cooking tapioca in a clean coffee grinder to give it an unobtrusive presence in my finished fruit pies. If you can't find the stuff or don't have a grinder, use an equal amount of tapioca starch. Just be warned that for some reason cornstarch—another go-to thickener—doesn't stand up well to juicy fruits.

A handful of what's fresh at the farmers' market in the spring

rhubarb
raspberries
leeks
mushrooms

Strawberry Basil Pie will keep for 2 to 3 days, covered, on the counter.

 ## MAKE 'EM TEENY PIES

In step 4, divide one disk of the dough into four equal balls and roll out each into a rough 6-inch circle. Lay each into a 5-inch pie tin, and trim any excess dough from the edge, being sure to leave a ½-inch overhang.

Give the filling one final stir and spoon an equal amount into each crust-lined teeny tin (roughly 1 cup each).

In step 6, divide the remaining dough into four equal pieces and roll out each into a rough 7-inch circle. Carefully lay the crusts over the filling, and trim any excess dough from the edge, leaving a ½-inch overhang. Tuck the overhanging dough under the overhanging bottom crust and crimp the two crusts together, pressing to seal. Cut a ½-inch slit in the top of each pie to allow steam to escape.

Place the Teeny Pies on a rimmed baking sheet and bake until the crusts are golden brown, 40 to 45 minutes.

HOW TO MAKE FRIENDS WITH PIE

1. Make pie every day for one year.
2. Move to a new city where you have no friends.
3. Bake half a dozen pies.
4. Invite potential new friends over for a pie party.
5. Eat pie and drink whiskey.
6. FRIENDS!

Strawberry Rhubarb Pie

PREP TIME: 20 MINUTES • **BAKE TIME:** 40 TO 50 MINUTES • **TOTAL TIME:** 1 HOUR 10 MINUTES • **MAKES:** ONE 9-INCH DOUBLE-CRUST PIE (6 TO 8 SLICES) OR FOUR 5-INCH DOUBLE-CRUST TEENY PIES

We used to grow our own strawberries when I was a kid. Considering how often my brother and I raided the strawberry patch, it's amazing my mom was able to gather enough for any pie at all, but when she did she always paired them with rhubarb. It took me a long time to enjoy the taste of rhubarb, but now it's one of my favorite pairings for berries. The tart bite of the rhubarb is just enough to temper the sun-soaked sweetness of the strawberries. I really like making strawberry rhubarb pie with people who have never had rhubarb; it's fun to offer them a small bite of the unsweetened rhubarb and watch their faces sour-pucker with disgust. Rhubarb is definitely puckerworthy when it's raw, but it's delicious once baked into a pie.

1. Preheat the oven to 400°F with a rack in the middle position.

2. Place the strawberries, rhubarb, and lemon juice in a medium bowl and toss to combine.

3. Stir together the sugars and tapioca in a small bowl. Sprinkle the sugar mixture over the fruit, tossing gently with your hands or a spoon to coat evenly. Set aside while you roll out the crust; the fruit will begin to juice.

INGREDIENTS

1 to 1½ pints strawberries, hulled and cut into ¼-inch-thick slices (2½ cups)

2 to 3 stalks rhubarb, diced (½-inch to 1-inch pieces, equal to 2 cups; see Note, page 169)

1 tablespoon freshly squeezed lemon juice

¼ cup granulated sugar

¼ cup packed light brown sugar

¼ cup quick-cooking tapioca, finely ground (see Note, page 165)

2 disks dough from Whole Wheat Crust (page 28)

Up to ¼ cup all-purpose flour, for rolling out the crust

4. Prepare the bottom crust: Place one disk of the dough on a floured work surface, and with a floured rolling pin, roll it into a rough 11-inch circle about ⅛ inch thick. Lay the crust into a 9-inch pie plate, gently press it in, and trim any excess dough from the edge with a paring knife, being sure to leave a ¾-inch overhang.

5. Give the filling one final stir to make sure the fruit is evenly coated, then spoon the mixture into the crust.

6. Prepare the top crust: On a floured work surface with a floured rolling pin, roll out the remaining dough disk into a rough 11-inch circle about ⅛ inch thick. Carefully lay the crust on top of the filling, and trim any excess dough from the edge, leaving a ¾-inch overhang. Tuck the overhanging dough under the overhanging edge of the bottom crust, and crimp the two crusts together. Cut a few small slits in the top crust with a sharp knife.

7. Set the pie on a rimmed baking sheet and bake until the filling is thickly bubbling and the crust is golden brown (cover it with foil if it begins to brown too quickly), 40 to 50 minutes.

Strawberry Rhubarb Pie will keep for 2 to 3 days covered, on the countertop.

NOTE: When buying rhubarb, look for firm, thick stalks with healthy leaves. Trim off and discard the leaves (they're mildly poisonous!) and chop the stalks crosswise as you would celery.

 MAKE 'EM TEENY PIES

In step 4, divide one disk of the dough into four equal balls and roll out each into a rough 6-inch circle about ⅛ inch thick. Lay each into a 5-inch pie tin, and trim any excess dough from the edge, being sure to leave a ½-inch overhang.

Give the filling one final stir and spoon an equal amount into each crust-lined teeny tin (roughly 1 cup each).

In step 6, divide the remaining dough into four equal pieces and roll out each into a rough 7-inch circle, about ⅛ inch thick. Carefully lay the crusts over the filling, and trim any excess dough from the edge, leaving a ½-inch overhang. Tuck the overhanging dough under the bottom crust and crimp the two crusts together, pressing to seal. Cut a ½-inch slit in the top of each pie to allow steam to escape.

Place the Teeny Pies on a rimmed baking sheet and bake until the crusts are golden brown, 40 to 45 minutes.

Banana Cream Pie with Vanilla Wafer Crust

PREP TIME: 30 MINUTES • **CHILL TIME:** 4 HOURS • **TOTAL TIME:** 4 HOURS
30 MINUTES • **MAKES:** ONE 9-INCH SINGLE-CRUST PIE (6 TO 8 SLICES)

My mom rarely made cream pies when I was growing up, always preferring fruit pies for our spring picnics. However, my very best friend, Kristen, grew up with banana cream being her favorite, and I wanted to make one especially for her before I left Chicago for good. So it was with a certain amount of trepidation that I attempted my first banana cream, which, as it happened, wasn't very good. I spent the whole weekend trying to get it right, whisking until my arm was dead and rearranging the recipe until I was finally satisfied. I sliced extra bananas into the vanilla cream, taking a certain amount of pleasure from swirling them into every bite. I topped the whole thing with piles of whipped cream and hoped the heartfelt banana cream would make the distance between Chicago and my new home in Washington, D.C., seem a little less vast.

The vanilla wafer crumb crust is a nod to Aaron's mom, who introduced me to the most spectacular banana pudding concoction I'd ever tasted. She'd adapted an incredible recipe from Magnolia Bakery in New York, and it includes layer after layer of Nilla Wafers cookies, whipped cream, and rich banana pudding chock-full of thick banana pieces. I'd never had banana

INGREDIENTS

½ cup granulated sugar

3 tablespoons packed cornstarch

½ teaspoon salt

2 cups whole milk

4 medium egg yolks

2 tablespoons unsalted butter

1 teaspoon banana extract (optional; see Note)

2 bananas

1 prebaked 9-inch Vanilla Wafer Crust (recipe follows)

1 batch Homemade Whipped Cream (page 45)

cream pie in anything but a regular prebaked pie crust, but that pudding inspired me to make a toasty vanilla wafer crust on the double. It's a delicious twist that makes this pie super special, but you can also make it in a traditional prebaked pie shell (pages 29–31) if you prefer—it'll still be Kristen-worthy.

1. Whisk together the sugar, cornstarch, and salt in a medium saucepan with a wire whisk. Add the milk and egg yolks and whisk together until there are no lumps.

2. Place the saucepan over medium heat and cook, whisking constantly, until the mixture comes to a low simmer and begins to thicken, about 7 minutes. Continue cooking, whisking constantly and being sure to scrape the bottom of the pan to prevent scorching, until the mixture begins to boil, about 2 minutes. Still whisking constantly, let it boil for a full minute, then immediately remove it from the heat.

3. Add the butter and banana extract (if using), and whisk until the butter has melted and the mixture is smooth.

4. Peel the bananas and thinly slice them directly into the cream. Stir gently with a spoon to incorporate.

5. Pour the banana cream into the prebaked pie shell and, while it is still hot, cover it with plastic wrap to prevent a film from forming on the top. Refrigerate the pie until the cream has set, at least 4 hours.

6. Before serving, remove the plastic wrap, top with the whipped cream, and serve cold.

Banana Cream Pie with a Vanilla Wafer Crust will keep for 2 to 3 days, covered, in the refrigerator.

NOTE: Because I add so many sliced bananas to my cream pie, I don't usually feel the need to add any extract. However, if you would like a slightly stronger banana flavor, you have a few options. Imitation banana flavoring from any grocery store is probably the most convenient and inexpensive option. I think it tastes a little too much like Laffy Taffy, so I like to go with a pure banana extract that you can buy at Whole Foods or similar shops that carry high-quality baking products. The third option is to use 1 teaspoon of banana liqueur . . . but using only a teaspoon at a time means you'll have the bottle for quite a while (good for banana daiquiris, perhaps?).

Vanilla Wafer Crust

PREP TIME: 10 MINUTES • **BAKE TIME:** 5 TO 7 MINUTES • **TOTAL TIME:** 15 MINUTES • **MAKES:** ONE 9-INCH SINGLE CRUST

INGREDIENTS

1½ cups vanilla wafer crumbs (from about 45 cookies)

7 tablespoons unsalted butter, melted

1. Preheat the oven to 350°F with a rack in the middle position.

2. Transfer the cookie crumbs to a medium bowl, pour the melted butter over them, and stir to combine. The crumbs should clump easily when pressed together.

3. Spoon three quarters of the crumb mixture into a 9-inch pie plate and using your fingers, press the mixture up the side of the plate until you have a ¼-inch-thick shell all the way around. Spoon the rest of the crumb mixture into the plate and press it to form the bottom of the shell, making sure the bottom and side are joined.

4. Bake the shell until it is lightly browned, 5 to 7 minutes. Remove from the oven, let cool, and fill.

PieLab
Greensboro, AL

I arrived in the tiny town of Greensboro, Alabama, in April, ready to begin my monthlong, six-day-a-week apprenticeship at PieLab. Every fixture in the gorgeous shop had been donated, repaired, or found. This refurbished design, full of distressed metal and old wooden pieces, each with its own history, was not only smart in a financial sense but it also lent the space a homey and hardworking feel. Large sheets of cleaned-up corrugated metal gave a few of the walls texture and personality, while another dividing wall was a puzzle of reclaimed two-by-fours of different lengths and colors.

PieLab is front and center on Greensboro's main thoroughfare

Most of the girls I worked with at PieLab were participants in work programs that helped underprivileged youth and those in the community without high school diplomas or college degrees. My time there was a nice mix of learning and teaching. And pie was the string that tied us all together.

Many of the pie specialties that I'd specifically gone south to master were made at the shop. Lemon icebox, chocolate chess, classic pecan, buttermilk pumpkin, and deep-dish apple all made an appearance on the rotating daily menu board as I whisked together eggs, butter, and plenty of sugar along with my fellow bakers. For four weeks I was fully ensconced in small-town living. I spent my days baking at PieLab and my evenings reading borrowed romance novels from the town's one-room library. Shanijah, the head baker during my apprenticeship, was quick to show me the ropes when I first arrived, and together we kept the shop chock-full of pie. On the weekends the shop became flooded with out-of-towners who had heard about PieLab from *Southern Living* or the *New York Times* and came for a slice of their Southern favorite.

But it was the regulars, who came and went like clockwork, who were perhaps my favorite part about working in such a small town. Their constant visits to the pie shop and their extravagant stories kept us in good spirits while we worked. Once they found out why I was in town, they began to arrive at the shop bearing their mothers' and grandmothers' old recipe cards, each representing a pie of the past. I carefully copied down the worn and butter-stained

Alabama baking ladies

pieces of pie-baking history while I listened to their stories of Greensboro and of homemade, heartfelt pies. Each recipe prompted its own story, and I was constantly reminded of the tradition tied to old family recipes and the timeless techniques that are passed down from generation to generation.

In the last few years I've noticed a new wave of appreciation for the handmade desserts of our parents' and grandparents' generation. Today's bakers are rediscovering and reclaiming the beautiful art of baking. Nowhere was that more apparent to me than at PieLab. I thought of my mom's and grandmother's favorite recipes, tucked away in their well-loved recipe boxes, and I was proud to be a part of their baking legacy.

1317 Main Street
Greensboro, AL 36744
334-624-3899
pielab.org

Next Stop: Davie, FL (page 194)

Their gorgeous interior is entirely "found, donated, or refurbished."

PieLab's Snickerdoodle Pie

PREP TIME: 45 MINUTES • **BAKE TIME:** 45 MINUTES • **TOTAL TIME:** 1 HOUR 30 MINUTES •
MAKES: ONE 9-INCH SINGLE-CRUST PIE (6 TO 8 SLICES)

⟫⟫

When I first heard about PieLab I went to its website to check out the menu, and this was the pie that I absolutely lost my mind over. I adore snickerdoodle cookies, and the idea that someone had turned them into a pie set my heart aflutter. Each time this pie ended up on the day's to-do-list my fellow bakers practically had to remove me forcibly from the shop to prevent me from devouring the whole thing straight out of the oven.

Because of the brown sugar syrup and the cookie-like filling, this pie is almost a shoofly pie masquerading as a snickerdoodle. It's one of the more complex pies in this book, because of all the components. But the resulting pie is somewhere between a cookie and a sugar pie, each of the steps making it a worthwhile endeavor.

FOR THE CRUST

1 disk dough from Buttery All-Purpose Crust (see headnote, page 30)

Up to 3 tablespoons all-purpose flour, for rolling out the crust

1 tablespoon raw sugar

½ teaspoon ground cinnamon

1 tablespoon unsalted butter, melted

FOR THE BROWN SUGAR SYRUP

¼ cup (½ stick) unsalted butter, at room temperature

½ cup packed light brown sugar

2 tablespoons light corn syrup

¼ teaspoon ground cinnamon

½ teaspoon pure vanilla extract

FOR THE FILLING

¼ cup (½ stick) unsalted butter, at room temperature

½ cup granulated sugar

¼ cup confectioners' sugar

1 teaspoon baking powder

½ teaspoon salt

¼ teaspoon cream of tartar

1 large egg

1 teaspoon pure vanilla extract

½ cup whole milk

1¼ cups all-purpose flour

1. Prepare the crust: Place the disk of dough on a floured work surface and with a floured rolling pin roll it into a rough 11-inch circle about ⅛ inch thick. Lay the crust into a 9-inch pie plate, gently press it in, and trim any excess dough from the edge with a paring knife, being sure to leave a ¾-inch overhang. Tuck the overhang under itself and crimp all the way around.

2. Stir together the raw sugar and the cinnamon in a small bowl. Brush the melted butter over the crust, then sprinkle it with 1 teaspoon of the cinnamon sugar. Set aside the remaining cinnamon sugar; cover the crust lightly with plastic wrap and refrigerate it.

3. Preheat the oven to 350°F with a rack in the middle position.

4. Make the brown sugar syrup: Combine the butter, brown sugar, corn syrup, cinnamon, and 3 tablespoons water in a medium saucepan over medium heat and cook, stirring to dissolve the sugar, until the mixture comes to a boil. Boil gently for 2 minutes and then remove the mixture from the heat. Stir in the vanilla and set aside.

5. Prepare the filling: In the bowl of a stand mixer fitted with the paddle attachment, or in a large bowl using a handheld electric mixer, beat the butter on medium speed for 30 seconds. Beat in the granulated sugar, confectioners' sugar, baking powder, salt, and cream of tartar until well combined and the mixture is light and fluffy.

6. Scrape down the side of the bowl with a rubber spatula and beat in the egg and vanilla. Scrape down the side of the bowl again and then gradually beat in the milk until combined. Add the flour all at once, and mix it in slowly, stopping as soon as everything comes together.

7. Remove the crust from the refrigerator, unwrap it, and set it on a rimmed baking sheet. Scrape the filling into the crust and spread evenly with a rubber spatula.

8. Give the brown sugar syrup one final stir and slowly pour it over the filling. Sprinkle with the remaining cinnamon sugar. Cover the edges of the crust with aluminum foil.

9. Bake the pie for 25 minutes, then carefully remove the foil. Continue to bake until the top of the pie is puffed and golden brown and a toothpick inserted near the center comes out clean, about 20 minutes more. Remove from the oven and allow the pie to cool for 30 minutes on a wire rack. Serve warm.

PieLab's Snickerdoodle Pie will keep for 2 to 3 days, covered, on the countertop.

Chess Pie

PREP TIME: 20 MINUTES • **BAKE TIME:** 1 HOUR • **TOTAL TIME:** 1 HOUR 20 MINUTES
MAKES: ONE 9-INCH SINGLE-CRUST PIE (6 TO 8 SLICES)

Peter Horn, a familiar face during my apprenticeship at PieLab, gave me his mother Sylvia's recipe for chess pie, which was actually only a partial recipe, a few of the baking tips worn away with time and the paper smudged with ingredients. The night before I left Alabama a friend and I baked a lemon chess pie in honor of Sylvia, and it was a lovely combination of sweet and sour—a lemon bar masquerading as a pie.

This recipe makes a traditional chess pie, with its cornmeal custard filling, but if you'd like to transform it into a lemon chess pie, simply use lemon extract in place of the vanilla and add 1 to 2 teaspoons grated lemon zest and 1 to 2 tablespoons freshly squeezed lemon juice along with the milk and eggs.

1. Preheat the oven to 350°F with a rack in the middle position.

2. Place the sugar, flour, and cornmeal in a medium bowl and stir with a wire whisk or a fork to combine.

3. In a large bowl whisk, together the milk, eggs, and vanilla until combined and slightly frothy, about 1 minute. Gradually add the dry mixture, whisking until there are no clumps.

4. Slowly add the melted butter, whisking continuously until everything is well combined. Set aside.

INGREDIENTS

1½ cups granulated sugar

1 tablespoon all-purpose flour, plus up to 3 tablespoons extra, for rolling out the crust

1 tablespoon cornmeal

¾ cup whole milk

3 large eggs

1 teaspoon pure vanilla extract

4 tablespoons (½ stick) unsalted butter, melted and cooled

1 disk dough from Whole Wheat Crust (page 28)

Chess Pie will keep for 3 to 4 days, covered, in the refrigerator.

5. Prepare the crust: Place the disk of dough on a floured work surface and with a floured rolling pin roll it into a rough 11-inch circle about ⅛ inch thick. Lay the crust into a 9-inch pie dish, gently press it in, and trim any excess dough from the edge with a paring knife, being sure to leave a ¾-inch overhang. Set the crust on a rimmed baking sheet.

6. Give the filling one final stir, pour it into the crust, and transfer it, on the baking sheet, to the oven. Bake until the crust and top are golden brown, about 1 hour.

JUS' PIE

Chess pie is a distinctly Southern pie, and like most sugar pies, it's filled to the brim with sweet and—what else?—sugary goodness. Sugar pies are very common in the South, and often the main ingredients—flour, butter, sugar, and eggs—stay the same and the pie is tweaked slightly with the addition of chocolate, nuts, or some other type of flavoring. Buttermilk pie, chess pie, sugar pie, vinegar pie, lemon chess pie, chocolate chess pie, and pecan pie . . . they all fall under the "sugar pie" umbrella.

Chess pie is set apart from the others by the addition of cornmeal to the filling, though it's often considered interchangeable with vinegar pie because of the similarity of its ingredients. As the story goes, it got its name after a newcomer tried it for the first time, and asked, "What kind of pie is this?" The pie maker (or server or store clerk—no one knows for sure) replied in her Southern drawl that it was "jus' pie." But with that drawl the phrase sounded much more like "chess pie"—and there you have it.

Shoofly Pie

PREP TIME: 30 MINUTES • **BAKE TIME:** 50 TO 60 MINUTES • **TOTAL TIME:** 1 HOUR 30 MINUTES • **MAKES:** ONE 9-INCH SINGLE-CRUST PIE (6 TO 8 SLICES)

Shoofly pie is one of those pies that I'd always heard of but never actually tasted, or even known what it was made with, for that matter. It's a traditional pie among the Pennsylvania Dutch, and it is supposedly a descendant of the English treacle tart (which I'm pretty sure I remember being featured in *Harry Potter*). Treacle tarts have a filling made with golden syrup, whereas shoofly pie has a molasses-based filling and brown sugar crumble that, when baked, result in a slightly cakey, incredibly rich pie. It's because of that molasses that the pie got its quirky name: Back in the day, pies were often set on the windowsill to cool. The sweet, sugary molasses of these pies drew the flies, necessitating a sharp lookout and a shooing motion to bat the pests away.

But I digress . . . I made my first shoofly pie when I was down in Georgia, and I couldn't get over how funny the whole process was: The baking soda emits a soft fizz when you add the boiling water, and for whatever reason, that moment never got old. This is a pie that I absolutely cannot eat without a strong cup of black coffee to accompany it because of the intensity of the molasses. It's a rich way to sweeten up your spring.

INGREDIENTS

1¼ cups all-purpose flour, plus up to 3 tablespoons extra for rolling out the crust

¾ cup packed light brown sugar

¼ teaspoon ground cinnamon

4 tablespoons (½ stick) cold unsalted butter

1 teaspoon baking soda

⅔ cup boiling water

¾ cup dark molasses

1 large egg

1 disk dough from Whole Wheat Crust (page 28)

1. Preheat the oven to 375°F with a rack in the middle position.

2. Make the brown sugar crumble: Combine the flour, brown sugar, and cinnamon in a medium bowl and whisk together to combine thoroughly.

3. Cut the butter into small cubes, add them to the flour mixture, and toss to coat. With a pastry cutter, a fork, or your fingers, cut the butter into the flour mixture until the butter is the size of small peas. There will be more dry mixture than there is butter, so don't worry if the mixture doesn't stick together. Set aside.

4. Place the baking soda in a large heatproof bowl and pour the boiling water over it. (Hear the little fizz?) Whisk until the baking soda dissolves completely. Add the molasses and whisk to incorporate.

5. Lightly whisk the egg in a small bowl. Add the egg to the molasses mixture and whisk until it's fully incorporated. Set aside.

6. Prepare the crust: Place the dough on a floured work surface and with a floured rolling pin roll it into a rough 11-inch circle about ⅛ inch thick. Lay the crust into a 9-inch pie dish, gently press it in, and trim any excess dough from the edge with a paring knife, being sure to leave a ¾-inch overhang. Tuck the excess dough under itself and crimp. Set the crust on a rimmed baking sheet.

7. Give the molasses mixture one final stir and pour it into the crust. Slowly sprinkle on the reserved crumble, one handful at a time, until it is spread evenly over the top of the pie. Some of the crumbs will sink into the liquid, which is what gives the pie its cakey texture.

8. Transfer the pie, on the baking sheet, to the oven and bake until the crust is golden brown and the pie is set in the center and doesn't wobble when you jiggle it, 50 to 60 minutes. Let it cool at room temperature until the filling has set completely, at least 1 hour.

Shoofly Pie will keep for 4 to 5 days, covered, on the countertop.

Coconut Cream Pie

PREP TIME: 30 MINUTES · **CHILL TIME:** 4 HOURS · **TOTAL TIME:**
4 HOURS 30 MINUTES · **MAKES:** ONE 9-INCH SINGLE-CRUST PIE
(6 TO 8 SLICES) OR FOUR 5-INCH SINGLE-CRUST TEENY PIES

Not being a big cream-pie-making sort of family meant that when we went out to a restaurant that happened to have coconut cream on the menu, I was guaranteed to order it. Cream pies were a special restaurant treat and coconut cream was always my favorite. I'm a coconut lover. Scattered all over my kitchen are tiny canning jars filled to the brim with toasted coconut. Why? Because I happen to think it's the perfect snack. And to this day, if I see coconut cream on the menu I'm tempted to order it. But I usually refrain because I know that if I wait, and make it at home, I'll get all the extra toasted coconut to myself.

1. Combine the sugar, cornstarch, and salt in a medium saucepan and whisk together. Add the milk and egg yolks and whisk together until there are no lumps.

2. Place the saucepan over medium heat and cook, whisking constantly, until the mixture comes to a low simmer and begins to thicken, about 7 minutes. Continue cooking, whisking constantly and being sure to scrape the bottom of the pan to prevent scorching, until the mixture begins to boil, about 2 minutes. Still whisking constantly, let it boil for a full minute, then immediately remove it from the heat.

INGREDIENTS

½ cup granulated sugar

3 tablespoons packed cornstarch

½ teaspoon salt

2 cups whole milk

4 large egg yolks

2 tablespoons unsalted butter

1 teaspoon pure vanilla extract

1 cup sweetened shredded coconut flakes

1 prebaked 9-inch Buttery All-Purpose Crust (page 30)

Homemade Whipped Cream (page 45), for serving

3. Add the butter and vanilla, whisking until the butter has melted and the mixture is smooth. Add ¾ cup of the coconut and stir with a spoon to fully incorporate.

4. Pour the coconut cream into the prebaked pie crust and, while still hot, cover it with plastic wrap to prevent a film from forming on the top. Refrigerate until the cream has set, at least 4 hours.

5. While the cream is setting (at least 30 minutes before you wish to serve the pie), preheat the oven to 350°F.

6. Spread the remaining coconut on a rimmed baking sheet and toast, flipping halfway through with a spatula, until it is light brown, 7 to 10 minutes. Remove the coconut from the oven and let cool for a few minutes.

7. Remove the plastic wrap from the pie, top with the whipped cream, and sprinkle with the toasted coconut. Serve cold.

Coconut Cream Pie will keep for 2 to 3 days, covered, in the refrigerator.

 ## MAKE 'EM TEENY PIES

Prepare and prebake the crusts in four 5-inch teeny tins as directed. In step 4, divide the filling among the crusts, and proceed with the recipe as directed.

Lemon Meringue Pie

PREP TIME: 1 HOUR • COOLING TIME: 1 TO 2 HOURS • TOTAL TIME: 3 HOURS • MAKES: ONE 9-INCH SINGLE-CRUST PIE (6 TO 8 SLICES)

A lovely lemon meringue pie was what I baked for my final exam in home economics class in high school. I was determined to learn how to make a perfect meringue, and it took a few tries before I got my sky-high lemon meringue pie just right. The tart lemon filling and the altogether unique, "light-as-air" texture of the meringue made it well worth the effort. I got an A in the class, naturally.

The meringue should be put on top of the filling when the filling is still hot to prevent the meringue from shrinking and weeping once it cools. Once you've toasted the meringue you can let the pie sit out at room temperature for at least an hour to help the filling set before you place it in the fridge to chill.

1. Make the lemon curd: Place the sugar and cornstarch in a medium saucepan and stir to combine. Whisk the egg yolks lightly with 1½ cups water in a small bowl. Pour the egg mixture into the saucepan and whisk until there are no lumps and everything is incorporated.

2. Place the saucepan over medium heat and cook, whisking constantly, until the mixture comes to a low simmer and begins to thicken, about 10 minutes. Continue cooking, whisking constantly and being sure to scrape the bottom of

INGREDIENTS

FOR THE LEMON CURD FILLING

1½ cups granulated sugar

⅓ cup plus 1 tablespoon packed cornstarch

4 large egg yolks (reserve the whites for the meringue)

2 tablespoons unsalted butter

2 tablespoons freshly grated lemon zest

½ cup freshly squeezed lemon juice

FOR THE MERINGUE

4 large egg whites

¼ teaspoon cream of tartar

6 tablespoons granulated sugar

¼ teaspoon pure vanilla extract

1 prebaked 9-inch Whole Wheat Crust (page 28)

the pan to prevent scorching, until the mixture begins to boil, about 1 minute. Still whisking constantly, let it boil for a full minute, then immediately remove it from the heat.

3. Add the butter, lemon zest, and lemon juice and whisk until the butter is completely melted and everything is smooth. Set aside in the saucepan to keep warm.

4. Preheat the oven to 350°F with a rack in the bottom position.

5. Prepare the meringue: In the very clean bowl of a stand mixer fitted with the whisk attachment, or in a large, very clean bowl using a handheld electric mixer, beat the egg whites at medium-low speed until they are foamy.

6. With the mixer still running, add the cream of tartar. Add the sugar one tablespoon at a time, making sure it is incorporated before adding the next. When soft peaks form and the whites become a soft white color, 1 to 2 minutes, add the vanilla. Increase the speed to medium-high and beat to stiff, glossy peaks, about 30 seconds. Set aside.

7. Give the lemon curd one final stir and pour it into the prebaked pie crust. Top with the meringue, spreading it to the edge of the crust with a rubber spatula to seal in the filling. If you wish, use the back of a spoon to create peaks in the meringue.

8. Bake until the meringue is a light golden brown, 7 to 10 minutes. Let the pie sit at room temperature until it sets, 1 to 2 hours, then serve it at room temperature or refrigerate it until chilled if you prefer to serve it cold.

Lemon Meringue Pie will keep for 2 to 3 days, covered, in the refrigerator.

Zested Lime Curd Pie

PREP TIME: 30 MINUTES • **SETTING TIME:** 2 TO 4 HOURS • **TOTAL TIME:**
4 HOURS 30 MINUTES • **MAKES:** ONE 9-INCH SINGLE-CRUST PIE
(6 TO 8 SLICES) OR FOUR 5-INCH SINGLE-CRUST TEENY PIES

Key lime was Aaron's favorite pie of all time when he was growing up, so when I started this whole business of pie baking I was determined to make him the perfect Key lime pie. However, when I looked up a few recipes here and there I noticed that all of them called for sweetened condensed milk. And while I don't begrudge anyone their condensed-milk Key lime recipes, I wondered if there wasn't a fresh alternative. I began searching for recipes for curd, hoping a tart lime curd could come close to competing with the typical condensed-milk filling. I came across Ina Garten's lime curd recipe, and after adapting it slightly to suit my pie needs, I had a vibrant green curd to test on Aaron's discerning taste buds. And you know what? We like it better. The lime curd is just tart enough, the small flecks of zest are adorable, and nestled into a sweet graham cracker crust it tastes just like Key lime pie.

1. Make the lime curd: Place the eggs in a medium saucepan and whisk to combine. Add the sugar, salt, lime juice, and zest, whisking to combine after each addition.

2. Add the butter and whisk constantly over medium heat until the butter melts and the mixture begins to develop body and

INGREDIENTS

4 large eggs

1½ cups granulated sugar

¼ teaspoon salt

½ cup freshly squeezed lime juice

1 tablespoon freshly grated lime zest

½ cup (1 stick) unsalted butter, at room temperature

1 prebaked 9-inch Graham Cracker Crust (page 35)

Homemade Whipped Cream (page 45), for serving (optional)

thicken, 5 to 10 minutes. (Watch closely to make sure
the mixture doesn't boil, which can cause it to separate.)
Immediately remove it from the heat and pour it into the
prebaked graham cracker crust.

3. Let the pie sit at room temperature to set and cool completely,
   at least 1 hour. Refrigerate the pie, uncovered, until you
   are ready to serve. Serve with or without whipped cream,
   whatever you prefer.

 **MAKE 'EM TEENY PIES**

Prepare and prebake the crusts in four 5-inch teeny tins
as directed. In step 2, divide the filling among the crusts,
and proceed with the recipe as directed.

*Tested Lime Curd Pie will keep
for 2 to 3 days, covered, in the
refrigerator.*

PIE FLAMBÉ IS *NOT* A THING

The road to pie isn't always smooth. I've had my fair share of pie disasters, but I like to think that I've learned from each mistake and managed to move forward to become a better and more confident baker (after nursing my wounded pride for several days, of course). I've concluded that despite the frustration and occasional cupboard slam that accompanies each failed effort, it's usually all for the betterment of the baker.

There are days when absolutely nothing bakes right and I resign myself to taking large swigs of the bourbon reserved for baking and eating handful after handful of semisweet chocolate chips and toasted coconut (it's a very sad version of trail mix). I've watched a gluten-free pie crust melt right off the pie and puddle in buttery defiance on the floor of the oven, where it promptly burned to a crisp and filled my kitchen with billowing smoke. (Turns out burnt crust smells exactly like the opposite of what you want your kitchen to smell like after baking a homemade pie.) I've had pies that didn't work until the sixth or seventh try, and it's usually because of some silly something or other that I'd overlooked or miscalculated, which is just the *worst*! And I've had days go by without being able to manage a single decent crust. Those are the days that I buy extra vodka because a Bloody Mary nearby usually helps.

My favorite pie disaster, however, wasn't even my fault (maybe that's why it's my favorite). In fact, Aaron was the cause of this particular pie disaster, and he may hate me for including it in this book, but he comes out pretty cool by the end, so I think it's all right. I also happen to think it's a pie disaster that everyone can learn from.

Aaron managed to light a pie on fire. Then he promptly put it out, so nobody panic. This isn't a story where someone is burned or maimed and then they learn their lesson. It's a story where someone is dumb, but then they get to be heroic, and then everyone learns a lesson.

I had baked a sweet potato pie in a disposable tin and had left it to cool on a back burner on the stovetop, imagining that Aaron would enjoy having a breakfast pie the following day. Very early the next morning Aaron, essentially still asleep, thought he was turning on the burner underneath the kettle to boil water for coffee, and instead turned on the burner under the pie. And then four minutes later there was fire . . . real fire: flames ten feet high, burning with the passion of a thousand suns.

Or at least that's what I like to imagine; I didn't actually get out of bed despite the terrible sounds coming from the kitchen and the smoke slowly filling the apartment, so I wouldn't actually know. Aaron, fully awake now and in superhero mode, fought the flames without a single third-degree burn, and managed to Frisbee the scorched pie into the sink,

where it couldn't do any further damage. He brushed the pie crumbs from his hands, cleaned a few scorch marks off the counter, and boiled the water as originally intended. Through the smoky haze, Aaron and I were able to admire the beams of sunlight flooding the room while we drank our morning coffee. Truth be told, it was a fairly successful Sunday morning, with the only downside being that we had to bid farewell to our breakfast pie.

I don't think scorched pie will ever become a thing, but like I said, I do think we learned some very valuable lessons. We learned that a pie in an aluminum pie tin is extremely flammable. (Flames ten feet high, a thousand burning suns, etc.) We learned that if for any reason educational media doesn't work out for Aaron, he may have a second calling as a firefighter. And we learned that when it comes to smelling smoke and sensing danger, I'll most likely stay in bed, listen to the crashes and curses of imminent danger, and keep my fingers crossed for coffee. Lesson learned.

Bob Roth in the grove

Bob Roth's New River Groves
Davie, FL

The first week of May found me in Florida at Bob Roth's New River Groves, where I had traveled to learn the secrets of Key lime pie. Carrying on the legacy of his late wife, Terry, through pie, owner Bob Roth set me up in the kitchen where I would learn to whip together her famous pies, literally. All of the batches of Key lime filling are actually whipped together in a long line of stand mixers—the deafening whir of the mixers becoming commonplace after the first few days. Like tiny Key limes themselves, the kitchen was exceptionally small, with the mixers on one wall and a row of large refrigerators lining the other. A long table sat in the center of the room where multitudes of pies could be filled, topped with swirls of whipped cream, and boxed while the next round of fillings whirred away in the mixers.

Within the walls of that small kitchen I helped make all the variations of Key lime pie the Groves had to offer: Traditional Key lime, mango Key lime, orange Key lime, and pumpkin Key lime were all on the menu. Being new to the Key lime business, I was encouraged to try each of the flavors as they went into the weekly rotation. Orange

Key lime was by far my favorite, the sweet orange juice tempering the tart bite of the lime, but the pumpkin Key lime pie was perhaps the most intriguing. Pumpkin Key lime is a purely seasonal offering at Bob Roth's and apparently flies out the door faster than they can whisk them together. I expected to hate it, thinking the flavors would never go together in a harmonious and delicious way, but I was happily proven wrong. The more subtle pumpkin flavor enveloped the bright Key lime and the end result was a very balanced pumpkin pie with just a hint of citrus. I was sold after a single slice.

Alla, the Groves' full-time baker, had learned the art of Key lime pie from Terry herself and had taken over pie production in 1995. Every morning she brewed decaffeinated coffee in her electric percolator, and we would sip the fragrant brew and pretend it was helping us stay awake. She often told hilarious stories of one mishap or another while we whisked together

Bourbon bacon pies made an appearance in Florida.

the pie fillings. After we topped up row after row of graham cracker crusts with the tart mixture, Alla would swirl the whipped cream atop each pie with a practiced hand and we'd box everything up before beginning the whole cycle again. Bob was always prowling around the grounds and popping in to make sure I was having a good time and learning enough. Occasionally his kids and grandkids would stop by, sampling the fragrant oranges or the freshly made fudge, and on rare, but wonderful, occasions Bob's father, boasting of his recent one-hundred-second birthday, would visit. It was a true family affair.

While a lot of my experiences during the Tour of Pie involved learning to make a large variety of pies and other baked goods, my time at Bob Roth's New River Groves was all about perfecting the varieties and subtleties of a single type of pie. Day in and day

A slice of Terry's famous pie

Whipped perfection

out we made nothing but Key lime pie and its various iterations, and, while that might seem rather monotonous, it was ideal at that point on the tour. Finally given the time to focus on this one pie, I began to notice an efficiency to my work that hadn't been there before. There's something very powerful about engaging in a repetitive activity over an extended period of time: You begin to notice the most minute details about how you work, how the tools you're using work, and how everything comes together in a fluid and familiar way.

In the rush of having to fill an order that includes twelve different pies, it's easy to forget to pay attention to the smaller details, but in the long run, they can make all the difference. Taking the time to do something to the best of your ability, regardless of how routine it may seem, is an incredibly valuable way of developing your skills and pushing yourself to new heights. My time in Florida brought with it a new perspective and appreciation for learning by rote. If done with the right attitude, monotony can breed mastery.

5660 Griffin Road
Davie, FL 33314
954-581-8630
newrivergroves.com

Next Stop: Atlanta, GA (page 216)

Terry's Famous Key Lime Pie

PREP TIME: 15 MINUTES • **CHILL TIME:** 3 TO 4 HOURS • **TOTAL TIME:** 4 HOURS 15 MINUTES •
MAKES: ONE 9-INCH SINGLE-CRUST PIE (6 TO 8 SLICES)

Just as its name suggests, this is Terry's famous recipe, sold at Bob Roth's New River Groves. Terry's husband and children still run the Groves and oversee the making of her ever-famous pies. If you happen to be in Davie, Florida, you can stop into the Groves and pick up a bottle or two of Terry's Key Lime Pie Juice for all of your Key lime needs. Otherwise you can order as much as you'd like from their website (see opposite). If you are in the area, though, a quick trip is well worth it to see firsthand a family continuing their matriarch's pie legacy.

1 can (14 ounces) sweetened
   condensed milk

6 ounces frozen whipped topping

½ cup Terry's Key Lime
   Pie Juice

1 prebaked 9-inch
   Graham Cracker
   Crust (page 35)

Homemade Whipped Cream
   (page 45), for topping

1. In the bowl of a stand mixer fitted with the whisk attachment, or in a large bowl with a handheld electric mixer, beat together the condensed milk and the whipped topping on medium-high speed until it's light and fluffy, about 4 minutes.

2. Add Terry's Key Lime Pie Juice and whisk until the juice is fully incorporated.

3. Pour the filling into the prebaked graham cracker crust and refrigerate, uncovered, for at least 3 hours or up to 4 days. Top the pie with the whipped cream and serve cold.

Terry's Famous Key Lime Pie will keep for 4 days, covered, in the refrigerator, or up to 10 days frozen.

YOU CAN CALL IT A KENTUCKY PIE, YOU CAN CALL IT A MAY DAY PIE, JUST DON'T CALL IT DERBY PIE.

Derby pie was an invention of the Kern family in Prospect, Kentucky, in the 1950s, and its name was supposedly pulled out of a hat (a *derby*, naturally). The pie has since become so quintessentially Kentuckian that it's served at the Kentucky Derby horse race every year, where it's enjoyed by people drinking mint juleps and wearing—what else?—large hats. The Kern family trademarked the name "Derby pie" in 1968 and has aggressively guarded it and the secret recipe ever since. The Kern Kitchen has filed no fewer than twenty-five lawsuits to have "Derby pie" removed from various cookbooks and magazines in the last forty-five years. It seems hard to believe that a little walnut chocolate pie could cause so much trouble, but the Kern family is determined to defend its secret recipe, and I suppose I have to commend them for that.

Derbyish Pie

PREP TIME: 30 MINUTES • **BAKE TIME:** 40 TO 50 MINUTES • **TOTAL TIME:** 1 HOUR 20 MINUTES • **MAKES:** ONE 9-INCH SINGLE-CRUST PIE (6 TO 8 SLICES) OR FOUR 5-INCH SINGLE-CRUST TEENY PIES

Because the name "Derby pie" is so aggressively protected (see opposite) and I'd rather not have this recipe removed forcibly from my cookbook, I'm calling this pie "Derbyish" and adding a butterscotch twist. A Derby pie is rather like a pecan pie with walnuts in place of the pecans, with a sweet addition of chocolate to round things out. Traditionally, it doesn't have butterscotch pieces, but since this is my very own Derbyish pie, who's to say it can't? It's the perfect Kentucky Derby treat, so be sure to bake this pie on the first Saturday of May in honor of those sure-footed Thoroughbreds . . . just don't call it Derby pie.

1. Preheat the oven to 350°F with a rack in the middle position.

2. Melt the butter in a small saucepan over medium heat and bring it to a low simmer. Begin whisking it gently and let it cook until it turns amber and small dark specks of sediment begin to form on the bottom of the pan, 5 to 7 minutes. Remove the butter from the heat and continue whisking for an additional 3 minutes to prevent overcooking. Set aside to cool completely.

INGREDIENTS

½ cup (1 stick) unsalted butter

½ cup all-purpose flour, plus up to 3 tablespoons more, for rolling out the crust

¾ cup granulated sugar

½ teaspoon salt

2 large eggs

2 tablespoons Kentucky bourbon (I like Jim Beam)

1 teaspoon pure vanilla extract

1¼ cups chopped walnuts

½ cup semisweet chocolate chips

½ cup butterscotch chips

1 disk dough from Whole Wheat Crust (page 28)

3. Place the flour, sugar, and salt in a large bowl and stir to combine. Add the eggs and the cooled butter, and stir briskly until everything is incorporated and smooth.

4. Add the bourbon and vanilla, and stir until smooth. Gently fold in the walnuts, chocolate chips, and butterscotch chips with a rubber spatula until they are fully incorporated. Set aside while you roll out the pie crust.

5. Prepare the crust: Place the disk of dough on a floured work surface and with a floured rolling pin roll it into a rough 11-inch circle about ⅛ inch thick. Lay the crust into a 9-inch pie dish, gently press it in, and trim any excess dough from the edge with a paring knife, being sure to leave a ¾-inch overhang. Tuck the overhang under itself and crimp all the way around.

6. Set the crust on a rimmed baking sheet. Give the filling one final stir and pour it into the unbaked pie shell.

7. Transfer the pie, on the baking sheet, to the oven and bake until the crust is golden brown, the middle no longer wobbles, and a knife inserted in the center comes out clean, 40 to 50 minutes. Let the pie cool at room temperature until set, at least 45 minutes, before serving.

Derbyish Pie will keep for 4 to 5 days, covered, on the countertop.

MAKE 'EM TEENY PIES

In step 5, divide the dough into four equal balls and roll out each into a rough 6-inch circle about ⅛ inch thick. Lay each into a 5-inch pie plate, and trim any excess dough from the edge, being sure to leave a ½-inch overhang. Tuck the excess dough under itself and crimp.

Place the crusts on a rimmed baking sheet. Give the filling one final stir and divide it among the crusts (about ¾ cup per crust).

Bake the Teeny Pies until the crusts are golden brown, 40 to 45 minutes. Let cool to set, at least 45 minutes, before serving.

DAY DRINKING AT THE DERBY

Mint juleps, another Derby Day tradition, make a delightful pairing with my Derbyish pie.

SERVES YOU (OR SOMEONE YOU LOVE)

INGREDIENTS

3 ounces Kentucky bourbon (such as Jim Beam)

Leaves from 4 to 6 sprigs fresh mint, plus extra for garnish

Granulated sugar to taste

1. Muddle a tablespoon or two of the bourbon with the mint leaves and sugar in a small tumbler, using the back of a spoon to smash the mint leaves a bit. Let stand for a few minutes while the leaves release their flavor.

2. Strain the mixture into a separate tumbler, and rotate the glass to coat the sides with the liquid. Top with crushed ice and the rest of the bourbon, and garnish with a fresh sprig of mint. Serve with pie.

INGREDIENTS

FOR THE FILLING AND CRUST

2 tablespoons olive oil

1½ pounds lamb stew meat, cut into 1-inch cubes

1 medium onion, peeled and diced into ½-inch cubes

4 garlic cloves, diced

1 tablespoon chopped fresh rosemary leaves

1 tablespoon chopped fresh mint

¾ cup white wine

2 teaspoons salt

½ teaspoon ground black pepper

2 medium white potatoes, peeled and diced into 1-inch cubes

2 disks dough from Savory Pie Crust (page 32)

Up to a ¼ cup all-purpose flour, for rolling out the crust

FOR THE RASPBERRY SAUCE

1 cup fresh or frozen raspberries

2 tablespoons white wine

2 tablespoons granulated sugar

2 tablespoons chopped fresh mint

Lamb, Mint, and Raspberry Teeny Potpies

PREP TIME: 3 HOURS • **BAKE TIME:** 45 TO 55 MINUTES • **TOTAL TIME:** 4 HOURS • **MAKES:** SIX 5-INCH DOUBLE-CRUST TEENY PIES

Toward the end of the winter leg of the tour, as spring was just starting to warm the weather and lengthen the days, I began my search for the quintessential spring savory pie. Lamb was my first choice of main ingredients, as it seemed appropriately spring-ish. I started making lamb curries and putting them into my whole wheat crust, hoping that one of them would be the be-all and end-all of lamb pies. But after each incarnation Aaron shook his head, stating sadly that while it was good, it wasn't "it." The curries were just too heavy for the bright flavors I was hoping to infuse into the pie, and they didn't echo the lightness of the season. I was rather at a loss until Aaron suggested making mint and a hint of tart raspberries part of the equation. Game for anything, and grateful for the new flavors to play with, I came up with this recipe, and finally we found the spring savory we'd been searching for.

If you'd prefer a stronger raspberry mint flavor, you can set the sauce aside and use it as a drizzle on the finished pies, rather than baking it with the rest of the filling.

1. Heat the olive oil in a large skillet over medium heat. Line a plate with paper towels.

2. Pat the lamb dry with paper towels and add it to the hot oil. Sear the meat, turning occasionally, so it's browned on all sides. Remove it from the pan to the prepared plate.

3. Add the onion, garlic, rosemary, and mint to the skillet and cook over medium heat until the onion becomes translucent and begins to brown, 5 to 10 minutes. Add the ¾ cup white wine to deglaze the skillet, and use a wooden spoon to scrape up any bits of browned meat from the bottom of the pan. Return the lamb to the skillet, add 1 cup water, the salt and pepper, and bring everything to a simmer, about 10 minutes.

4. Reduce the heat to low, cover the skillet, and simmer, stirring occasionally, until the meat begins to fall apart easily, about 1½ hours. If the liquid gets too low (you want at least ¼ cup) while it's cooking, add an additional ¼ to ½ cup water.

5. Meanwhile, prepare the bottom crusts: Divide the dough into twelve equal balls and return six to the refrigerator. On a floured surface with a floured rolling pin, roll the first six balls into 6-inch circles about ⅛ inch thick. Lay each into a 5-inch pie plate, gently press them in, and trim any excess dough from the edge, being sure to leave a ½-inch overhang. Transfer the crusts to a rimmed baking sheet, loosely cover with plastic wrap, and place them in the refrigerator.

6. Prepare the top crusts: Roll out the remaining dough balls into 6-inch circles about ⅛ inch thick and place them on a plate, separated by parchment paper. Cover and return them to the refrigerator.

7. Make the raspberry sauce: Place the raspberries, wine, and sugar in a small saucepan over medium heat and cook until the sugar dissolves and the raspberries begin to fall apart, about 7 minutes. Remove from the heat, stir in the chopped mint, and set aside to cool.

8. When the lamb is very tender, add the potatoes and simmer until they are cooked through, about 15 minutes. Remove from the heat and set aside to cool completely.

9. Preheat the oven to 375°F with a rack in the middle position.

10. When the lamb has cooled, remove the crusts from the refrigerator. Spoon the filling into the crust-lined tins, dividing it evenly, and top each with a few tablespoons of the raspberry sauce. Place the top crusts on each pie, tuck the excess dough under itself, and crimp all the way around to seal. Cut a steam vent, about ½ inch long, in the top crust of each pie.

11. Set the Teeny Pies on a rimmed baking sheet and bake until the crusts are golden brown and the insides are bubbling, 45 to 55 minutes. Serve immediately.

Lamb, Mint, and Raspberry Teeny Potpies will keep for 2 to 3 days, covered, in the refrigerator. To reheat them, bake in a 325°F oven for 20 minutes.

Breakfast Pie with a Hash Brown Crust

PREP TIME: 30 MINUTES • **BAKE TIME:** 30 TO 40 MINUTES • **TOTAL TIME:** 1 HOUR 10 MINUTES • **MAKES:** ONE 9-INCH SINGLE-CRUST PIE (6 TO 8 SLICES)

Breakfast is my favorite meal of the day. It generally trumps any and all lunches or dinners. I usually leave Aaron to the breakfast making; with his phenomenal egg sandwiches, piled high with kale and topped with Sriracha sauce, he has yet to disappoint. Since he so readily makes breakfast most of the time, I thought it only fair that I come up with a breakfast pie for those weekend days when I'm in charge of the meal.

Leeks in the spring are positively massive and are the perfect accompaniment to the earthy mushrooms you can find at any farmers' market. If you don't want to shred your own potatoes for the crust, you can always cheat and buy preshredded hash browns from the store, as long as you have three and a half cups.

I usually make this in a pie plate, but a cast-iron pan works, too (just be sure to grease it before pressing in the hash brown crust).

1. Preheat the oven to 350°F with a rack in the middle position.

2. Heat the olive oil in a large skillet over medium heat. While the skillet heats, combine the shredded potatoes

INGREDIENTS

3 tablespoons olive oil

3½ cups peeled, shredded hash brown potatoes (I like russets)

Salt and ground black pepper

1 tablespoon chopped fresh rosemary leaves

2 tablespoons unsalted butter

1 large leek, halved lengthwise, cleaned, and whites and light greens thinly sliced into half-moons

About 8 ounces mushrooms, stemmed and cut into ¼-inch slices (to equal ¾ cup)

5 large eggs

¾ cup heavy (whipping) cream

1 cup grated Parmesan cheese

with 2 teaspoons salt, ½ teaspoon pepper, and the rosemary in a large bowl and toss to combine.

3. Add the seasoned potatoes to the hot skillet, spread them into a single layer, and cook, flipping once with a spatula, until they are crispy on both sides, about 10 minutes. Remove from the heat and let cool.

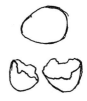

4. Melt the butter in a small skillet over medium heat. Add the leeks and mushrooms and cook until they are soft and lightly browned, 15 to 20 minutes. Remove from the heat and let cool.

5. Meanwhile, combine the eggs and cream in a large bowl and whisk together. Add salt and pepper and half the grated cheese and whisk until incorporated.

6. Press the cooled hash browns into the bottom and up the side of a 9-inch pie plate. Spread the leeks and mushrooms over the bottom of the crust, and top with the remaining cheese. Pour in the egg mixture.

7. Bake until the filling is cooked through and the top is nicely browned, 30 to 40 minutes. Serve immediately.

Breakfast Pie with a Hash Brown Crust will keep for 3 to 4 days, covered, in the refrigerator. To reheat, cover with foil and bake at 350°F until warm in the center, 10 to 15 minutes.

CHAPTER 6

Summer

Pies to Picnic With

For a pie baker, summertime is warm. In fact, I'd go so far as to say summertime for a pie baker is sweltering! But a baker's warm weather travails are well worth it—friends perk up considerably when they spot a homemade pie at a picnic or a barbecue, and there's no better way to beat the heat than a decadent slice of juicy, sweet-tart pie topped with a generous scoop of ice cream.

Home is where the cherry is.

Blueberries finally lose their early-season bite and become my favorite way to temper the last stalks of the season's rhubarb. Stone fruits like peaches and cherries are finally ripe for the picking and need nothing more than a bit of sugar and spice before being tucked into a flaky crust and baked to a golden brown.

The summertime stops on the Tour of Pie were scheduled to start in July, when I would be apprenticing at Pie Shop in Atlanta, Georgia, during the height of peach season. From there I would head west to spend August in Los Angeles, working for the small but fierce I Heart Pies. And I'd cap off the entire tour where it truly had begun: with a visit to my mom's kitchen in Littleton, Colorado. There I would again be learning at my mother's apron strings, this time as an adult with a greater sense of purpose (and, hopefully, a more mature attention to detail!). I had those three final stops to fully embrace my traveling apprenticeship before an entirely new adventure would begin, because the end of summer also meant the end of my year of vagabond baking. I had no idea what would happen after September, but I was excited to begin the final season of the tour.

Pie Shop was just barely into its second year when I began my monthlong stay. The owner, Mims Bledsoe, opened the shop in 2010, and she was determined to give Atlanta a delicious dose of homemade pie. The shop used to be an old bread bakery, and it's located, rather sneakily, on the backside of a few shops in Buckhead. It's worth the hunt. Mims has a passion for pie, especially the more traditional pies, some of which I'd only ever seen pictures of in my mom's ancient *Betty Crocker Cookbook.* Our daily menus included everything from a simple peach pie to a more intriguing raspberry chiffon pie, decked high with fluffy whipped cream. Mims was especially good about taking my apprenticing in hand, continually checking in with me to make sure I was getting as much as I could out of my visit and introducing me to new pies that I'd never made before. I worked hard at Pie Shop and was sorry to say good-bye at the end of July, but it was time to return to the West Coast.

My monthlong apprenticeship at L.A.'s I Heart Pies was spent working with the married owners, Emily and Nick Cofrancesco. Rather than having a storefront, Emily and Nick offer a pie delivery service in addition to having a stall at a farmers' market where customers can pick up pies on the weekends. They welcomed me graciously, and now that I was fully able to competently roll out a crust and carry on a conversation at the same time, it took only half a day to get over my "new-place-nerves." Emily and Nick were both easy company and didn't seem to mind my tendency to blather on about my pie adventures, as long as the work got done. My four-week stay seemed to pass in an instant. All of a sudden it was time for my official "last stop."

Returning to my mom's kitchen was—literally—like going home. I had traversed the country learning from the best of the best, but I still had much to learn from the lady who had first taught me to love pie. I went home to Colorado for my final apprenticeship, and my heart was full as the familiar mountains came into view. My mom had recently finished remodeling her kitchen, replacing the tacky linoleum with warm wood, ripping out the drab dark cupboards and putting light, glass-fronted cabinets in their place, and painting the entire room a bright and welcoming white. It was the ideal time to cover everything from top to bottom with flour. We spent our days turning through old family recipes, baking off our favorites and experimenting with new ideas, and reveling in four weeks of uninterrupted time together. It was the perfect way to end the Tour of Pie.

Sour Cherry Pie, aka My Favorite

PREP TIME: 25 MINUTES • **BAKE TIME:** 45 TO 55 MINUTES • **TOTAL TIME:** 1 HOUR 20 MINUTES • **MAKES:** ONE 9-INCH DOUBLE-CRUST PIE (6 OR 8 SLICES) OR THREE 5-INCH DOUBLE-CRUST TEENY PIES

Cherry pie has been a longtime favorite in my family. Both my brother and I requested it every year for our birthday pies, and my mom was always happy to oblige. We had large choke cherry bushes in our backyard and most of the fruit was picked and put directly into a pie. But toward the end of the year, when the fall frost threatened to zap the rest of our cherries, we would pick as many as we could find to freeze them for the winter (see page 225). My brother and I would fight over who got to turn the crank on the cherry pitter, as my mom washed, dried, and froze baking sheet after baking sheet of the tart red fruit. To this day, I still use only her recipe. Maybe it's because I really love tart pies, but the simplicity of the sour cherries tempered with sweet sugar and a hint of almond makes it the best.

1. Preheat the oven to 400°F with a rack in the middle position.

2. Stir together the sugar and cornstarch in a small bowl.

3. Place the cherries (or thawed cherries and juice) in a medium saucepan and cook over medium-low heat until they begin to juice. Stir occasionally until you have ¼ to ½ cup of juice in the saucepan.

INGREDIENTS

¾ cup granulated sugar

4 tablespoons cornstarch (6 tablespoons if using frozen fruit)

4 cups fresh or frozen sour cherries, pitted (see box, page 214)

1 teaspoon almond extract

2 disks dough from My Mom's All-Shortening Crust (page 29)

Up to ¼ cup all-purpose flour, for rolling out the crust

4. Turn up the heat to medium-high and add the sugar mixture, stirring until it's fully incorporated and there are no lumps; the liquid will be milky and very thin and watery. Cook, stirring constantly and being sure to scrape the bottom of the pan to prevent scorching, until the juice thickens and deepens in color, becoming shiny and translucent, but the fruit is still intact, 15 to 20 minutes. Transfer the filling to a heatproof bowl and stir in the almond extract. Set aside and let cool while you prepare the pie crust.

5. Prepare the bottom crust: Place one disk of the dough on a floured work surface and with a floured rolling pin roll it into a rough 11-inch circle about ⅛ inch thick. Lay the crust into a 9-inch pie plate, gently press it in, and trim any excess dough from the edge with a paring knife, being sure to leave a ¾-inch overhang.

IT'S ALL IN THE BITE

Sour cherries are different from the sweet cherries you typically find at the supermarket: They are much more acidic and, similar to rhubarb, they're much too sour to eat by themselves. But when sprinkled generously with sugar and tucked into a flaky, buttery crust they become addictively sweet and sour. They have a quick grow season, so most likely you will have to buy them at your local farmers' market or frozen from the grocery store. If you can't find them near you, you can purchase frozen ones online from Friske Orchards (friske.com).

When using frozen cherries in this recipe, thaw them and save all of their juices, and place both in the saucepan in step 3.

6. Give the cooled filling one final stir to combine and pour it into the crust.

7. Prepare the lattice crust: On a floured work surface with a floured rolling pin, roll out the remaining dough disk into a rough 11-inch circle ⅛ inch thick. Cut the dough into strips and weave them into a lattice as directed on page 24. Tuck the overhanging dough strips under the bottom crust and crimp together, pressing to seal.

8. Set the pie on a rimmed baking sheet and bake until the filling is thickly bubbling and the crust is golden brown (cover the crimp with foil if it begins to brown too quickly), 45 to 55 minutes.

Sour Cherry Pie will keep for up to 3 days, covered, on the countertop.

MAKE 'EM TEENY PIES

In step 5, divide one disk of the dough into four equal balls and roll out each into a rough 6-inch circle about ⅛ inch thick. Lay each into a 5-inch pie tin, and trim any excess dough from the edge, being sure to leave a ½-inch overhang.

Give the filling one final stir and spoon an equal amount into each crust-lined teeny tin (roughly 1 cup each).

In step 7, divide the remaining dough into four equal balls and roll out each into a rough 7-inch circle about ⅛ inch thick. Cut each dough circle into strips and weave them into a lattice over each pie as directed on page 24. Tuck the overhanging dough strips under the bottom crusts and crimp together, pressing to seal.

Bake the Teeny Pies until the crusts are golden brown, 30 to 40 minutes.

Pie Shop "to-dos"

Early morning crust-rolling

Pie Shop
Atlanta, GA

ARRIVED IN GEORGIA in the middle of a Southern summer, and the heat and humidity came as quite a shock. I hadn't been back to the South since my spring in Alabama, and July in Georgia meant temperatures well into the nineties with 70- to 80-percent humidity.

In a word: hot. The daily afternoon thunderstorms did little to cool things down, and to top it all off, I soon realized that the best way to commute to my apprenticeship was not by public transportation but by biking through Atlanta's rather bike-unfriendly streets. Once again, my lovely and gracious hosts came to the rescue.

Patrick and Kay Golan stepped up and lent me their son Sean's road bike. Sean, being slightly taller than I at six foot two (I'm five foot five . . . I suppose the height difference is more than slight), had a bike that was a bit large for me, but once I lowered the seat and stretched my toes, it was a beautiful ride. The mornings were cooler than the afternoons, and soon I began to relish waking up at five in the morning to make my daily commute to Pie Shop simply because it meant I didn't have to bike in the glaring sunlight.

Five very early mornings a week I would arrive at Pie Shop, where I was apprenticing under owner and baker Mims Bledsoe and baking alongside Katy, the head baker, and Belinda, a fellow apprentice who'd just finished pastry school. Belinda and I each arrived by six, taking small, desperate sips of hot coffee in an attempt to wake up enough to roll a respectable crust. Each day Katy compiled the list of pies to be baked by the time the shop opened at eleven o'clock, and handed half to each of us. I would start on my list of to-do's and Belinda would start on hers and we would gossip and bake our way to the end; we always finished our shifts rolling out our daily quota of pie crusts. Some days we were rolling circles to fill pie tins, crimping the crusts all the way around, and stacking them five high before putting them in the freezer for baking the following day. Other days we were simply rolling out one small round crust after another, which were to be filled and formed later into the hundreds of hand-pies that were sold at the local farmers' market. Belinda and I stood across from each other at the beautiful wooden worktables and talked while we rolled, slowly being dusted from head to toe with flyaway flour.

My aching shoulder muscles and my tired feet belied any ideas that the first few years of owning a pie business were going to be easy. I had always understood that it was never going to be a breeze, especially in the first five years, when staying afloat is as crucial as it is incredibly difficult. But at Pie Shop, during those endless hours of rolling, I realized that even a job that you love with your whole heart is occasionally still a job like any other. There will be days when I dread waking up at four in the morning and weekends when all I want to do is play, rather than work. There are going to be days, pursuing this dream of pie, when I will

be mentally and physically exhausted, not to mention overwhelmingly anxious for everything to work out. But the hard work and the worries are well worth a future filled with pie.

Chicken potpies waiting for their rosemary

Standing there, rolling out pie crust after pie crust with Belinda, it finally sank in that I was an official pie baker. I knew what I was doing, and not only that, I was finally really good at it. I was no longer paralyzed by uncertainty each time I moved temporarily to a new city: I relished the idea of making new friends, and I'd slowly but surely been readying myself for my future. I didn't have any misconceptions about how hard it was going to be, and I still had a pretty healthy dose of fear that came along with thoughts of the future, but I knew that every single day I came home floury from a day's work was going to be worth it.

3210 Roswell Road
Atlanta, GA 30305
404-841-4512
the-pie-shop.com

Next Stop: Los Angeles, CA (page 232)

Georgia Peach Pie

PREP TIME: 30 MINUTES • **BAKE TIME:** 45 TO 55 MINUTES • **TOTAL TIME:** 1 HOUR 30 MINUTES • **MAKES:** ONE 9-INCH DOUBLE-CRUST PIE (6 TO 8 SLICES)

Peach pie was one of the reasons I was so excited to have a stop in Georgia on the Tour of Pie, and the peaches did not disappoint. I was in town for the month of July and the sweet, juicy peaches were at the height of the season. I was staying with Kay and Patrick, the generous parents of my old college friend and Atlanta native Sean, who had volunteered his parents' guest room after hearing about my travels. In late July, Kay invited a few of her friends over for a pie party. Each of the ladies brought their own peaches, I provided the crust ingredients, and they all learned how to make peach pie. Sipping on iced tea and eating a warm slice of Georgia peach pie was the perfect way to end my visit.

1. Preheat the oven to 400°F with a rack in the middle position.

2. Place the peaches in a medium bowl. In a separate small bowl, stir together the sugar, cinnamon, and cornstarch until incorporated.

3. Sprinkle the sugar mixture over the peaches and toss them gently with your hands to coat. Set aside while you roll out the bottom crust; the fruit will begin to juice.

INGREDIENTS

7 to 8 peaches, peeled and cut into ½-inch slices (6 cups; see Note, page 220)

½ cup granulated sugar

½ teaspoon ground cinnamon

6 tablespoons cornstarch

2 disks dough from Whole Wheat Crust (page 28)

Up to ¼ cup all-purpose flour, for rolling out the crust

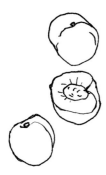

4. Prepare the bottom crust: Place one disk of the dough on a floured work surface and with a floured rolling pin roll it into a rough 11-inch circle about ⅛ inch thick. Lay the crust into a 9-inch pie dish, gently press it in, and trim any excess dough from the edge with a paring knife, being sure to leave a ¾-inch overhang.

5. Set the pie dish on a rimmed baking sheet. Give the fruit a quick stir, then use a slotted spoon to spoon the peaches into the crust.

6. Prepare the top crust: On a floured work surface with a floured rolling pin, roll out the remaining dough disk into a rough 11-inch circle about ⅛ inch thick. Carefully lay the crust on top of the filling, and trim any excess dough from the edge, leaving a ¾-inch overhang. Tuck the overhanging dough under the overhanging edge of the bottom crust, and crimp the two crusts together. Cut a few small slits in the top crust with a sharp knife to allow steam to escape.

7. Transfer the pie, on the baking sheet, to the oven and bake until the filling is thickly bubbling and the crust is a golden brown (cover the crimp with foil if it begins to brown too quickly), 45 to 55 minutes.

NOTE: The easiest way to peel peaches is to blanch them: Score the bottom of each peach with a small X using a sharp paring knife and drop the peaches into boiling water for a few minutes. Remove the peaches with a slotted spoon and rinse them under cold water to cool, then simply slip the skins off with your fingers.

Georgia Peach Pie will keep for up to 3 days, covered, on the countertop.

FAMILY DINNER

One of the most wonderful things I discovered while on the Tour of Pie is just how many people have some sort of connection with the pastry. Whether it was a story or a favorite recipe, there were countless people I met along the way who seemed to light up at the mention of pie. One of my favorite instances of this was when I was in Florida, staying with Lisa and Doug Weiner. Lisa and Doug are the parents of my friend Jenny, and they were willing to host an apprentice pie baker for the month of May on one condition: that I participate in their Sunday night family dinners.

Sunday night family dinners at the Weiner house are an event. That's not to say they are particularly fancy or overblown; in fact, the opposite is true: It's a very homey and warm evening filled with family and friends. Lisa spends the afternoon assembling the main dish while aunts, cousins, grandparents, and a rotating roster of close friends arrive between six and seven o'clock bearing appetizers, salads, and side dishes. Doug, the resident dessert maker, bakes the cakes and pies to the delight of his family and scoops the accompanying ice cream.

For my first family dinner, it was decided that my duty was to teach Doug how to make a homemade pie crust and he, in turn, would teach me his "blueberry dream" recipe. Without hesitation, he had himself a deal. I measured the flour, cut in the butter, and showed him how to roll out and crimp the crust while he rinsed the berries and whisked together the sugar and lemon that we would pour atop everything. The smell of baking blueberries filled the kitchen as the Weiner family began to trickle in. We raised our glasses and toasted to family and friends, old and new, before we dove into the delightful meal of brown sugar–crusted salmon and roasted veggies. Once dinner was over and it was time for dessert, Doug and I grinned gleefully at each other as the thick slices of our collaborative handiwork were devoured.

Summer's Best Blueberry Pie

PREP TIME: 30 MINUTES • **BAKE TIME:** 50 TO 60 MINUTES • **TOTAL TIME:**
1 HOUR 30 MINUTES • **MAKES:** ONE 9-INCH DOUBLE-CRUST PIE
(6 OR 8 SLICES) OR FOUR 5-INCH DOUBLE-CRUST TEENY PIES

INGREDIENTS

5 cups fresh blueberries

1 tablespoon freshly
squeezed lemon juice

¼ cup fresh mint leaves,
roughly chopped
(optional)

½ cup granulated sugar

3 tablespoons quick-
cooking tapioca,
finely ground
(see page 165),
or tapioca starch

2 disks dough from
Whole Wheat Crust
(page 28)

Up to ¼ cup all-purpose
flour, for rolling out
the crust

A few summers ago I asked my friend Effie what kind of
pie she wanted for her birthday and she replied with a
resounding "blueberry!" Her birthday plans were to go for a
morning bike ride and end up in the park to picnic. Being the
proud parent of a tiny mint plant growing contentedly on my
windowsill, I'd taken to throwing a few leaves into everything
I was baking or cooking that summer, and Effie's blueberry pie
was no exception. I roughly chopped a quarter cup of mint and
tossed it in with the fresh summer berries and lemon juice, and it
perked her picnic pie right up. The mint is optional in this recipe,
but if you're feeling adventurous, toss in a few leaves and enjoy
the cool breeze with the burst of berries.

1. Preheat the oven to 400°F with a rack in the middle position.

2. Place the blueberries in a medium bowl, add the lemon juice
   and mint (if using), and toss gently to coat.

3. Stir together the sugar and the ground tapioca in a separate
   small bowl to combine. Sprinkle it over the blueberries and

toss gently to coat evenly. Set aside while you roll out the crust; the fruit will begin to juice.

4. Prepare the bottom crust: Place one disk of the dough on a floured work surface and with a floured rolling pin roll it into a rough 11-inch circle about ⅛ inch thick. Lay the crust into a 9-inch pie dish, gently press it in, and trim any excess dough from the edge with a paring knife, being sure to leave a ¾-inch overhang.

5. Set the crust on a rimmed baking sheet. Give the fruit a quick stir, then pour the filling into the crust.

6. Prepare the top crust: On a floured work surface with a floured rolling pin, roll out the remaining dough disk into a rough 11-inch circle about ⅛ inch thick. Carefully lay the crust on top of the filling, and trim any excess dough from the edge, leaving a ¾-inch overhang. Tuck the overhanging dough under the overhanging edge of the bottom crust, and crimp the two crusts together. Cut a few small slits in the top crust with a sharp knife.

7. Transfer the pie, on the baking sheet, to the oven and bake until the filling is thickly bubbling and the crust is golden brown (cover the crimp with foil if it begins to brown too quickly), 50 to 60 minutes.

Summer's Best Blueberry Pie will keep for 4 to 5 days, covered, on the countertop.

 MAKE 'EM TEENY PIES

In step 4, divide one disk of dough into four equal balls and roll out each into a rough 6-inch circle about ⅛ inch thick. Lay each into a 5-inch pie plate, and trim any excess dough from the edge, being sure to leave a ½-inch overhang.

Give the filling one final stir and spoon an equal amount into each crust-lined teeny tin (roughly 1 cup each). In step 6, divide the remaining dough into four separate pieces and roll out each into a rough 7-inch circle about ⅛ inch thick. Carefully lay the crusts over the filling, and trim any excess dough from the edge, leaving a ½-inch overhang. Tuck the overhanging dough under the bottom crust and crimp the two crusts together, pressing to seal. Cut a ½-inch slit in the top of each pie to allow steam to escape.

Bake the Teeny Pies until the crusts are golden brown, 40 to 45 minutes.

A jumble of sugared berries

FREEZING BERRIES FOR THE OFF-SEASON

Summer can last only so long, and when it fades, the glorious fruit that it brings with it becomes unavailable. It's usually a few months into winter when I start craving blueberry and blackberry pie again, but I refuse to resign myself to buying the bitter and flavorless fruit then on offer at the grocery store. Having the foresight to freeze a few of your favorite berries during their peak will save you from going crazy during those long, berry-less winter months.

Measure out three cups of ripe berries, rinse them well, and pat them dry (if you're freezing strawberries, hull them). Spread the berries on a baking sheet (if they are still damp, let them sit until dry), and put them uncovered in the freezer. Once they are frozen through—a few hours—take the berries out of the freezer, and transfer them to freezer-safe ziplock bags. Write the quantity and date on the bags and return the fruit to the freezer.

If you freeze the berries this way, you'll know exactly how many cups are in each bag and they won't stick together in one large clump. They should last at least six months frozen and will definitely help see you through the winter.

Lemony Blueberry Crumb Pie

PREP TIME: 20 MINUTES • **BAKE TIME:** 45 TO 55 MINUTES • **TOTAL TIME:**
1 HOUR 20 MINUTES • **MAKES:** ONE 9-INCH SINGLE-CRUST PIE (6 TO 8 SLICES)

INGREDIENTS

4 cups fresh blueberries
(5 cups if reserving
some for topping)

Freshly grated zest of
1 lemon (1 to
2 tablespoons)

⅔ cup granulated sugar

7 tablespoons cornstarch

½ teaspoon ground
cinnamon

1 tablespoon freshly
squeezed lemon juice

1 disk dough from
Whole Wheat Crust
(page 28)

Up to 3 tablespoons
all-purpose flour, for
rolling out the crust

1 batch Oat-and-Nut
Crumble (page 43), for
topping (optional)

There are several options for topping this brightly flavored blueberry pie. If you like a crumb top, I highly recommend using the Oat-and-Nut Crumble on page 43. If you'd prefer your blueberries loud and clear, leave the pie naked and top it straight out of the oven with fresh blueberries and a tart lemon drizzle.

If you do decide to make the lemon drizzle, you'll want to prepare it in advance and refrigerate it while you assemble and bake the pie. Simply whisk together 1 tablespoon of confectioners' sugar and 2 tablespoons of freshly squeezed lemon juice in a small bowl until it's smooth.

When I go the fresh berry–topped route, I also like to cut out fun shapes from the extra pie crust dough, bake them separately as crust cookies (see page 25 for instructions), and stick them on top later to create decorative scenes. Either way, it's a wonderful summer pie!

1. Preheat the oven to 400°F with a rack in the middle position.

2. Place the 4 cups blueberries in a large bowl, add the lemon zest, and toss to combine. In a medium bowl, stir together the sugar, cornstarch, and cinnamon to combine.

3. Add the lemon juice to the sugar mixture along with 1 tablespoon water and whisk until smooth. (If the cornstarch and sugar still clump, you can add an additional tablespoon of water.) Pour over the blueberries and toss gently to coat. Set aside.

4. Prepare the crust: Place the disk of dough on a floured work surface and with a floured rolling pin roll it into a rough 11-inch circle about ⅛ inch thick. Lay the crust into a 9-inch pie plate, gently press it in, and trim any excess dough from the edge with a paring knife, being sure to leave a ¾-inch overhang. Tuck the overhanging dough under itself and crimp. Place the lined pie plate on a rimmed baking sheet.

5. Pour the blueberries into the unbaked pie crust. If you're using the crumble, sprinkle it evenly over the filling.

6. Bake until the filling is thickly bubbling and the crust and crumble are golden brown (cover the crimp with foil if it begins to brown too quickly), 45 to 55 minutes. If you've kept the pie naked, scatter the remaining cup of fresh berries over the hot filling and let it cool, then drizzle with the reserved lemon drizzle and serve. If you've topped the pie with crumble, let it cool before serving.

Lemony Blueberry Crumb Pie will keep for 3 to 4 days, covered, on the countertop.

Bluebarb Pie

PREP TIME: 30 MINUTES • BAKE TIME: 45 TO 55 MINUTES • TOTAL TIME:
1 HOUR 30 MINUTES • **MAKES:** ONE 9-INCH DOUBLE-CRUST PIE (6 TO 8 SLICES)
OR FOUR 5-INCH DOUBLE-CRUST TEENY PIES

Bluebarb pie was a happy accident. I had an abundance of rhubarb in the refrigerator but the farmers' market strawberries were on their last legs. I scanned the market stalls, hoping for inspiration, and the first blueberries of the season were looking particularly gorgeous. I took a chance on the new combination, and the result was outstanding! I'm not the biggest fan of baked blueberries because of how sweet they tend to get, but the rhubarb with its inherent tartness turned out to be the ideal counterpart. It's always a crowd pleaser because while most people have had strawberry rhubarb pie, they likely haven't experienced the wonder that is bluebarb.

I like to use a double crust for this stunning pie, but I often use the top crust dough to make fun crust cookies that I place on top of the baked, cooled pie. See page 25 for instructions.

1. Preheat the oven to 400°F with a rack in the middle position.

2. Place the blueberries and rhubarb in a medium bowl and toss together to combine.

3. Stir together the sugar and cornstarch in a small bowl. Sprinkle the mixture over the fruit and toss gently to coat. Set aside; the fruit will begin to juice.

INGREDIENTS

4 cups fresh blueberries

2 to 3 stalks rhubarb, diced (½-inch pieces, to equal 1½ cups; see Note, page 169)

½ cup granulated sugar

6 tablespoons cornstarch

2 disks dough from Whole Wheat Crust (page 28)

Up to ¼ cup all-purpose flour, for rolling out the crust

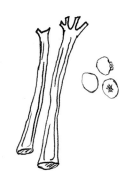

4. Prepare the bottom crust: Place one disk of the dough on a floured work surface and with a floured rolling pin roll it into a rough 11-inch circle about ⅛ inch thick. Lay the crust into a 9-inch pie dish, gently press it in, and trim any excess dough from the edge with a paring knife, being sure to leave a ¾-inch overhang.

5. Set the lined pie dish on a rimmed baking sheet. Give the fruit a quick stir, then pour the filling into the crust.

BLUEBARB BLISS

One evening in June, as I waited for the last leg of the tour to start, Aaron and I hosted a dinner party with an invite list that included a large number of friends, all of whom were in town for one reason or another. The meal itself was a triumph of epic proportions as we ate our way through fish tacos with homemade slaw and guacamole piled high with jalapeño peppers. After eating our fill, we whiled away the evening with whiskey and game after game of Mexican train dominoes, determined to complete a full thirteen-round game so an ultimate dinner party champion could be named. Halfway through the heated tournament we decided to break for dessert. The day had been rainy and I'd gladly escaped to the kitchen a few hours earlier to throw together a quick bluebarb pie.

Perhaps we were all so relaxed from the magnificent meal we had just finished or maybe the whiskey was making us all feel warm and fuzzy, but as we cut into that pie we could only marvel at its absolute perfection. The crust was flaky and tasted of butter, and it had that distinctly nutty flavor that only can come from whole wheat flour. That ever-elusive balance between tart and sweet had been achieved and the dark blueberries and the light rhubarb were held in perfect suspension within each and every triangular slice, staining our teeth a deep purple as we smiled through our bliss.

6. Prepare the top crust: On a floured work surface with a floured rolling pin, roll out the remaining dough disk into a rough 11-inch circle about ⅛-inch thick. Carefully lay the crust on top of the filling, and trim any excess dough from the edge, leaving a ¾-inch overhang. Tuck the overhanging dough under the edge of the bottom crust, and crimp the two crusts together. Cut a few small slits in the top crust with a sharp knife.

7. Place the pie, on the baking sheet, in the oven and bake until the filling is thickly bubbling and the crust is golden brown (cover the crimp with foil if it begins to brown too quickly), 45 to 55 minutes.

Bluebarb Pie will keep for up to 3 days, covered, on the countertop.

 ## MAKE 'EM TEENY PIES

In step 4, divide one disk of dough into four equal balls and roll out each into a rough 6-inch circle about ⅛ inch thick. Lay each into a 5-inch pie tin, and trim any excess dough from the edge, being sure to leave a ½-inch overhang.

Give the filling one final stir and spoon an equal amount into each crust-lined teeny tin (roughly 1 cup each).

In step 6, divide the remaining dough into four equal balls and roll out each into a rough 7-inch circle about ⅛ inch thick. Carefully lay the crusts over the filling, and trim any excess dough from the edge, leaving a ½-inch overhang. Tuck the overhanging dough under the overhanging bottom crust and crimp the two crusts together, pressing to seal. Cut a ½-inch slit in the top of each pie to allow steam to escape.

Bake the Teeny Pies until the crusts are golden brown, 40 to 45 minutes.

I Heart Pies' owners,
Emily and Nick

I Heart Pies
Los Angeles, CA

Baking with Emily and Nick Cofrancesco at L.A.'s I Heart Pies was a true lesson in how to build something from the ground up. They don't own their own space, which means they don't have their own kitchen. Instead, they share a co-packing kitchen with other bakers and food makers. Emily and Nick have their own little room where most of their prep takes place, but the stovetop and the ovens were in the shared communal space. On any given day there are one or two other companies baking, cooking, or packaging their wares. My favorite days in the space were the ones we shared with the cookie lady, when the smells of pie and cookies would comingle and fill the air with their sweet warmth.

Emily and Nick keep all of their dry ingredients at the kitchen and bring everything else as needed for that week's particular roster of pies—pies to fill orders and to take to the market. Their menu changes seasonally, which, of course, I love, and nearly all of their ingredients are from local farms and the occasional friend. Saturdays are spent selling three sizes of pies at the Autry Farmers Market in L.A.'s

Griffith Park, and the rest of the week is spent alternating between baking at the kitchen to fill orders and delivering those orders in Emily's zippy little Mini Cooper. She traverses the entirety of L.A. with a trunkful of pie.

Because Emily and Nick didn't spend every day in the kitchen, my schedule was pretty light midweek. Fridays were always the busiest, so Emily would blast the music and fill the tiny kitchen with an energy that made the day fly by. Once all the pies were baked and well on their way to being completely cooled, we started packaging them up. Folding boxes, cutting ribbon, and punching holes in stickers all had to be done before we could box the bigger pies and bag the smaller ones. The tiniest pies (which were my favorite, of course) were put in small see-through baggies and secured with a sticker and a perfect red ribbon before being taken to the market.

At every stop on the Tour of Pie I learned something different, and I Heart Pies taught me, among other things, to trust my instincts. His operations most closely resemble what I imagined my nascent pie business would be. Whenever I envisioned my first steps as a business lady, I returned to the idea of baking from a communal kitchen for the first few years, selling wholesale to my favorite local restaurants, and finding a home at the farmers' market. And I Heart Pies has made that model

Darling packaging for super tasty pies

work! Through their personable door-to-door delivery service and their weekly appearance at the farmers' market, Emily and Nick have managed to build up a strong and dedicated customer base without having to worry about the capital it takes to open an actual shop. When they finally do have everything in place to open a storefront, they won't have to struggle to find customers, seeing as they already have a community of people devoted to their pie.

Just before leaving the last of my "official" pie apprenticeships, I asked Emily what she would recommend to a pie vagabond seeking the courage to take the next step. Her advice was simple: "Just start. You know what you need to know, and now you just need to start."

323-744-1632
iheartpies.com

Next Stop: Littleton, CO—aka Home (page 248)

I Heart Pies' Apple Crumb Pie

PREP TIME: 45 MINUTES • **BAKE TIME:** 1 HOUR • **TOTAL TIME:** 1 HOUR 45 MINUTES •
MAKES: ONE 9-INCH SINGLE-CRUST PIE (6 TO 8 SLICES)

This was one of the first pies that I Heart Pies offered, and it has since become a customer favorite. Emily and Nick have been told that it has changed the way people think about pie! The company prides itself on seasonal baking, so I urge you to make Emily and Nick proud by baking this in the fall or wintertime (I included it in the summer chapter because that's when I visited I Heart Pies). Keep an eye out for when the Jonagold apples look their best and you'll know it's time to get baking.

I made this recipe for Aaron last fall and we decided that it's the epitome of apple pie: It's what you imagine apple pie should be. The limited sugar in the filling lets the flavor of the apples really shine through, while the crumble totally satisfies your sweet tooth. I recommend using an all-purpose flour crust for this pie; since I Heart Pies closely guards their recipe, I suggest either Buttery All-Purpose Crust (page 30) or Mom's All-Shortening Crust (page 29). Both recipes make two crusts, so you can freeze the additional disk of dough for another pie.

FOR THE CRUMB TOPPING

½ cup plus ⅛ cup
    all-purpose flour

½ cup packed light brown sugar

1 teaspoon ground cinnamon

⅛ teaspoon salt

6 tablespoons (¾ stick) cold unsalted butter,
    cut into small cubes

FOR THE FILLING AND CRUST

1¾ pounds Jonagold apples, peeled, cored,
    and cut into 8 slices each

⅛ cup granulated sugar

½ teaspoon ground cinnamon

¼ teaspoon ground nutmeg

2 tablespoons cornstarch

1 disk dough from all-purpose flour crust dough (see headnote)

Up to 3 tablespoons all-purpose flour, for rolling out the crust

Vanilla ice cream, for serving (optional)

1. Preheat the oven to 350°F with a rack in the middle position.

2. Make the crumb topping: Stir together the flour, brown sugar, cinnamon, and salt in a medium bowl. Using your fingers, incorporate the butter into the flour mixture until crumbs form.

3. Make the filling: Toss together the apples, sugar, cinnamon, nutmeg, and cornstarch in a large bowl until the apples are well coated. Set aside.

4. Prepare the crust: Place the dough on a floured work surface and with a floured rolling pin roll it into a rough 11-inch circle about ⅛ inch thick. Lay the crust into a 9-inch pie dish, gently press it in, and trim any excess dough from the edge with a paring knife, being sure to leave a ¾-inch overhang. Tuck the overhanging dough under itself and crimp. Place the lined pie dish on a rimmed baking sheet.

5. Layer the filling (including any juices) into the crust, fitting the apples together snugly. Sprinkle the topping over the filling, making sure to cover all the apples and the spaces between.

6. Bake the pie, on the baking sheet, until the filling is bubbling and the crust is golden brown, about 1 hour. Enjoy warm with a scoop of vanilla ice cream!

I Heart Pies' Apple Crumb Pie will keep for up to 3 days, covered, on the countertop.

Blackberry Pie

PREP TIME: 15 MINUTES • **BAKE TIME:** 45 TO 55 MINUTES • **TOTAL TIME:** 1 HOUR 15 MINUTES * **MAKES:** ONE 9-INCH DOUBLE-CRUST PIE (6 TO 8 SLICES) OR FOUR 5-INCH DOUBLE-CRUST TEENY PIES

Blackberry pie was one of the first pies I made on the Tour of Pie, when I was apprenticing at High 5 Pies in Seattle. Sure, I had made blackberry pies when I was growing up, but they didn't really stick in my memory the way sour cherry pie or strawberry rhubarb pie had. My Seattle hosts had a slew of frozen blackberries in their freezer, so when I showed up on their doorstep, we set to work. The pie was incredible: The dark berries were juicy and sweet and my whole wheat crust added a distinctly nutty flavor, which gave the pie a warm and homey taste. Aaron came to visit a few weeks later, and a single slice of blackberry pie was a revelation for him. Up until that point his favorite pie of all time had been Key lime (see page 197), but everything changed when he took that first bite. He gleefully finished his slice and blackberry pie became his new summertime favorite. I've included the recipe here so you can take advantage of summer's bounty of fresh blackberries.

1. Preheat the oven to 400°F with a rack in the middle position.

2. Place the blackberries in a medium bowl. Stir together the sugar and cornstarch in a separate small bowl to combine.

INGREDIENTS

4 cups fresh blackberries

¼ cup granulated sugar

¼ cup cornstarch

2 disks dough from Whole Wheat Crust (page 28)

Up to ¼ cup all-purpose flour, for rolling out the crust

Sprinkle the sugar mixture over the blackberries and toss gently to coat. Set the berries aside while you roll out the crust; the fruit will begin to juice.

3. Prepare the bottom crust: Place one disk of the dough on a floured work surface and with a floured rolling pin roll it into a rough 11-inch circle about ⅛ inch thick. Lay the crust into a 9-inch pie plate, gently press it in, and trim any excess dough from the edge with a paring knife, being sure to leave a ¾-inch overhang.

4. Set the crust on a rimmed baking sheet. Give the fruit a final stir, then pour the filling into the crust.

5. Prepare the top crust: On a floured work surface with a floured rolling pin, roll out the remaining dough disk into a rough 11-inch circle about ⅛ inch thick. Carefully lay the crust on top of the filling, and trim any excess dough from the edge, leaving a ¾-inch overhang. Tuck the overhanging dough under the edge of the overhanging bottom crust, and crimp the two crusts together. Cut a few small slits in the top crust with a sharp knife.

6. Place the pie, on the baking sheet, in the oven and bake until the filling is thickly and bubbling and the crust is golden brown (cover the crimp with foil if it begins to brown too quickly), 45 to 55 minutes.

Blackberry Pie will keep for up to 3 days, covered, on the countertop.

 ## MAKE 'EM TEENY PIES

In step 3, divide one disk of dough into four equal balls and roll out each into a rough 6-inch circle ⅛ inch thick. Lay each into a 5-inch pie tin, and trim any excess dough from the edge, being sure to leave a ½-inch overhang.

Give the filling one final stir and spoon an equal amount into each crust-lined teeny tin (roughly 1 cup each).

In step 5, divide the remaining dough into four equal balls and roll out each into a rough 7-inch circle ⅛ inch thick. Carefully lay the crusts over the filling, and trim any excess dough from the edge, leaving a ½-inch overhang. Tuck the overhanging dough under the overhanging bottom crust and crimp the two crusts together, pressing to seal. Cut a ½-inch slit in the top of each pie to allow steam to escape.

Bake the Teeny Pies until the crusts are golden brown, 40 to 45 minutes.

S'mores Pie

PREP TIME: ABOUT 1 HOUR • **CHILL TIME:** 4 HOURS • **TOTAL TIME:** 5 HOURS •
MAKES: ONE 9-INCH SINGLE-CRUST PIE (6 TO 8 SLICES) OR FOUR 5-INCH
SINGLE-CRUST TEENY PIES

INGREDIENTS

FOR THE FILLING

¾ cup granulated sugar

¼ cup unsweetened cocoa
powder

3 tablespoons cornstarch

¼ teaspoon salt

1½ cups whole milk

½ cup heavy (whipping)
cream

4 large egg yolks (reserve
2 egg whites for the
marshmallow topping)

1 cup semisweet chocolate
chips

FOR THE CRUST
AND TOPPING

1 prebaked 9-inch
Graham Cracker Crust
(page 35)

¾ cup granulated sugar

½ cup light corn syrup

⅛ teaspoon salt

2 egg whites (reserved
from the filling, above)

¼ teaspoon cream of
tartar

We went camping all the time when I was little; growing up in Colorado meant driving to Nebraska to find a decent (albeit man-made) lake where we would park our motor home and stay for the week. My brother loved the water, my mom worked hard for her tan, and I would take bags of books to read on the beach. In the evening we would all come together around the campfire. My brother and I had long sticks crafted into marshmallow skewers, and while my brother's idea of roasting marshmallows was simply to set them on fire, I was a bit more of a perfectionist. I would roast all the way around the mallow, occasionally going so far as to flip it around on my stick to make sure I got the bottom. That elusive golden hue was what I was after, and only the most perfectly toasted marshmallow was allowed to top my s'more.

Because I have such fond memories of those campfire confections, I decided to re-create them without the open flame. This recipe makes a rich chocolate cream pie with a salty-sweet graham cracker crust, topped with a generous mound of fluffy marshmallow that you brown under the broiler. It takes a little while to put together, and you need a stand mixer or a handheld electric mixer as well as a candy thermometer for part of it, but it's worth it. The best part? You can toast the marshmallow any way you like. I won't say a word.

1. Make the chocolate filling: Whisk together the sugar, cocoa powder, cornstarch, and salt in a large saucepan.

2. Whisk together the milk, cream, and egg yolks in a separate, small bowl until smooth. Add the milk mixture to the sugar mixture in the saucepan and whisk until frothy and the mixture resembles chocolate milk.

3. Cook over medium heat, whisking constantly, until the mixture comes to a low simmer and begins to thicken, 7 to 12 minutes. Continue cooking, whisking constantly and being sure to scrape the bottom of the pan to prevent scorching, until the mixture begins to boil, about 1 minute. Let boil for a full minute, then remove it from the heat.

4. Add the chocolate chips and whisk until they melt completely and the mixture is smooth.

5. Pour the chocolate filling into the prebaked graham cracker crust and, while the filling is still warm, cover with plastic wrap to prevent a film from forming on the top. Refrigerate until set, at least 4 hours.

6. Once the pie has set, make the marshmallow topping: Whisk together the sugar, corn syrup, salt, and ¼ cup water in a medium saucepan. Cook, stirring occasionally, over medium heat until the syrup comes to a simmer and reaches 240°F on a candy thermometer, about 10 minutes. Remove the pan from the heat.

7. Meanwhile, in the very clean bowl of a stand mixer fitted with the whisk attachment, or in a large bowl using a

handheld electric mixer, beat together the egg whites and cream of tartar on medium speed until the egg whites become frothy and stiff, 5 to 10 minutes. Continue to beat until the mixture becomes glossy white and soft peaks begin to form, 5 to 10 minutes more. Turn off the mixer (you may need to wait for the syrup to come up to temperature).

8. Once you've removed the syrup from the heat, turn the mixer back on to low speed and drizzle 3 to 4 tablespoons of the syrup along the inside of the bowl, a tablespoon at a time, to temper the egg whites (if you pour in the hot liquid all at once, the whites will scramble, so take your time).

9. Slowly pour the remaining syrup into the bowl, increase the speed to medium high, and whisk until the whites are glossy and begin to form stiff peaks, 5 to 7 minutes.

10. Preheat the oven to 350°F with a rack in the bottom position. Remove the pie from the refrigerator.

11. Spread the marshmallow topping evenly over the chocolate filling, heaping on as much as you like, and swirl it with the back of a spoon.

12. Bake until the marshmallow begins to turn golden brown, 5 to 7 minutes. Let the pie rest for 10 minutes, then serve.

 **MAKE 'EM TEENY PIES**

Prepare and prebake the crust in four 5-inch teeny tins as directed. In step 5, divide the filling among the crusts, and proceed with the recipe as directed.

S'mores Pie will keep for 2 to 3 days, covered, in the refrigerator.

SHARE AND SHARE ALIKE

Since the idea of plunging blindly into pie-shop ownership complete with rent, equipment, employees, and more usually sent me into a bit of tizzy, I realized it seemed much saner to work from a communal cooking space to start. (That's not to say I won't someday want a space or storefront of my own, but come on! Baby steps.) As I found out in L.A. by working alongside the lovely people of I Heart Pies, a communal cookspace offers that in-between transition space where you've graduated from baking at home but don't have to commit to a million-year lease in a city you're not sure you'll be living in five years from now. A communal kitchen also comes with a certified food-prep "stamp of approval." Well, it's not an actual stamp, but it does give you the legal cred to sell your comestibles at local farmers' markets and through wholesale. In other words, it makes a full-fledged pie business an actual possibility.

I've been lucky enough to find a new communal baking home here in D.C. at a place called Union Kitchen, which has allowed me to open my very own small business! Union Kitchen is a true testament to how stellar the communal kitchen scene can be. I couldn't be happier with the opportunity to build my business with them.

Strawberry Lime Tarts

PREP TIME: 20 MINUTES • **BAKE TIME:** 45 TO 50 MINUTES • **TOTAL TIME:** 1 HOUR 10 MINUTES • **MAKES:** 2 TARTS (4 TO 6 SLICES EACH)

These rustic tarts are a fun and fast way to combine two of my summertime favorites: strawberries and lime. They are "easy as pie" to put together and perfect as an appetizer or light dessert. This recipe, rather ridiculous in its simplicity, allows the true strawberry flavor to shine with a bit of lime to liven up each bite. I like to have a slice (or two) for breakfast, because it's the perfect amount of sweet and pastry to start my day.

1. Preheat the oven to 400°F with a rack in the middle position. Line a large baking sheet with aluminum foil.

2. Place the strawberries in a large bowl and pour half the lime juice over them. Toss gently with your hands to coat. Stir together the sugar and cornstarch in a small bowl to combine.

3. Pour the sugar mixture over the strawberries and stir lightly with your hands or a large spoon until the berries are evenly coated. Set aside while you roll out the tart crusts.

4. Make the crusts: Divide the dough into two equal disks. On a lightly floured surface with a lightly floured rolling pin, roll out the first disk into a rough circle about 12 inches in diameter ⅛ inch thick. Place the circle on the baking sheet. Roll out a second dough disk in the same way and place

INGREDIENTS

About 1½ pints strawberries, hulled and sliced ¼ inch thick (to equal 3 cups)

¼ cup freshly squeezed lime juice

½ cup granulated sugar

6 tablespoons cornstarch

1 tablespoon confectioners' sugar

1 disk dough from Whole Wheat Crust (page 28)

Up to 3 tablespoons all-purpose flour, for rolling out the crust

it next to the first on the baking sheet. (Don't worry if the circles overlap slightly; there will be enough room for both tarts once they are formed.)

5. Arrange 1½ cups of the strawberry filling (including any juices) in the center of the first dough circle, leaving a 1½-inch edge. Starting on one side, fold the extra crust over the edge of the filling on each of the tarts. Moving your way around the circle, continue to fold up the extra crust, pleating all the way around. The crust does not have to meet in the center; the edges just have to be tucked up toward the filling. The look you're going for is a very rustic tart.

6. Repeat the filling and folding with the remaining strawberry filling and crust.

7. Stir together the remaining lime juice and the confectioners' sugar in a small bowl to combine. Set aside.

8. Bake the tarts until the filling is thickly bubbling and the crust is golden brown (cover the crimp with foil if it begins to brown too quickly), 45 to 50 minutes. Drizzle the lime syrup over the filling of both tarts and serve warm.

Strawberry Lime Tarts will keep for 3 to 4 days, covered, on the countertop.

Me and my Mamma

Home Sweet Home
Littleton, CO

The invention of rosemary caramel apple

MY MOM IS the best pie baker I know. It's not because she's particularly fancy or technical about any of it, it's just that for her, baking a pie is the simplest thing in the world. When I was growing up, she worked full-time as a nurse, so any minute we were able to spend in the kitchen together was treasured. We would wear our matching aprons and whatever she was baking that day I would bake in miniature. Most often, that meant pie. I would stand on a stool at her elbow and she would show me how to roll out my tiny pie crusts with care. More often than not I would snatch up the scraps of dough with my floury fingers and "secretly" snack on them, while my mom's back was turned. She pretended not to see the telltale dusting of flour all over my face as she helped me fill my crust-lined tins with heaping spoonfuls of fruit filling. The tiniest of sour cherry or apple pies would sit proudly next to her full-size ones.

Years later, when my pie passion reignited and I started baking several pies a week, I constantly peppered my mom with phone calls full of pie queries. She knew how to solve the problem of a soupy strawberry rhubarb or a weepy meringue, and she was always happy to pull out those old family recipes and rattle them off over the phone whenever I was in need of a new pie to play with. Pie became a lovely new reason for us to be in touch.

Given that my mom is a true pie master, it was clear at the outset of my Tour of Pie that I'd need to apprentice with her. An added (and enormous) bonus was that I got to go home for a month to do nothing but bake pie at her side. As an adult I haven't had the opportunity to go home nearly as often as I would like, and when I am there we always make big baking plans, only to find ourselves constantly out of time. It was really nice to be at home with the intention of baking together for the pure joy of it and then being able to make that happen. We have a wonderful ease around each other that helped us become quite the pie pair during my monthlong "apprenticeship." My mom was pretty bossy about the whole thing, as only moms can be, and it was exactly what I needed. Each morning I would sleepily stumble into the kitchen, in search of the coffee that my mom's husband, Dave, had graciously brewed for all of us before he left for work. There I would find my mom perched on a kitchen stool consulting countless family recipes. The question every morning was always, "What are we baking today?" Similarly clad in old jeans and T-shirts that we didn't mind staining with butter, we made lists of pies we wanted to try, planned trips to the grocery store every other day, and looked toward those family recipes for inspiration.

Mother and daughter baking

Her passion for making as many pies as possible was catching and soon the counters of her newly remodeled kitchen were covered.

We had cream pie days and meringue days, fruit pie days and only one day when we filled the kitchen with pie disasters rather than successes. We zested lemon and thickened homegrown cherries in their own juices on the stovetop while the kitchen filled with the best smells those pies could offer. By the end of any given baking day we were dusted with flour, sticky from the sugar, and sated with the knowledge that we'd accomplished that day's pies. Essentially, we baked ourselves silly.

Perhaps drawn by the aromas, my brother, Jay, would pop over on a consistent basis and happily eat several slices of whatever pie we put in front of him. In fact, we all ate countless slices on any given day and when we couldn't possibly fit in another bite, my mom and Dave would take the leftovers to work, where they were demolished within an hour of their arrival. Pie after pie was presented to coworkers,

Mom keeping me from scorching the cream

old friends, and whatever family members we managed to trap in our cave of pies, formerly known as my mom's kitchen.

It was such a comfort to be together with my mom in the kitchen. There were never any pie disasters that were insurmountable, there wasn't anything that wasn't worth trying at least once, and best of all, I had my number-one cheerleader by my side the whole time. My mom has never doubted anything I've ever done in my entire life. She's always encouraged me to do my best and championed every decision, regardless of how nutty my ideas may be, and because of that support I've always felt like I could do anything. Her proclivity toward pie and the ease with which she taught me to bake made me feel like I had a place among other bakers. Because of her love and unwavering confidence in me, I was able to take that first step toward an uncertain future without hesitation.

It will always be true, however, that the best place to perch in the kitchen is still at her elbow, although I no longer need the stool, and between the two of us there's never a single scrap of pie crust dough left.

HOW TO BUILD YOUR OWN CAVE OF PIES

1. Make one million pies.
2. Cover all light sources with filmy scarves and curtains to create a dark and shadowy ambience.
3. Turn on the faucet just a little bit, so it drips occasionally . . . like stalactites dripping to the cave floor.
4. Invite all of your friends over and beckon them into your pie cave.

My Mom's Rhubarb Strawberry Custard Pie

PREP TIME: 30 MINUTES • **BAKE TIME:** 55 MINUTES • **TOTAL TIME:** 1 HOUR 30 MINUTES •
MAKES: ONE 9-INCH DOUBLE-CRUST PIE (6 TO 8 SLICES)

This lattice pie is one of my mom's summertime favorites. We grew our own strawberries and rhubarb, so at the earliest sign of having enough of each, my mom would head to the backyard to pick them. Most strawberry rhubarb pies have the strawberries front and center while the rhubarb takes a backseat to its sweeter counterpart, but this pie does the opposite. The rhubarb is the spotlight ingredient with just a hint of strawberry and a simple custard-like filling to help temper the rhubarb's acidity. When I was growing up, I couldn't comprehend how my mom actually *enjoyed* the unique flavor rhubarb has to offer, let alone make an entire pie out of it. My brother and I clamored endlessly for her famous tart cherry pie, but in between the constant cherry demands she would bake one of these pies . . . and she wouldn't share a slice. Now that I've been swayed to her way of thinking, I beg her to bake these—and I make her share.

1 cup hulled, sliced strawberries (sliced about ¼-inch thick)

4 cups diced rhubarb (from 3 to 4 stalks; see Note, page 169)

1½ cups granulated sugar

5 tablespoons all-purpose flour, plus extra for rolling out the crust

2 large eggs

2 disks dough from Buttery All-Purpose Crust (page 30) or Mom's All-Shortening Crust (page 29)

1. Preheat the oven to 450°F with a rack in the middle position.

2. Place the strawberries and rhubarb in a large bowl and toss gently to combine.

3. Whisk together the sugar and flour in a small bowl. Add the eggs and whisk until the mixture is smooth. Set aside.

4. Prepare the bottom crust: Place one disk of the dough on a lightly floured surface and with a floured rolling pin roll it into a rough 11-inch circle about ⅛ inch thick. Lay the crust into a 9-inch pie plate, gently press it in, and trim any excess dough from the edge with a paring knife, being sure to leave a ¾-inch overhang.

5. Place the strawberries and rhubarb in the crust. Give the egg mixture another stir and pour it evenly over the fruit.

6. Prepare the lattice crust: On a floured work surface with a floured rolling pin, roll out the remaining dough disk into a 11-inch circle about ⅛ inch thick. Cut the dough into strips and weave them into a lattice as directed on page 24. Tuck the overhanging dough strips under the bottom crust and crimp together, pressing to seal.

7. Set the pie on a rimmed baking sheet and bake for 10 minutes, then reduce the heat to 325°F and bake until the crust is golden brown, an additional 45 minutes. Allow the pie to cool and set before serving.

My Mom's Rhubarb Strawberry Custard Pie will keep for 3 to 4 days, covered, on the countertop.

Reuben Potpies with a Rye Crumble and Caraway Crust

PREP TIME: 45 MINUTES • **BAKE TIME:** 20 TO 30 MINUTES • **TOTAL TIME:** 1 HOUR 15 MINUTES • **MAKES:** SIX 5-INCH SINGLE-CRUST TEENY PIES

To me one of the best summer lunches around is a good Reuben sandwich with a pickle and stellar fries on the side. Because of my love for actual Reuben sandwiches I was determined to make this recipe incredible. The pies had to stand up to the high bar raised by the sandwich—there was no room for mediocrity—so I tested a LOT of recipes before perfecting this one. It's an adapted recipe for Reuben mac and cheese, courtesy of Aaron's mom, minus the pasta. This is one of the few pies for which my whole wheat crust doesn't work at all because the flavor competes with the crumble, so I came up with an all-purpose crust studded with caraway seeds as a substitute. (Note that you'll want to make the crust dough at least an hour before assembling the rest of the pie.) After you taste these pies, you'll probably want to eat one every night for the rest of your life. It happens.

1. Prepare the crust: Stir together the flour, salt, and caraway seeds in a large bowl. Cut in the butter and the shortening using a pastry cutter until each piece is the size of a small pea and coated in flour.

INGREDIENTS

FOR THE CARAWAY CRUST

2½ cups all-purpose flour, plus up to 3 tablespoons extra for rolling out the crust

2 teaspoons salt

1 teaspoon caraway seeds

¾ cup (1½ sticks) cold unsalted butter, cut into small pieces

¼ cup (4 tablespoons) cold shortening

¼ cup (4 tablespoons) cold vodka

6 tablespoons ice water, plus extra as needed

FOR THE FILLING

1 tablespoon unsalted butter

2 tablespoons all-purpose flour

¾ cup whole milk

½ teaspoon salt

½ teaspoon ground black pepper

2 tablespoons spicy brown mustard

¾ cup (3 ounces) grated Gruyère cheese

1 pound thinly sliced corned beef, roughly chopped

½ cup sauerkraut (not canned)

FOR THE RYE CRUMBLE

3 slices rye bread (seeded or not)

1 tablespoon unsalted butter, at room temperature

¼ cup fresh parsley leaves

1 teaspoon paprika

2. Pour the vodka and ice water over the dry ingredients a few tablespoons at a time and, using a rubber spatula, press the dough together to form a large ball. The dough should be fairly wet and sticky, but if it seems dry, you can add a little extra ice water a tablespoon at a time until everything comes together easily. (Be careful to work the dough as little as possible, otherwise it may become tough.) Separate the dough into six equal balls, press each into a 1-inch-thick disk, wrap each in plastic wrap, and refrigerate for at least 1 hour or up to 2 days.

3. When you are ready to assemble the pies, preheat the oven to 350°F with a rack in the middle position.

4. Remove the dough from the fridge, unwrap it, and on a lightly floured work surface with a floured rolling pin, roll out each disk into a rough circle about 6 inches in diameter and ⅛ inch thick; transfer each to a 5-inch pie tin and gently press it in. Trim off any excess dough with a paring knife, being sure to leave a ½-inch overhang. Tuck the overhang under itself and crimp.

5. Prebake the pie crusts as directed on page 25. When baked, take them out of the oven, remove the weights and liners, and set aside to cool. Leave the oven on.

6. While the crusts cool, make the filling: Melt the butter in a medium saucepan over medium heat. Whisk in the flour and cook, stirring, until it's fully incorporated, about 1 minute. Add the milk, salt, and pepper and continue to whisk until

A Reuben pie with a finely ground crumble

the sauce thickens to the consistency of heavy cream and coats the back of a spoon, 5 to 7 minutes. Remove from the heat and whisk in the mustard and the cheese.

7. Stir together the corned beef and sauerkraut in a large bowl. Add the cheese sauce ½ cup at a time and stir well until everything is combined. (I don't always use all of the cheese sauce, so just eyeball it. If it seems like enough sauce after ¾ cup, don't feel obligated to use all of it.) Set aside.

8. Make the rye crumble: Toast and butter the bread slices. Coarsely chop the bread and place it in the bowl of a food processor along with the parsley and paprika. Pulse a few times until the bread pieces are the size of large peas.

9. Place the prebaked crusts (still in their tins) on a rimmed baking sheet. Scoop an equal amount of filling into each of the crusts, and sprinkle each pie with enough crumble to cover the top. Bake until the crust and crumble are golden brown, 20 to 30 minutes. Serve warm.

Reuben Potpies with a Rye Crumble and Caraway Crust will keep for 2 to 3 days, covered, in the refrigerator.

Teeny Summer Squash Pies with a Cracker Crust

PREP TIME: 40 MINUTES • **BAKE TIME:** 30 TO 40 MINUTES • **TOTAL TIME:** 1 HOUR 20 MINUTES • **MAKES:** SIX 5-INCH SINGLE-CRUST TEENY PIES

This is a really light and easy savory pie. My friend Krissy works for the Westminster Bakers Company in Rutland, Vermont, which specializes in all sorts of crackers. She and I wanted to come up with a simple summer recipe that would utilize a cracker crust, and after receiving a massive box filled to the brim with every imaginable type of cracker, this is what we came up with. The Westminster Bakers Company's multigrain snack crackers are very tasty, but any type of multigrain cracker could work in its place. I grind them down to a fairly fine meal in a food processor until the crumbs are similar to the consistency of graham cracker crumbs. The salty crackers and Parmesan cheese pair delightfully with the fresh vegetables in the filling, making for a simple, summery meal.

1. Make the cracker crust: Stir together the cracker crumbs and melted butter in a large bowl until the butter is evenly distributed. The mixture will darken slightly and should clump easily when pressed together.

INGREDIENTS

FOR THE CRACKER CRUSTS

1½ cups multigrain cracker crumbs (from about 40 crackers; see headnote)

7 tablespoons unsalted butter, melted

FOR THE FILLING

2 tablespoons olive oil

1 medium onion, peeled and thinly sliced

2 yellow summer squash, quartered and thinly sliced

2 zucchini, quartered and thinly sliced

2 large eggs

¼ cup heavy (whipping) cream

2 teaspoons salt

2 teaspoons ground black pepper

1 teaspoon chopped fresh rosemary

2 cups (8 ounces) grated Parmesan cheese

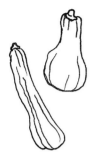

2. Distribute the cracker crumbs evenly into six 5-inch pie tins. Press the mixture up the side and into the bottom of each tin to make a ¼-inch-thick shell all the way around. Set aside on a rimmed baking sheet while you assemble the filling.

3. Preheat the oven to 350°F with a rack in the middle position.

4. Make the filling: Heat the olive oil in a large skillet over medium heat. Add the onion and cook, stirring occasionally, until translucent and beginning to caramelize, about 10 minutes.

5. Add the summer squash and zucchini and cook, stirring, until the veggies are tender, 10 to 15 minutes. Remove from the heat, and set aside to cool.

6. Whisk together the eggs, heavy cream, salt, pepper, rosemary, and 1 cup of the Parmesan cheese in a medium bowl. Add the vegetables and stir gently to combine.

7. Spoon an equal amount of filling into each of the crusts and top each pie with the remaining Parmesan cheese.

8. Bake the pies on the baking sheet until the cheese on top is browned and bubbling, 30 to 40 minutes. Serve immediately.

Teeny Summer Squash Pies with a Cracker Crust will keep for 2 to 3 days, covered, in the refrigerator.

The End, Which Is Actually a Beginning

think there is a moment, when trying to change your life, that you realize the change has already occurred. Or, at the very least, has started to happen. Or the change within yourself has grown so great that it's finally time to move on to the next step. Whatever it is, I think there's a moment. It didn't happen in a flash; I didn't wake up one day and realize that in a split second everything had finally coalesced and that I was an official baker, ready in all aspects to open up a pie

My first D.C. market

shop. But something certainly shifted, and in the midst of having a perfectly lovely time at my L.A. apprenticeship, I realized I was ready, almost antsy, to move on.

Being one of those people who craves being home, after an entire year of vagabond living, I was a little weary of travel. As much fun as the adventure had been and as grateful as I was for the people who'd hosted me, I was tired of baking in borrowed kitchens and sleeping in unfamiliar beds. And as much as I had learned during that year of intense pie study, I felt as though my time as an unpaid pie apprentice was coming to a close. It was now time to move forward and take a new leap of faith. I'd spent the past year earning my lady bakership, and while I didn't have a piece of paper declaring it, I knew with absolute certainty that I was a baker.

Since the start of the Tour of Pie, Aaron had gone to grad school, earned his master's degree, and managed to land his absolute dream job in Washington, D.C. There he was waiting for me, and my newly acquired pie skills, to join him. I moved to D.C. full of relief, excitement, and just the right amount of heart-pounding fear. After a year of being a pie wanderer I finally felt settled, at home, and ready to find out what it meant to pursue pie full time, in one place, for the long term.

During the Tour of Pie I had baked my way through nine states and accumulated a considerable amount of practical pie knowledge. And I learned exactly which pies I love (I'm looking at you, Blackberry and

Teeny Pie Love

Rosemary Caramel Apple), which pies I don't love (sorry, Lemon Shaker . . . you just didn't make the cut), and which pies require a large cup of black coffee to accompany them (any and all pies I made in the South). I found a few wonderful pie mentors who have remained constants in my life. They provide continual support and inspiration regardless of where I am in the country. Every time I talk to them I'm renewed in my dream to be like them: a vibrant participant in a community of people who take pride in what they make with their own two hands, and share with others. My year of pie apprenticing was an adventure of epic proportions and I couldn't be happier or more proud of myself for simply *going*. I reveled in the good times and took the bad times in stride (mostly), and at the end of the day I'm still wholeheartedly, undeniably in love with pie.

And the best part is, I'm nowhere near finished. Aaron has yet to grow tired of his daily slice of breakfast pie, and I'm still delighted to be the one baking it. I've written a cookbook full of my favorite pie recipes, with the sincerest hope that anyone who owns it feels like a fellow pie baker. And I've finally (and very excitedly) become a small business owner. I've gotten settled in at Union Kitchen, the vibrant up-and-coming communal kitchen space where I've carved out a little baking home for myself amongst the other small businesses. The environment is lovely and engaging and I'm surrounded by people who are all in the same boat and therefore overwhelmingly happy to offer support and help. I've partnered with my local CSA, Norman's Farmers' Market, and have begun selling Teeny Pies at their roadside stands and CSA pickups on the weekends. And I've made custom pies by the hundreds for everything from weddings to corporate events.

Everything has happened very quickly in the last few months—it's thrilling to realize that my year of vagabond pie living truly prepared me for the next steps. Someday soon I'll take another leap of faith and open my own shop. It will be a lovely place filled with warmth, good people, good music, good coffee, and *great* pie.

The most beautiful logo in the whole world

Lady Bakership Lesson #9

PURSUE PERFECTION

I don't think perfection is possible, which is why I think it's so important to continue to chase it. I never want to stop trying for the perfect pie. There will always be another lady bakership lesson to be learned and another pie to perfect, and I plan on enjoying the pursuit.

Index

Note: Page references in *italics* indicate photographs.

A

Aaron's Chicken Potpies with Kale and Cannellinis, 97–101, *98*
Abrams, Samantha, 90–91
Alabama, 162, 163
all-purpose flour, 13–14
Almond Pie, Sweet Roasted, 94–95
apple pie
  Apple and Pork Potpies, 102–104
  Green Chile Apple Pie with Cheddar Cheese Crust, 56–58
  I Heart Pies' Apple Crumb Pie, 234–235
  Rosemary Caramel Apple Pie, *60*, 61–63
  Sweet and Simple Apple Pie, 53–54
Atlanta, Georgia, 210–211, 216–217
Autry Farmers Market, 232

B

Bacon Pecan Pie, Bourbon, *80*, 81–84
baker's apprentice, xii–xiii
baking
  messiness of, 133
  seasonal, xv–xvi
Banana Cream Pie with Vanilla Wafer Crust, 171–173
beets
  Pickled Beet and Goat Cheese Tarts with Candied Walnuts, *156*, 157–159
  Pickled Beets, 159
berries
  Blackberry Compote, *136*, 140
  Blackberry Pie, *236*, 237–239
  Bluebarb Pie, *228*, 229–231
  Emmy's Berry Cobbler, 92–93
  Espresso French Silk Pie with Blackberry Compote, 137–138
  freezing, 225

Lamb, Mint, and Raspberry Teeny Potpies, 202–204
Lemony Blueberry Crumb Pie, 226–227
My Mom's Rhubarb Strawberry Custard Pie, 251–252
Sour Cherry Pie, aka My Favorite, 213–215
Strawberry Basil Pie, 164–166
Strawberry Lime Tarts, 245–246
Strawberry Rhubarb Pie, 167–170
Summer's Best Blueberry Pie, 222–224
blackberries, 69–70
  Blackberry Compote, 140
  Blackberry Pie, *236*, 237–239
Bledsoe, Mims, 210–211, 216–217
blueberries
  Bluebarb Pie, *228*, 229–231
  Lemony Blueberry Crumb Pie, 226–227

Summer's Best Blueberry Pie, 222–224

Boston, Massachusetts, 106–107

Bourbon Bacon Pecan Pie, *80*, 81–84

bowls, 6

Breakfast Pie with a Hash Brown Crust, 205–207, *206*

Browned Butter Pecan Pie, 85–88

bulk ingredients, 96

butter, 14

Buttery All-Purpose Crust, 30–31

C

candy thermometer, 62

caramel
    Rosemary Caramel Apple Pie, *60*, 61–63
    tips for, 62

Chai Cream Pie, 150–151

Cheddar Cheese Crust, 59

Cherry Pie, aka My Favorite, Sour, *212*, 213–215

Chess Pie, 179–180

Chicago, Illinois, 106–108, 131, 142–143

Chicken Potpies with Kale and Cannellinis, Aaron's, 97–101, *98*

chilled ingredients, 12–13

chocolate
    Chocolate Cream Pie, 131–132
    Derbyish Pie, 199–201
    Espresso French Silk Pie with Blackberry Compote, *136*, 137–138, *139*
    French Silk Pie, 134–135
    Peanut Butter Brownie Pie with a Pretzel Crust, 129–130
    S'Mores Pie, 240–243, *241*

Cinnamon Crumble, 42–43

Cobbler, Emmy's Berry, 92–93

Coconut Cream Pie, *184*, 185–186

communal kitchens, 244, 261

Community Supported Agriculture (CSA), 53

Cone, Dani, 51–52, 64–65

Confrancesco, Emily, 211, 232–233

Confrancesco, Nick, 211, 232–233

cream pies
    Banana Cream Pie with Vanilla Wafer Crust, 171–173
    Chai Cream Pie, 150–151
    Coconut Cream Pie, *184*, 185–186
    Earl Grey Cream Pie in a Sugar Cookie Crust, 147–149, *148*
    S'Mores Pie, 240–243

crimping, 19–20

Crisco, 14

crowd-funding, 125

crumbles
    Cinnamon Crumble, 42–43
    Oat-and-Nut Crumble, 43–44
    Stuffing Crumble, 44–45

crust. *See* pie crust

crust cookies, 25

crust cover, 6

custard pies
    My Mom's Rhubarb Strawberry Custard Pie, 251–252
    tips for, 74

D

Davie, Florida, 163, 194–196

deorating, 23, 25

Derbyish Pie, 199–201

Derby pie, 198

docking, 25

double crusts
    Buttery All-Purpose Crust, 30–31
    Mom's All-Shortening Crust, 29–30
    Savory Pie Crust, 32–33

dough
    dry, 40
    freezing, 25–26
    gluey, 41
    melty, 40–41

mixing methods, 15–16
overworked, 13
rolling out, 16–18, 21
shrinkage, 41
troubleshooting, 40–41
wet, 40

E

Earl Grey Cream Pie in a
    Sugar Cookie Crust,
    147–149, *148*
eggs
    Breakfast Pie with a Hash
        Brown Crust, 205–207
    raw, 138
egg washes, 25
electric mixer, 5–6, 16
Emmy's Berry Cobbler, 92–93
Emmy's Organics, 51, 52,
    90–91
Espresso French Silk Pie with
    Blackberry Compote, *136*,
    137–138, *139*
Espresso Whipped Cream, 48

F

fall season, 50–52
family dinners, 221
Farmer Ground Flour, 91
farmers' markets, 54, 108
fats, 14–15
Felicia's Atomic Longe, 91
fine grater, 7

Florida, 162, 163, 194–196
flours, 13–14
food processor, 5–6, 16
footwear, 160
fork crimp, 20
freezing
    berries, 225
    dough, 25–26
    pie, 26–27
French rolling pins, 87
French Silk Pie, 134–135
    Espresso French Silk
        Pie with Blackberry
        Compote, *136*, 137–138,
        139
fruit pies
    See also specific types
    freezing, 26–27
Fuel Coffee, 51

G

Gaffney, Ian, 90–91
Georgia Peach Pie, *218*,
    219–220
Ginger Pie, Honey, 88–89
Gluten-Free Crust, 33–35
goat cheese
    Pear and Goat Cheese
        Tart, 109–111, *110*
    Pickled Beet and Goat
        Cheese Tarts with
        Candied Walnuts, *156*,
        157–159
Golan, Kay, 216, 219

Golan, Patrick, 216, 219
Graham Cracker Crust, 35–36
Grapefruit and Pomegranate
    Pie, *122*, 123–125
grater, 7
Green Chile Apple Pie with
    Cheddar Cheese Crust, 56–58
Greensboro, Alabama, 85, 163,
    174–175

H

hairdos, 76
Hale Empowerment and
    Revitalization Organization
    (HERO), 163
Hatch, New Mexico, 56
High 5 Pie, 51–52, 64–65, 87,
    237
High 5 Pie's Marionberry Pie,
    66–68
Homemade Whipped Cream,
    45–47
Honey Ginger Pie, 88–89
Horn, Peter, 179

I

I Heart Pies, 210, 211, 232–233
I Heart Pies' Apple Crumb Pie,
    234–235
Indiegogo, 125
ingredients
    bulk, 96
    chilling, 12–13

choosing, 12
fats, 14–15
flours, 13–14
key, 13–15
liquids, 15
mixing methods, 15–16
vodka, 15
Ithaca, New York, 13, 52, 77,
90–91

K

Kern family, 198
Key lime pie, 194–196
Terry's Famous Key Lime
Pie, *195*, 197

L

lady bakership lessons, xii–xiii,
76, 87, 96, 115, 133, 152, 160,
244, 262
Lamb, Mint, and Raspberry
Teeny Potpies, 202–204
lard, 14–15
lattice, 24–25
leeks
Breakfast Pie with a Hash
Brown Crust, 205–207,
206
leftovers, crust, 25
lemons
Lemon Meringue Pie,
187–188

Lemony Blueberry Crumb
Pie, 226–227
Lemon Zested Whipped
Cream, 47
limes
Strawberry Lime Tarts,
245–246
Terry's Famous Key Lime
Pie, *195*, 197
Zested Lime Curd Pie,
189–191, *190*
liquids, 15
Littleton, Colorado, 210, 211,
248–250
London, England, 147
Los Angeles, California, 210,
211, 232–233

M

Magnolia Bakery, 171
Marionberry Pie, High 5 Pie's,
66–68
McLeod, Renee, 107, 116
measuring cups, 6
measuring spoons, 6
mini pie plates, 4–5
mint juleps, 201
mixing methods, 15–16
Mom's All-Shortening Crust,
29–30
My Mom's Rhubarb
Strawberry Custard Pie,
251–252

N

Nathan, Sharin, 108, 142–143
New River Groves, 162, 163,
194–196
Norman's Farm Market, 261
nuts
Bourbon Bacon Pecan Pie,
81–84
Browned Butter Pecan Pie,
85–88
Derbyish Pie, 199–201
Oat-and-Nut Crumble,
43–44
Sweet Roasted Almond Pie,
94–95

O

Oat-and-Nut Crumble, 43–44
Orange Cream Pie, 126–127
Orange Zested Whipped
Cream, 48

P

pastry cutter, 5, 15
Peach Pie, Georgia, *218*,
219–220
Peanut Butter Brownie Pie
with a Pretzel Crust,
129–130
pears
Pear and Goat Cheese
Tart, 109–111, *110*

picking, 113
Poached Pear Pie with
  Cinnamon Crumble,
  112–114
Sweet Sensations'
  Browned Butter Pear
  Pie, 144–146
pecan pie
  Bourbon Bacon Pecan Pie,
  80, 81–84
  Browned Butter Pecan Pie,
  85–88
pecans, 106
Peppermint Whipped Cream,
  47
perfection, 262
Petsi Pies, 106–107, 116–118,
  162
Petsi Pies' Sweet Potato Pie,
  119–121
Pickled Beet and Goat Cheese
  Tarts with Candied Walnuts,
  156, 157–159
pie beads, 7
pie birds, 7
pie crust
  Buttery All-Purpose Crust,
  30–31
  Cheddar Cheese Crust,
  59
  cookies, 25
  crimping, 19–20
  decorating, 23–24
  egg washes, 25

experimentation with, 10–11
Gluten-Free Crust, 33–35
Graham Cracker Crust,
  35–36
ingredients, 13–15
lattice, 24–25
laying on top, 22
leftovers, 25
lining pie plate, 18–19, 21
mixing methods, 15–16
Mom's All-Shortening
  Crust, 29–30
prebaking, 25–26
Pretzel Crust, 36–37
rolling out, 16–18, 21
Savory Pie Crust, 32–33
Sugar Cookie Crust,
  37–39
Teeny Pies, 21
tips for, 12–13
troubleshooting, 40–41
Vanilla Wafer Crust, 173
venting, 23
Whole Wheat Crust,
  28–29
pie disasters, 192–193
PieLab, 85, 162–163, 174–175,
  179
PieLab's Snickerdoodle Pie,
  176–178
pie plates, 4–5
  lining, 18–19
Pie Shop, 210–211, 216–217
Pike Place Market, 51

Poached Pear Pie with
  Cinnamon Crumble, 112–114
Pomegranate Pie, Grapefruit
  and, *122*, 123–125
Pork Potpies, Apple and,
  102–104
potatoes
  Breakfast Pie with a Hash
  Brown Crust, 205–207,
  206
potpies
  Aaron's Chicken Potpies
  with Kale and
  Cannellinis, 97–101, *98*
  Apple and Pork Potpies,
  102–104
  Lamb, Mint, and
  Raspberry Teeny
  Potpies, 202–204
  Reuben Potpies with a Rye
  Crumble and Caraway
  Crust, *254*, 253–256, *256*
prebaking pie shell, 25–26
Pretzel Crust, 36–37
Prospect, Kentucky, 198
Pumpkin Pie, 71–74, *72*
pumpkin seeds, toasted, 75

R

receipts, 115
Reuben Potpies with a Rye
  Crumble and Caraway Crust,
  253–256, *254*, *256*

rhubarb
    Bluebarb Pie, *228*, 229–231
    My Mom's Rhubarb
        Strawberry Custard Pie,
        251–252
    Strawberry Rhubarb Pie,
        167–170, *168*
rod rolling pins, 2–3
roller rolling pins, 3–4
rolling pins, 2–4, 87
Rosemary Caramel Apple Pie,
    60, 61–63
Rosewater Whipped Cream, 48
Roth, Bob, 162, 163, 194–196
Rutland, Vermont, 257

S

Savory Pie Crust, 32–33
savory pies
    Aaron's Chicken Potpies
        with Kale and
        Cannellinis, 97–101, *98*
    Apple and Pork Potpies,
        102–104
    Breakfast Pie with a Hash
        Brown Crust, 205–207,
        206
    Lamb, Mint, and
        Raspberry Teeny
        Potpies, 202–204
    Reuben Potpies with a Rye
        Crumble and Caraway
        Crust, 253–256, *254, 256*

Teeny Summer Squash
    Pies with a Cracker
    Crust, 257–258
Thanksgiving Dinner Pies,
    153–155
seasonal baking, xv–xvi
Seattle, Washington, 51, 64–65,
    69–70
sheeters, 117–118
Shoofly Pie, 181–183
shortening, 14
S'Mores Pie, 240–243, *241*
Snickerdoodle Pie, PieLab's,
    176–178
Somerville, Massachusetts,
    107, 116–118, 162
Sour Cherry Pie, aka My
    Favorite, *212*, 213–215
spring season, 162–163
strawberries
    My Mom's Rhubarb
        Strawberry Custard Pie,
        251–252
    Strawberry Basil Pie,
        162, 164–166
    Strawberry Lime Tarts,
        245–246
    Strawberry Rhubarb Pie,
        167–170, *168*
Stuffing Crumble, 44–45
Sugar Cookie Crust,
    37–39
sugar pies, 180
    Chess Pie, 179–180

PieLab's Snickerdoodle
    Pie, 176–178
Shoofly Pie, 181–183
Summer's Best Blueberry Pie,
    222–224
summer season, 210–211
Summer Squash Pies with
    a Cracker Crust, Teeny,
    257–258
Sweet and Simple Apple Pie,
    53–54
sweet potatoes
    baking, 121
    Petsi Pies' Sweet Potato
        Pie, 119–121
    Sweet Potato Pie, 77–79
Sweet Roasted Almond Pie,
    94–95
Sweet Sensations' Browned
    Butter Pear Pie, 144–146
Sweet Sensations Pastry,
    106–108, 142–143

T

tarts
    Pear and Goat Cheese
        Tart, 109–111
    Pickled Beet and Goat
        Cheese Tarts with
        Candied Walnuts,
        157–159
    Strawberry Lime Tarts,
        245–246

techniques
    crimping, 19–20
    decorating crust, 23
    lattice making, 24–25
    laying top crust, 22
    lining pie plate, 18–19
    mixing methods, 15–16
    rolling out dough, 16–18
    venting, 23
Teeny Pies
    adaptations for, 55, 74, 79,
        84, 87, 114, 127, 132,
        135, 138, 151, 166, 170,
        186, 191, 201, 215, 224,
        231, 239, 243
    rolling out and lining, 21
Teeny Pies blog, xiii, 141
Teeny Summer Squash Pies
    with a Cracker Crust, 257–
    258
Terry's Famous Key Lime Pie,
    195, 197
Thanksgiving Dinner Pies,
    153–155
Tipsy Pecans, *106*
tools
    crust cover, 6
    electric mixer, 5–6, 16
    food processor, 5–6, 16
    grater/zester, 7

measuring cups, spoons,
    bowls, 6
pastry cutter, 5, 15
pie beads, 7
pie birds, 7
pie plates, 4–5
rolling pins, 2–4
top crust
    decorating, 23–24
    laying on, 22
    venting, 23
treacle tarts, 181
turkey
    Thanksgiving Dinner Pies,
        153–155

U
Union Kitchen, 244, 261

V
Vanilla Wafer Crust, 173
V crimp, 20
vodka, 15

W
Walden Pond, 128
Washington, D.C., 11, 53, 260

Weiner, Doug, 221
Weiner, Lisa, 221
Westminster Bakers Company,
    257
whipped cream
    Espresso Whipped Cream,
        48
    Homemade Whipped
        Cream, 45–47
    Lemon Zested Whipped
        Cream, 47
    Orange Zested Whipped
        Cream, 48
    Peppermint Whipped
        Cream, 47
    Rosewater Whipped
        Cream, 48
Whole Wheat Crust, 28–29
whole wheat flour, 13–14
winter season, 106–108

Z
Zested Lime Curd Pie, 189–191,
    190
zester, 7

Conversion Tables

APPROXIMATE EQUIVALENTS

1 stick butter = 8 tbs = 4 oz = ½ cup

1 cup all-purpose presifted flour or dried bread crumbs = 5 oz

1 cup granulated sugar = 8 oz

1 cup (packed) brown sugar = 6 oz

1 cup confectioners' sugar = 4½ oz

1 cup honey or syrup = 12 oz

1 cup grated cheese = 4 oz

1 cup dried beans = 6 oz

1 large egg = about 2 oz or about 3 tbs

1 egg yolk = about 1 tbs

1 egg white = about 2 tbs

Please note that all conversions are approximate but close enough to be useful when converting from one system to another.

WEIGHT CONVERSIONS

US/UK	METRIC	US/UK	METRIC
½ oz	15 g	7 oz	200 g
1 oz	30 g	8 oz	250 g
1½ oz	45 g	9 oz	275 g
2 oz	60 g	10 oz	300 g
2½ oz	75 g	11 oz	325 g
3 oz	90 g	12 oz	350 g
3½ oz	100 g	13 oz	375 g
4 oz	125 g	14 oz	400 g
5 oz	150 g	15 oz	450 g
6 oz	175 g	1 lb	500 g

LIQUID CONVERSIONS

U.S.	IMPERIAL	METRIC
2 tbs	1 fl oz	30 ml
3 tbs	1½ fl oz	45 ml
¼ cup	2 fl oz	60 ml
⅓ cup	2½ fl oz	75 ml
⅓ cup + 1 tbs	3 fl oz	90 ml
⅓ cup + 2 tbs	3½ fl oz	100 ml
½ cup	4 fl oz	125 ml
⅔ cup	5 fl oz	150 ml
¾ cup	6 fl oz	175 ml
¾ cup + 2 tbs	7 fl oz	200 ml
1 cup	8 fl oz	250 ml
1 cup + 2 tbs	9 fl oz	275 ml
1¼ cups	10 fl oz	300 ml
1⅓ cups	11 fl oz	325 ml
1½ cups	12 fl oz	350 ml
1⅔ cups	13 fl oz	375 ml
1¾ cups	14 fl oz	400 ml
1¾ cups + 2 tbs	15 fl oz	450 ml
2 cups (1 pint)	16 fl oz	500 ml
2½ cups	20 fl oz (1 pint)	600 ml
3¾ cups	1½ pints	900 ml
4 cups	1¾ pints	1 liter

OVEN TEMPERATURES

°F	GAS MARK	°C	°F	GAS MARK	°C
250	½	120	400	6	200
275	1	140	425	7	220
300	2	150	450	8	230
325	3	160	475	9	240
350	4	180	500	10	260
375	5	190			

Note: Reduce the temperature by 20°C (68°F) for fan-assisted ovens.